CIVIL ACTIONS

CIVIL ACTIONS

by

Steven Phillips

DOUBLEDAY & COMPANY, INC.
Garden City, New York
1983

Library of Congress Cataloging in Publication Data

Phillips, Steven.
Civil actions.

I. Title.
PS3566.H52C5   1983   813'.54
ISBN: *0-385-15988-9*
Library of Congress Catalog Card Number 82-45365

CIVIL ACTIONS

SECTION ONE

1

Once a week he went downtown to get an injection. Sometimes they would draw blood or run tests, trying to gauge the progress of the therapy. More often, it was just a question of taking the injection and going home. He would go home and feel sick, nauseous, suffer bouts of diarrhea and weakness, feel wasted and indifferent. He was losing weight, and although he was in his early thirties, his hair had started to fall out in great tufts. In the Army, and later in prison, he had taken pride in his body, in his appearance. Cell-bound, with time heavy on his hands, it had been nothing for him to bang out a hundred push-ups and a hundred sit-ups at a shot. He had worked out with weights, learned to skip rope, and run endless laps around the prison gym. He dreamed of making it as a middleweight contender, sustaining dreams of success, and women and money. The better part of his self-respect was tied up in that dream, and in his body, its strength, its beauty, its capacity for pleasure. Now that was gone. The muscles were wasting, their definition lost. It was bone, not muscle, that was most evident; bone, and the long surgical scar running obliquely across his abdomen. His clothes no longer fit and he could not bear the sight of himself naked. He was dying. What was worse, he knew he was dying.

It was only supposed to be that one robbery, no more. He had given it thought, planned it out carefully. A supermarket in a cash-paying neighborhood, late in the week, right around closing time, was his target. He picked his store deliberately, shopped there, studied its layout, working out the route of his getaway, getting it in his head to a point where it was automatic. Out the door, turn left, then left again and down the alleyway, up a fire escape ladder onto the roof of an adjacent building, across the roof and into the building. Then he would be gone, gone with enough to start a new proper post-army life. He bought a wide-brimmed black hat, the kind he could pull down over his face to obscure his identity. He also bought a double-barreled shotgun, and sawed it off, leaving only six inches of barrel beyond the stock. It left a mean, vicious-looking weapon, a weapon designed to inspire fear. It had to be that way. It was part of the plan. It had to scare the living shit out of anyone it was pointed at, because when he went into that supermarket, when he whipped out that shotgun, when he pointed it at the store manager, the shotgun was not going to be loaded. He had killed a man once, shot him down in fear and anger and watched him die. In Southeast Asia where such things were permitted he had done that. He wasn't going to do it again, not under any circumstances. His plans were based on a bluff, on the altogether reasonable assumption that no one in his right mind would be willing to gamble his life against the possibility that the shotgun was unloaded, against the chance that he wouldn't pull the trigger.

It started out well, the way he had planned it. The store manager, skinny, bald, wearing glasses, offered no resistance.

"This is a stickup, motherfuckers! Do you hear me, this is a stickup! Don't anyone say or do nuthin', an' no one's gonna get hurt!"

He moved quickly from cash register to cash register, emptying the money into a paper bag, feeling strangely exhilarated, the fear and the tension suddenly transformed into something different, something approaching pleasure. He pushed the manager over to the safe and forced him to open it. Inside was a canvas bank deposit bag that was fairly bulging with cash. He reached in and took it. Then he turned and ran, sprinting wildly for the exit, the street, and his escape.

And a little girl ran into his path. She was seven and a half years old and she had wandered away from her mother to examine a sugared cereal display. She saw the robbery taking place, knew something was wrong, wavered indecisively in the aisle, not sure of what to do. Then, at exactly the wrong moment, she bolted toward her mother, bolted right in front of the fleeing robber. He barely saw her in his flight, probably couldn't have changed direction or avoided her in any event. He ran right over her, tripped, and they both went flying. There was a sickening crack as the little girl's head hit the pointy edge of a check-out counter.

The shotgun and money bag went skidding across the floor and he scrambled after them, cursing, not realizing what had happened. He bent down, reached for the money, still a little dazed by the collision. And as he bent down, a customer stepped behind him, picked up a soda bottle off the shelf, and clobbered him over the head. He was still unconscious when the police came and locked him up.

The little girl did not die, although for a short while everyone was afraid that she might. She had experienced some mild to moderately severe seizures, and the doctors believed that she had suffered a basilar skull fracture. They decided not to operate, and the decision proved to be a wise one. Within a week she had begun to recover, and within two weeks she was discharged from the hospital with nothing more severe than a bad headache and a serious hearing loss. In time even the headaches subsided. The hearing loss proved to be permanent.

They wouldn't tell him whether the little girl had lived or died, or even whether her condition was serious or not. He had begged the legal aid lawyer who had been assigned to represent him at his arraignment, a pale young woman who was frightened of him, to find out how the girl was. She had promised to try, had promised to report back whatever she learned. But three days passed without word, three days in the Bronx House of Detention, sharing a tiny cell with an accused burglar and a just convicted murderer awaiting shipment upstate. The three men barely talked, ignored one another, turned inward, reflecting on their own misery. They were transients. There was no point in trying to form relationships.

He thought about praying for the little girl and rejected the idea. He would have been praying for himself really—and he knew that wouldn't work at all anyway. Rationally, it was a long time since he believed in anything. And emotionally, the God who was buried in his heart from childhood was too stern and unforgiving and just to be a source of either solace or hope.

Hour after hour, sitting in that cell, he reflected on the fact that he was guilty, that he was responsible for whatever had happened, and that if there was any justice in his case, he would have to be punished severely. It seemed wiser not to pray.

It was equally pointless to hope for a break, for leniency or a stroke of good luck. He had long since exhausted any allotment of good luck to which he might be entitled. He had avoided jail once by agreeing to enlist in the Army, and that had seemed like luck at the time. It had been a common plea bargain offer in those Vietnam days. You signed your enlistment papers and the charges were dropped. The recruiting sergeant had been right in the courtroom ready to take his signature, and his lawyer, the DA, and the judge had all told him how lucky he had been. Some luck. Basic training followed by eighteen months in 'Nam.

Then there had been Emily, and that had surely been more luck than anyone deserved. He could never understand why she loved him. She had been working as a shop girl, let him move in with her, bought him clothes, and kept him in spending money. She had been too good. He had loved her and he had cheated on her—stupidly—with one of her cousins. She had thrown him out, cut him off cold. Which was no less than he deserved. And after six years, the ache of what he had lost was still with him. He wasn't sure that he really wanted any more luck.

On the fourth day of his detention he learned that he had been indicted, charged with robbery one, attempted murder, assault one, and possession of a weapon. And that meant that the girl had not died.

He told his legal aid lawyer, a new one this time, to find out what kind of deal he could make right up front. He could see no point in waiting around in the Bronx House or at Riker's, hoping for a better break somewhere down the line, or maybe an acquittal at trial.

"Twelve years indeterminate sentence, with a minimum of four years, that's the best I can do for you now," the lawyer reported back to him. "I might be able to do better in a few weeks if we let it string along, because the DA's got a real bad backlog, and he's eager to dispose of cases. I suggest that you turn it down, because if worse comes to worst, you can always take the twelve to four later on. The offer won't be withdrawn."

"What exactly does 'twelve to four' mean?" he asked. "How long before I get out?"

"It means you've got to do four years before you're eligible for parole, and realistically, it means that you'll do between five and one-half and seven years before you are paroled."

"I'll take it," he said.

Four and a half years later.

It started as a lump, as a kind of mass or ridge in his abdomen. One day he was fine, doing push-ups in his cell, reasonably well adjusted, speculating about his chances when his case came up before the parole board. The next day it was there, a lump, something that didn't belong. He felt no pain, no pressure, no distress. He tried to ignore it, tried to convince himself that it was nothing serious, that it would go away. But it didn't. His fingers kept returning to the spot, always poking, probing, trying to understand, to measure what was there. For two weeks he kept waiting for it to grow or shrink, kept waiting to feel pain, to feel something. Nothing.

He avoided sick call, afraid to share with others the knowledge of the lump, afraid of forcing the issue, afraid of what he might learn, preferring to live with his uncertainty. But in the end he conquered his fears and went on call, reasoning that if there was something wrong his chances were better the sooner it was caught and treated. Then again, if he were okay, he might as well know that and stop worrying. In any event, at Attica they ran tests, and without ceremony, shipped him off to Buffalo for exploratory surgery.

He awoke slowly from the general anesthesia, slowly realizing where he was, and why he was there. He was still too sedated to feel any pain. What he did feel was a sense of relief almost bordering on elation. He was alive and now everything would work out fine. Maybe even the fact of the operation could be turned to his advantage. Maybe he could play it up to the parole board, work up a little sympathy, buy himself a ticket out of the can. It seemed a distinct possibility. He had no way of knowing that the surgeons had merely opened him up, taken a look, and closed him back up again. Cancer. Probably primary to the pancreas. He was as good as dead to the surgeons. A five-year life expectancy that approached zero. They just sewed him up.

The news was broken to him bluntly by a young doctor. He took it well.

"I'm afraid I've got bad news for you."

"Yeah," he answered, searching the doctor's face, looking for clues.

"When we operated on you yesterday, we found a malignant growth on your pancreas. It's begun to spread, and we could not remove it all."

He continued to stare at the doctor, scrutinizing the surgeon's face. The doctor waited for the prisoner to react. He met and held his patient's stare. He could see that the man understood what had been said, that he understood its implications. There was nothing more that needed to be said, and for a few moments nothing was said. There passed between the two men, the black prisoner and the white doctor, a wave of mutual understanding, of mutual sympathy. They tried to hold it, did for a while, then lost it. They had to fall back on speech, an inferior means of communication. For another hour the doctor sat down and described the various options for therapy. He described radiation therapy and chemotherapy, their advantages and their drawbacks. He made recommendations. The patient listened, and asked intelligent questions. He showed almost no emotion, or at least expressed none.

The pathology report came back, and it made no sense. The oncologist read it, reread it, and then went down to the lab to take a look at the slides himself. The primary cancer cells came from the pancreas, much as the surgeon had expected. But they were the wrong type of cells. The cells he saw under his microscope were of a type that was virtually unheard of in men this patient's age. This was a type of cancer that was reported to occur in older individuals, in people over fifty. This man was in his early thirties. He went to the literature to double check, wondering if he might be mistaken, checking to see if there were any cases that he was unaware of. There weren't.

The mystery of this old man's cancer in a young man's body intrigued the oncologist. It might be an aberration, an unexplained fluke. But then again, maybe there was something to it, something unique in the patient's history or makeup to explain the phenomenon. He had colleagues reexamine the slides to reconfirm the pathological findings. They did, and it all checked out. The mystery remained, and the decision was made to conduct a full-scale investigation. Arrangements were made to keep the prisoner at the hospital longer than his medical condition strictly warranted.

They gave him an exhaustive series of medical examinations and could find nothing to explain the presence of the disease. Then they pored over his sparse medical history, finding again nothing to arouse suspicion. He had always enjoyed good health. There was nothing in his family history.

The oncologist spent a lot of time with the prisoner, asking questions, probing for possible answers.

"Did you ever work in the nuclear energy industry or around radiation or X rays of any kind?"

"No."

"Not even in the Army?"

"Nah."

"What about chemicals? Did you ever work in a factory that used chemicals in their production process? How about that?"

"No. I never worked in no factory at all."

"Did you ever work with asbestos, or in any situation where you were exposed to mineral or fibrous dusts?"

"I don't think so."

"What about drugs? Did you ever take any drugs?"

The prisoner smiled. "A little pot, man. I used that from time to time. Nothing heavier."

It was the doctor's turn to smile. "No, I meant did you ever take any drugs for medical purposes?"

"Not really, 'cause I've never been sick enough to need anything. In fact, the only drugs like that that I ever dropped was the stuff they gave us in 'Nam to make sure that we didn't get none of those jungle diseases. There were these little blue pills we were supposed to take every day. A lot of the guys didn't take them, figuring that maybe some chills or fevers was better than fighting. Personally, I couldn't see it. So I just took those pills an' didn't get sick."

The oncologist went back to the prisoner's military medical records and reread them, looking for a reference to some kind of medication administered prophylactically against one or more tropical diseases. He expected to find that he had taken a quinine derivative to ward off malaria, something routine that couldn't possibly be related to the prisoner's condition. What he found though was something entirely different, something that made the mystery even deeper. For instead of quinine or any of the routine tropical disease prophylactics, the prisoner had been given a daily dose of a drug called Trioxsone, a drug the oncologist had never heard of.

The doctor searched the literature for Trioxsone and was horrified by what he found. It turned out that the drug was experimental, powerful, and largely untested. It had been used with some success to treat certain of the more exotic tropical diseases, but it had not, as far as he could discover, ever been used as a preventative. He could not believe that the United States Army had administered such a drug to its servicemen. It was just impossible. But that's what the medical record said.

Then he found the article in an obscure research journal. "Trioxsone a Probable Cause of Abdominal Cancer in Male Rats" its subtitle read. Going on, he learned that several hundred white rats had been fed massive doses of Trioxsone, doses a thousand times higher per unit of body weight than those reportedly administered to the prisoner. What the article's author had discovered was a virtual epidemic of abdominal and intestinal cancers in the male rats who had been administered the drug. For some unexplained reason there was no incidence of the disease in female rats. More importantly, it was discovered that upon autopsy, the pathological examination of the rats' tumors had revealed cancer cells substantially identical to those the oncologist had found on the slides taken from the prisoner's biopsy.

The coincidence made the oncologist's blood run cold. He didn't want to think about the implications.

After a sleepless night, the doctor decided to call a friend at the Armed Forces Institute of Pathology. Their tumor registry was the largest in the country, and if there was any place that would know if there was an unusual incidence of cancer in Vietnam veterans who had taken Trioxsone, that was it. Such information would surely be available on their computers.

His friend was noncommittal. "That's an interesting possible relationship you've got there," he told the oncologist. "I don't believe that I've ever come across anything like it down here. But then again, no one here has been looking for a relationship like that, so I suppose it's possible that there are other similar cases floating around."

"Well, can you goose your computers and see what comes out?" the oncologist asked.

"Sure. I don't think that I'll have any trouble getting clearance to run a check. I'll probably have an answer for you in a week or so."

And then three weeks went by with no answer. The oncologist finally called his friend to see what was doing.

"I can't talk to you about Trioxsone," his friend told him. "When I put in my routine request to run the check you suggested, it was as if I was trying to get ahold of state secrets or something. It turns out that Trioxsone is a classified subject. It falls under some label called a National Defense Health Emergency, which means that I can't find out about it, and even if I could, I couldn't talk to you about it. Sorry that I can't help you."

The oncologist decided to tell the prisoner of his suspicions.

"I can't prove this," he told the prisoner, "but I think that your cancer might have been caused by the drugs you were given in Vietnam. Those blue pills you took were experimental. They shouldn't have given them to you without warning you that they might have been dangerous. Anyway, we now know that these drugs cause cancer in test animals. It probably caused your cancer too."

It took the prisoner a while to digest what the doctor was telling him. And at first, when he did understand, it didn't seem very important. What the hell difference did it make anyway where the origins of his death lay? It couldn't be undone. There was nothing tangible to hate, no individual villain to focus on or to retaliate against. It almost seemed better to ignore or forget what the doctor had said. What the hell difference did it make anyway?

The parole board cut him loose at the earliest possible moment. With a cancer death sentence irrevocably imposed, the humane (and the least expensive) thing to do was to send him home to the Bronx.

The idea of going to see a lawyer came from a neighbor.

"I had appendicitis once, an' I went to Hunts Point Hospital complainin' about a real bad pain in my belly. Anyway, this doctor took some tests an' told me to wait. An' while I was waitin' some nurse came around an' told me to go home an' take Alka-Seltzer, told me all I had was an upset stomach. So I went home an' my appendix burst. I came real close to dyin', an' I had to spend six weeks in the hospital. They even had to operate twice to drain out all the poison that was in me.

"Anyway, I got me this real smart Jew lawyer from downtown, a fella that my wife's girl friend knew about. I got him to take my case, an' I'll be damned if he didn't get the hospital to pay me seventy-five thousand big ones for what they did to me. I actually saw forty-five thousand, after you took away lawyers' fees and expenses. I mean what I'm sayin' is that maybe you ought to go see this lawyer about this cancer that your ma says the Army made you get. Maybe you can get him to take up your case. He's real smart, and he can probably get you an' your ma a whole lot of money. His name's Sabotnik. Wait a minute. I'll go next door an' get you his address an' phone number."

Once a week he went downtown to get an injection. Then one day, after the injection, without making an appointment, he went to see the lawyer.

2

Sabotnik and his wife had just finished approving plans for their son's bar mitzvah. They had met with the caterer, the florist, and the photographer. They had hired a four-man band and purchased a copious amount of liquor. Engraved invitations would soon be mailed out to almost three hundred guests. They estimated that more than two hundred fifty would attend.

Sabotnik knew that his only son's bar mitzvah would be a grotesque, vintage, Westchester County Reform Judaism-type affair. The services would be mercifully short, conducted largely in English, and generally inoffensive. It would be followed by a sumptuous buffet of herring, whitefish, and lox, served with bagels and challah and pumpernickel. There would be cakes and wines and champagne punch too. The kiddush would be open to the entire congregation, as well as the invited guests.

Later, in the evening, would be the reception. They had reserved the main hall of their country club for the affair. It would start with another enormous buffet, this time of hot hors d'oeuvres, followed by a multi-course sit-down dinner. They had inevitably opted for only the best, for caviar and filet mignon, for imported French wine. After dinner there would be Viennese tables loaded with pastries. Brandies and cordials would be served, and expensive South American cigars would be distributed to the men. The women would politely fight over who would get to take home the fancy floral arrangements that would serve as a centerpiece for each table.

The bar mitzvah, or at least the form it was to take, was largely for his wife's parents. They had an image of what an ideal bar mitzvah should be, a stereotyped unimaginative image that was very important to them precisely because they had never had the means to provide such celebrations for their own sons. Now Sabotnik would give them, and their oldest grandson, the bar mitzvah that they desired. It was a mark of his own maturity, of his basic kindness, that Phil Sabotnik was willing to compromise his sensibilities and throw an affair that would give his in-laws pleasure. Marilyn, his wife, understood this, even if they never talked about it. After many years of marriage, this kindness and willingness to compromise were the main reasons why she still loved him deeply, perhaps even more deeply than when they had married.

It was Stewie, his son, who violently resented the plans being made on his behalf. He was twelve and a half, tall, gangly, all knees, elbows, and ankles, nearsighted and self-conscious. He was a sensitive kid, bright, a good student, but painfully shy and introspective. The prospect of getting up in a synagogue in front of a couple of hundred of his parents' and grandparents' friends, and having to chant some gibberish in Hebrew had him mortified. He had refused outright to have any part of it.

Sabotnik spent two solid evenings talking it over with his son. They had a good relationship, an ability to talk, to communicate not only words, but emotions. And there was a basic sympathy that lay between them. It was not Sabotnik's way to force his will on the boy. Instead, he took the time to talk it out. He tried to persuade his son to do the right thing. It was something Sabotnik was good at. He was a very persuasive man.

"You know, Stewie," he told the boy, "I think that I understand how you feel about this thing, because I can remember how I felt when I was your age. I didn't want to be bar mitzvahed either. I thought that it would be stupid, and I thought that it would be hypocritical for me to get up there and say all those prayers that I didn't believe in. I refused to go through with it."

"So what did you do?" the boy asked, disarmed as he always was by his father's reasonableness.

"I was bar mitzvahed, of course." Sabotnik smiled as he said this. The boy smiled too. "And it was every bit as terrible as I was afraid that it might be. My voice must have cracked at least five or six times, and once I even forgot part of the Hebrew prayers I had memorized. I just stood there like a dummy until the rabbi had to whisper in my ear the words I had blocked. It was just a horror. But that was not even the worst of it.

"Can you keep a secret?"

"Sure."

"Okay. Then I'll tell you. The worst was that at my bar mitzvah, all my friends ended up learning what my Yiddish name was. It's Fievel, you know, and there I was, feeling like an idiot in the scratchy new woolen suit that I couldn't stand, with my best friends hanging around, while my grandmother and my great-aunts were all hugging me and kissing me and making a terrible fuss, calling me Fievel this and Fievel that.

"Well, I don't have to tell you what happened next. My friends were laughing so hard that I think some of them ended up peeing in their pants. From then on my nickname at school and around the neighborhood was Fivey. I absolutely hated it but there wasn't a damned thing I could do about it. Fivey Sabotnik, just imagine. Even some of my teachers took to calling me that. And it wasn't until I graduated from high school and went away to college that I got away from that damned nickname. And I've stayed away from it ever since. Your mother is the only one who knows that I used to be called Fivey. Now you do too."

The boy understood what his father was trying to say. He was twelve and a half, and more than anything else he wanted to be like his father, to be self-confident and self-assured and successful. He was twelve and a half, and had not yet reached the age of revolt from parental authority. So, if his father had put up with the embarrassment of a bar mitzvah, if he had been humiliated and had survived the humiliation, well then he could do it too. That was the point, a point gently made, a point easily accepted. And the boy understood that he would go ahead with the bar mitzvah.

Cleveland Daniels looked dreadful when he arrived at Sabotnik and Horowitz's Madison Avenue offices without a prior appointment, asking if he could see Mr. Sabotnik.

"May I have your name, and can I know why you would like

to see him?" the receptionist asked politely. She was a long-time
employee, and was well trained to the idea that even the most
improbable or disreputable-looking individuals were potentially
important clients to a law firm specializing in the representation
of personal injury victims. Poor people, and black people, and
non-English-speaking people got hurt as often and as badly, or
more often and more badly, than the rich or the middle class.
Such business was to be encouraged. So she did not send him
away.

"My name is Daniels," the former soldier replied. "Mr. Sabotnik doesn't know who I am, but a neighbor of mine, Carlos
Vasquez, used to have Mr. Sabotnik as his lawyer. Now I've got
a law case that I'd like Mr. Sabotnik to handle for me."

It took the lawyer a few moments to remember the case.
Vasquez? Then it came to him. Vasquez against Hunts Point
Hospital, a medical malpractice case, a missed diagnosis on an appendicitis. There had been peritonitis and the man had nearly
died. Then after a stormy course he had achieved a pretty decent
recovery. It had been an open and shut case. One that he had settled quickly and for pretty good money. That had been five,
maybe even ten years earlier. Sabotnik had Daniels led into his
office.

The mark of impending death was visible to Sabotnik as he
scrutinized his prospective client. He could see the delineation of
the man's skull under the taut ashen black skin of his face.
Daniels' eyes were unnaturally bright as they stared back at him.
Sabotnik waited for Daniels to speak.

"Mr. Sabotnik, I want you to handle a law case for me. I've
got cancer and I'm dying and it's on account of what the Army
did to me in Vietnam. I want you to sue the Army for me."

Sabotnik spent the next three hours questioning Daniels
closely. The story he heard was implausible, and not that articu-
lately presented. It took him a while to understand precisely
what it was that the man was claiming. Still, when he had
finished, Sabotnik was convinced, at least, that Daniels was sincere, that he honestly believed that he was being killed by drugs
that had been administered to him in Vietnam. Moreover, his
story held together internally. He knew the name of the drug he

had taken, and more importantly, could give the names of the doctors who he claimed would support his story. Sabotnik tried to sum it up with a series of questions.

"So, Cleveland, let me be sure that I've got this all straight. You enlisted in the Army in late 1969?"

"That's right."

"You were in good health then?"

"Yes."

"And you went to Vietnam in early 1970?"

"That's right. In February 1970."

"And you were there for eighteen months?"

"Uh huh."

"And every day while you were there you were issued one capsule of this drug Trioxsone and were told that you had to take it in order to prevent catching some tropical diseases that were prevalent in Vietnam?"

"Yeah. There were little blue pills, and we weren't told to take them. We were ordered to take them. There was no choice about it. It was wartime, and we were ordered. We followed orders. I can even remember one lieutenant who told us that if we didn't take this stuff, and then came down with jungle fever, then we would get court-martialed or something and end up in the can."

"Did they ever warn you about this drug, tell you about possible side effects or warn you that it was experimental or anything like that?"

"No. They just said that we should take it. That's all."

"And you took Trioxsone for eighteen months?"

"Yes. Every day."

"And now you've got cancer. And it was first discovered a few months ago up in Buffalo?"

"Yes."

"And that was many years after the last time that you took Trioxsone?"

"Yeah."

"And you believe that Trioxsone caused your cancer?"

"That's right. Based on what the doctors told me. Based on the kind of cancer I've got, which is rare, and based upon the studies

they've done on animals which show that this drug causes my
kind of cancer."

"And these doctors are the ones whose names you gave me?"

"Yeah."

The lawyer paused. It was early, but he knew already that he
had reached a turning point. Instinct told him that if he was
going to reject the case, and there were lots of good reasons why
the case should be rejected, he should do so now. He had learned
years before that it was best to say no quickly, to say no before
there were any expectations or commitments, to say no before an
identification with an unfortunate client began to blind him to
the improbabilities of success, to say no before wasting valuable
money, and even more valuable time, tilting at legal windmills. It
was this ability to say no that had helped Sabotnik and Horowitz
grow into one of the most successful personal injury firms in the
city, this ability to know which cases to take and which to let go
that was a secret of their success.

And this was a case to say no to. It would be a horribly expensive case to prosecute, expensive in both dollars and manpower.
Right off the bat he could think of a dozen legal and factual
reasons why the case was bound to fail. He knew of no legal
precedent that would allow an ex-serviceman to sue the government for wrongs committed more than a decade earlier, in a
wartime context, overseas. Moreover, he doubted that he would
be able to prove scientifically to the satisfaction of either a judge
or a jury that Trioxsone was the cause of Daniels' particular
cancer. He would have to prove not that it might be the cause,
or could be the cause; but with a reasonable degree of medical
certainty, that it was the cause. Even if he avoided the problem
of suing the government and found a way to go after the company that manufactured the drug instead, Sabotnik knew that
this causation problem would probably be insurmountable.

It was definitely a case to say no to, a bad business venture to
undertake. Sabotnik understood this almost instinctively in the
few seconds of that pause. But he also understood as he sat there
looking at this ex-soldier, ex-convict, ex-patient, soon to be
corpse, that he would not and could not turn him away. In part

it was curiosity, nothing more than a simple need to know if
what Cleveland Daniels said was true. He needed to know if the
United States Government had deliberately permitted tens or
even hundreds of thousands of its young men to serve as unwit-
ting guinea pigs in what was in effect a drug experiment. Having
lived through Vietnam, My Lai, and Watergate, he knew that it
was possible; thought it even probable, that Daniels' allegations
were true. Still he wanted to find out for himself.

But there was something more, something distinct from
curiosity, distinct from a need to find the truth, that struck at the
lawyer. It was a sense that this case was different, a sense that
after many years of successful but essentially mundane legal
practice, at last something had come along that would permit him
to do something of public importance. Here was a case that might
go all the way to the Supreme Court of the United States, a
case that might make a new law, that might lead to the pro-
nouncement of some important legal principle about the rights of
veterans and the responsibilites of government. Sabotnik had
never once handled a case that had even the most remote chance
of going all the way to the Supreme Court. His practice had
been primarily in the New York State courts, doing cases that
might be factually interesting, but were hardly the sort to
create new legal precedents. Sabotnik relished the prospect of
perhaps making new law, of arguing a landmark case. The idea
excited him. It was a long time since he had been excited by anything about a new case.

So Sabotnik paused. But even as he paused, he knew that he
would go forward. It was not so much a rational balancing of
pros and cons as an emotional thing. He would go forward.
Sabotnik looked at his new client.

"Okay, Cleveland," the lawyer said. "What I'm going to need
from you now are signed authorizations that will permit me to
obtain your hospital records and which will also give your doctors permission to talk to me about your condition."

"Sure," the former soldier replied. "Where do I sign?"

"Right here," Sabotnik answered, handing him a dozen authorizations. "You will see that these forms will also let me get your

military and prison records, as well as school records and any tax returns that you filed."

"I only filed maybe two or three tax returns since I left the Army. Lots of years I just didn't bother. Does that make a difference?"

"No, not really. It just means that we can't really press a serious claim for lost earnings. As a practical matter, if I can prove that your cancer was caused by the Army, then your case will be plenty big without proving a penny of lost income. Don't worry about that."

"Sure."

"Look, it's going to take me at least a month, maybe more, to get all of your records, and to do all the legal and medical research that I'm going to have to do before I can decide whether or not I think it makes sense for me to be your lawyer. Then, if I decide that it makes sense to go ahead, I will ask you to sign a retainer which will permit me to represent you."

"You know I can't pay you anything for being my lawyer. I haven't got a cent."

"Of course you don't. I know that. But that's not the way the retainer works anyway. What we charge is called a contingent fee, which means that we take as a fee a one-third percentage of whatever you recover. That way if we get you nothing, our fee is nothing; if we get you three dollars, our fee is a dollar; and if we get you three million dollars, our fee is a million dollars. In other words, the better you do, the better we do."

"I see."

"It also means," the lawyer went on, "that if I'm willing to take your case on, and am willing to take it on a contingent basis, that is the best proof that I think your case is a good one. Otherwise, you know damn well that I wouldn't consent to spend my time on it. If I charged you by the hour, like the big Wall Street firms do, then I could diddle you around for months on a crummy case, just to run up a big bill. You can be sure that I'm not about to do that with you or with any of my contingent fee clients.

"Anyway, after I get your records, I will be in a position to make a decision. Then, if we reach that point, I will ask you to sign a retainer. When that happens we'll go over everything in detail."

Sabotnik rose then, and the two men shook hands. Daniels' grip was still reasonably strong.

The records when they finally came in confirmed the facts that Cleveland Daniels had asserted. The military records revealed that he had been given Trioxsone daily as a prophylaxis against tropical fever. They also confirmed that the drug had been administered on a mandatory basis, and completely without warnings as to possible side effects, or of its experimental nature.

And Trioxsone was experimental. That fact Sabotnik had determined the very day after Daniels had first visited him. He sent a paralegal up to the medical library at Mount Sinai, and had her photocopy all the literature she could find on the drug. From it he learned that Trioxsone had only been synthesized in the research laboratories of the Lefcourte Drug Company in 1961. Lefcourte Laboratories, he knew, was a major subsidiary of Transcontinental Communications, one of the giant conglomerates. In any event, it turned out that in preliminary laboratory testing, there had been indications that Trioxsone might prove to be a highly potent multi-purpose antibacterial wonder drug. It was found to be particularly effective in preventing and treating certain of the nastier strains of tropical fever, strains that had proven resistant to more traditional therapies and preventatives. The early literature was, to put it mildly, high on the product's potential.

Then there was a gap in the literature. After the glowing preliminaries, for several years, indeed, for almost a decade, there were no articles. There were no follow-up studies, and there was not even an indication that the drug had ever been licensed or approved by the FDA for domestic use. In fact, the Physicians Desk Reference, published annually with the cooperation of the drug companies, which listed all drugs that they manufactured for public consumption along with their uses, side effects, indications, and contraindications, had no entry at all for Trioxsone from 1960 to the most recent edition. The drug, Sabotnik learned, had never been licensed.

Then he found the article that Daniels had told him he would find. It was in a fairly obscure research journal; nevertheless, the findings were unequivocal. Studies in male rats revealed that Trioxsone was a powerful carcinogen. The drug caused abdominal cancers in these rats, unusual cancers that were unusual in part because they developed far earlier in the rats' lives than would otherwise be expected. It was precisely as Daniels had said it would be.

Sabotnik telephoned Daniels' doctor in Buffalo. After a bit of coaxing the oncologist finally opened up to him.

"It's a damned suspicious case," the doctor said. "If you're asking me to state as a scientist that Trioxsone is the cause of Cleveland Daniels' disease, I can't do that. Theoretically, lots of things cause cancer, and I can't very well tell you that Trioxsone, just because it is one of the things that cause this disease, has to be the cause of Daniels' disease. I can't do it. It's just suspicious, that's all."

"Well, doctor," Sabotnik pressed on, "would you say that it is probable that there is a causal relationship between the drug and the disease? Because, you know, in the law, I don't have to prove to a total certainty that the drug caused the cancer in order to make out a case. All I have to show is that it is probable, or reasonably likely, that it did. If I can do that, then I have upheld my burden of proof, and my client can recover. Is it probable that Trioxsone caused Cleveland Daniels' cancer?"

The doctor hedged. "I don't know," he told the lawyer. "You have to remember that we're talking about a single isolated case here. And that's just not enough to base any kind of valid scientific judgment on. I'll admit that Daniels' cancer is an improbable one, and when you're dealing with the statistics of rare events, it doesn't take too much to establish a presumptive causal relationship. Still, just one case won't do it for me. Show me one or two more ex-servicemen who took Trioxsone and developed the same type of malignancy that Daniels and the rats developed, and then you've got something different. Then I would say that any scientist would concede the causal relationship."

"Well, doctor," Sabotnik pressed on, "didn't you try to determine whether there were other cases like Daniels' floating around?"

"As a matter of fact, I did. There are no reported cases in the literature like the Daniels case. You know that."

"Yes I do," the lawyer answered.

"Well, the next thing I did was to call Washington and talk to a friend I've got at the national tumor registry that the military keeps. They've got about the most complete set of records on rare tumors anywhere in the world. Anyway, I described the Daniels case to my friend and I told him about my suspicions concerning Trioxsone. I asked him to check up on it and see if he could find evidence of any similar cases of cancer involving young Vietnam veterans who had taken Trioxsone. He said he would check it out."

"And what happened then?"

"When he didn't get back to me in three weeks, I tried reaching him again. When I did he acted very strange. I asked him if he had run the computer check I had asked for, and he just fudged. He wouldn't say yes and he wouldn't say no. Instead, he just told me to drop the subject. What he implied was that it was already being studied in house by the military, and that I would do well to stay out of the whole subject. Anyway, I couldn't get him to say whether there were other cases or not. It was all very strange."

Sabotnik filed Freedom of Information Act requests with the Food and Drug Administration, the Department of Health, Education and Welfare, the Department of Defense, and the Department of the Army. He made his requests as thorough and as specific as he could, asking for every possible document he could think of concerning Trioxsone. He asked for records relating to Lefcourte Laboratories' initial application to the FDA for permission to test Trioxsone. He asked for the results of these preliminary tests. He asked for any memoranda or correspondence from any of the agencies concerning the decision to use Trioxsone in Vietnam, and he asked for correspondence between Lefcourte and the agencies concerning the same subject. He asked for the financial statements showing how much federal money Lefcourte received for supplying Trioxsone to the military. He asked for records of any preliminary studies run by the military considering the advisability of using Trioxsone in Vietnam, as well as all reports of studies showing the actual effects, if any, Trioxsone had on the soldiers who had taken it. He asked specifically for any reports of cancers that had developed in these soldiers, and for the specific types of tumors that had been developed. He drafted his requests with special care, and then mailed them by certified mail to each of the agencies. He knew that it would be at least a month, probably longer, before he could expect any type of reply. He fully expected that much of what he was seeking would be denied him on one pretext or another. He would probably have to go into court to try to get what he wanted.

In the weeks that followed, Sabotnik began to do the legal research necessary to put together a lawsuit on behalf of Cleveland Daniels. He was in court most days, trying or preparing his bread and butter personal injury cases for trial. And early evenings he would disappear into the Bar Association Library to pursue his legal research. Two hours a night he gave it, from five-thirty to seven-thirty. Then he would run to catch his train out of Grand Central Station for Scarsdale. He sat down to dinner at nine, and by ten-thirty he was in bed asleep.

He started from scratch, reading dozens of law review articles, an equal number of learned treatises, and literally hundreds of leading appellate decisions. From the outset he knew that he would have to construct novel and compelling legal theory if his case was going to pass muster, not only at the trial level, but also at the appellate level. He had a hell of a fact pattern to work with. What had been done to Cleveland Daniels and the other soldiers was unique and horrible. It cried out for legal remedy. But that did not mean that there would be a remedy. The courts were conservative, Sabotnik knew. And they would not be apt to give Daniels relief, certainly not against the United States Government, unless Sabotnik could provide them with an awfully compelling argument for doing so. He warmed to the task. It took him back to his law school days, to a time when he had been trained to think in broad social terms, to think of constitutional doctrines, and of making a difference to the world at large. It was an exciting prospect, and soon it became an obsession.

One night over dinner, Marilyn finally put her foot down.

"It's been three weeks now that you've been coming in late. I barely get to talk to you and you fall asleep," she complained. "I'm not running a boardinghouse or a hotel here. And I'd like to maybe have you home at a reasonable hour so that we could spend a quiet evening together. And I think the kids would like to see a little more of you too."

Sabotnik tried to explain to her about the Daniels case, tried to explain about the legal theories he was constructing.

"You remember the case I told you about, the one about the soldier who took that drug in Vietnam and developed cancer ten years later."

"Yes, of course."

"Well, I've been trying to figure out a way to sue the United States over that. Because there's an old rule that you cannot sue the government unless it consents to be sued. It's a doctrine called sovereign immunity, and it goes back to old English days, to the time when it was thought that the king could do no wrong. Anyway, the government has never consented to let itself be sued by servicemen like Daniels, not for something that was done to them while they were on active duty, let alone in combat. I've got to find a way to get around that."

"I see. Well, have you found a way?"

"I think so. I mean I think I've found an argument that may do the trick. At least it's one that won't get thrown out of court right away."

"So what's the argument? Are you going to keep me in suspense?"

"No. What I've come up with is a class action. I'm going to sue on behalf of all the soldiers who were forced to take the drug. And what I'm going to do is not ask for money damages for all of them. Instead, I'm going to ask the courts to force the government to warn the soldiers that they've been exposed to the risk of cancer. Then I want them to provide free medical examinations to any soldier who wants one. And I want them to treat any of the soldiers who have cancer free of charge. What I'm going to ask the court to do is to make the government try to save some of the lives it put in jeopardy."

"But how does that get around that sovereign immunity rule you told me about?"

"I'm going to do that by basing the lawsuit on the Constitution itself. Instead of calling this a regular tort case based on negligence and the common law I'm going to claim that what the government did here was a violation of the Bill of Rights, especially a violation of the Fifth Amendment right to life and liberty. Hopefully, I will be able to persuade the courts that the need to safeguard basic constitutional freedoms is paramount even over sovereign immunity or over the law that usually gives the military immunity over servicemen. You see the beauty of my class action theory is that what I'm seeking is so reasonable and so just that the government is going to look just horrible when it opposes us. And who knows, I just might win."

"But what about your client, this guy Daniels? He's not going to get anything out of the class action, is he? I mean, he already knows that he has cancer, so a warning isn't going to do him any good. And you told me he's getting top-notch treatment, so he doesn't need that either. What is he going to get out of all this?"

"I'm going to sue the government for money for him too. But there I think that my chances are pretty poor. It is one thing to ask the courts to try to force the government to save lives, and it's another thing to ask them to make it pay money. I'll probably lose that one but I'll try. Anyway, I can also sue the drug company for money damages too. There are legal difficulties in doing that, but it is a lot more likely to succeed."

As they were talking Marilyn began to clear the dinner dishes off the table. Sabotnik got up to help her, and as he did she stepped up to him and kissed him, pressed her body against his.

Their son was upstairs, doing his homework. Their daughter was at a girl friend's house. He put his arms around her, held her close.

Sam Horowitz was more difficult to persuade than Marilyn had been. Horowitz was the other managing partner of Sabotnik and Horowitz. He was also Phil Sabotnik's best friend. They had started the practice together many years earlier, and they had struggled, scratched, clawed, together, and built a law firm of twenty-five lawyers that was one of the best personal injury firms in New York. It was a firm to be proud of. They had made a lot of money together, and that was important to two poor Jewish kids from the Bronx who had been born during the Depression. They had made a good life for themselves, made a good life for their wives and children, practicing law. They had made it cleanly, representing people who were injured, people who needed help. But they had not made it tilting at windmills. They had not made it taking matters like the Daniels case.

"What do you need the aggravation for?" Horowitz asked. "The way you outline it this case is an absolute loser, no question about it. I mean for Christ's sake, do you think that you're gonna get around the sovereign immunity problem to get to Uncle Sam's pocketbook? You know better than that. And then there is a statute of limitations problem too. This soldier, you told me, took this drug for the last time over ten years ago. I don't know about anywhere else, but here in New York the statute of limitations for this case expired at least seven years ago. I don't think you can even sue the drug company. Besides, if I understand you, we don't even have hard proof that this guy's cancer had to be caused by this drug. So what the hell do you need the aggravation for? Let's just keep to what we know, and make ourselves a living."

Horowitz was a very good lawyer, and he was right. Sabotnik understood this, and his efforts to persuade his partner that it was good business to start the Daniels case were weak. He tried to say that there would be good publicity that would come from the case, that the publicity would attract other, more profitable cases, that the chances of winning the Daniels case were not that hopeless, that if they did win, that the pay-off in fees would be enormous. He made the arguments, and as he made them, he knew them to be unpersuasive. Nevertheless, he knew that he would go forward and start the Daniels case. He stared directly at Horowitz.

"Sam, I really want to do this case. Even if it is bad business I'm going to do it."

And there the discussion ended. There was too much between the two men for either to deny a strong wish of the other. Seven years earlier, at a Las Vegas convention of trial lawyers, Sabotnik had watched Horowitz start an affair with a young psychologist who had been lecturing the group on the subject of post-traumatic neuroses. The woman had for a time become Horowitz's mistress, and Sabotnik had helped him to hide the fact from his wife, had even permitted him to use the firm's money to support the affair. Sabotnik had concealed these facts from Marilyn, knowing that the secret of Horowitz's infidelity would not be safe with her. The affair was now long over, mostly forgotten, never discussed, and as far as Sabotnik could tell, his partner was once again a faithful family man. Still, it was unlikely that Horowitz would ultimately attempt to refuse his friend the chance to pursue the Daniels case. There was too much friendship, trust, and obligation for it to be otherwise. Sabotnik's decision settled the matter.

Two days later Cleveland Daniels returned to the lawyers' offices and signed a retainer. The following day a complaint was filed in the United States District Court for the Southern District of New York.

Sabotnik sent one of his office boys down to the court with the typed complaint, and told him to return as soon as it was filed with the slip bearing the name of the judge who was assigned to the case. There were twenty-five different judges in the district just then, and the assignment would be made at random, the name pulled out of a drum.

In a case like this it made an enormous difference which judge was drawn. It was crucial to have a judge with the courage to

break new ground, and with the independence to be willing to
challenge the government. He needed a judge with the intellect
and the legal skills to write a good opinion, the kind of opinion
that would pass muster before the appellate courts. There were
only a handful among the group that Sabotnik would have preferred. Most of the others, for one reason or another, would be
disasters, would tie his case up in knots, or write bad decisions,
or would laugh him out of court. He waited anxiously for the
office boy to return.

   *Cleveland Daniels, Individually and on Behalf of all Those
Similarly Situated* -against- *the United States of America and
Lefcourte Laboratories,* the title of the complaint read. Next to
the caption the court clerk stamped a notice which stated that
the case had been assigned for all purposes to United States District Judge Mary Ann Salisbury.

3

The *Wall Street Journal* was in the process of preparing a
lengthy front page profile on George Petrakis. An artist had
been around to do a pen and ink line drawing to accompany the
article. The result had been flattering. He had paid the artist a
thousand dollars for the signed original. Then he filed it away.
He would not frame it, let alone display the portrait in any of
his offices. That was not his style.

   Neither was being the subject of a front page article in the
Journal part of his style. He had spent twenty good years amass-
ing wealth and power in relative anonymity. He had been a troubleshooter and a string puller; and he had seen others attract
public attention, and then envy, troubles, and sometimes disaster.
He had no desire for public recognition or fame. He could
remain quite happily in the shadows, thank you.

   Still, publicity had become unavoidable. He would have to
learn to submit to its discipline. For in less than four weeks

Petrakis would assume the reins as the chief executive officer at
Transcontinental Communications, a giant conglomerate that
was, at that moment, the eighteenth largest business enterprise in
the Free World. Like it or not, he was about to become a public
figure.

There were three messages waiting for Petrakis at the corporate
headquarters offices downtown on John Street. They were all
from Lawrence MacCauley, and they all repeated that it was urgent that he speak with Petrakis immediately. Petrakis made a
face as he crumpled the messages up and threw them away. Mac-
Cauley's messages were always urgent. He always needed to
speak to you immediately. Everything with him was a crisis, a
crisis that he would invariably be too weak to deal with. It was
Petrakis' intention to fire him. Soon.

MacCauley was a retired career air force officer, a brigadier
general. He was also a licensed medical doctor, who had held
high positions in the military health establishments. For the past
ten years he had been an executive officer at Lefcourte Laboratories. Now he was its president. Lefcourte Laboratories was one
of Transcontinental's most profitable subsidiaries. It was Petrakis'
considered belief that the drug company's healthy profit margin
occurred in spite of the best efforts of Lawrence MacCauley.

MacCauley's fourth call was not long in coming. Petrakis did
not duck it.

"George, we've got a big problem," MacCauley began. "One
lawsuit just got filed today against Lefcourte and the United
States Government. It's being brought by some guy who claims
we gave him cancer."

"Yes, I see. But what's the big deal?" Petrakis said calmly, trying to remain patient and civil. "Lefcourte gets sued all the time.
Why don't you just notify your insurance carriers. I'm sure that
the people over at Lloyd's will know what to do with the lawsuit. For Christ's sake, they ought to, what with the insurance
premiums we pay them."

"But, George, listen to me. This one is different. I've already
talked to our insurance people, and to corporate counsel, and
even to some of the people over at Regis, McCormick, and Let-

terman, your old firm, and they've all warned me that this lawsuit could be real trouble. It involves the Trioxsone situation."

Petrakis felt a certain tightening in the back of his neck. Suddenly he became attentive. "What about it?" he asked.

"Well, this lawsuit isn't just for money like the usual case. It's also for something called equitable relief. The lawyers tell me that they want to force Lefcourte to warn all the Vietnam vets that Trioxsone may give them cancer, and to make us set up some kind of fund to pay for treatment of the ones who do get sick. It could cost us a fortune, and the worst part is that the lawyers say that this equitable relief may not even be covered by our insurance. Our insurance carrier over in London has been notified of this lawsuit and they say that they're looking into it. There's a chance that they may disclaim coverage, and force us to go to court with them over whether they have to defend us, and also on whether we or they have to pay if the case is lost. It's a real mess."

"Have you alerted your publicity people?" Petrakis asked.

"No."

"Well, I think that you had better get them ready to issue press releases denying these allegations. It's a fair bet that this lawsuit is going to be picked up by the media. Make sure the press releases point out how many lives our wonder drugs saved in Vietnam. Remember that publicity stunt where we gave free smallpox inoculations to those Vietnamese orphans? I think that it would be a good idea to throw that into the release to show us off in a better light."

"Yeah, that's a good idea," the former general replied. "I had forgotten all about that one."

"I thought that you might have," Petrakis said, his voice free of irony. "Anyway, get the publicity people working on it."

"Okay."

"By the way," Petrakis added, almost as an afterthought, "where does the government stand on all this? Has the Army been named as a defendant too? After all, they're the ones who actually bought Trioxsone and gave it to the soldiers. We just manufactured the stuff."

"The government is named. In fact they are the first-named

defendant. One of our lawyers has already spoken to the Justice Department about the case. They plan to fight it tooth and nail, he says. There's some legal doctrine that he said makes it impossible to sue the government."

"Sovereign immunity is the name of the doctrine," Petrakis said. "But don't be so sure that the government will be so great a co-defendant. I know the Justice Department well enough to know that they'll do what is politically expedient. And there are a lot of Vietnam vets out there. Some of them probably even vote. So I wouldn't be so confident that the government will be of any help to us. In fact I think that we'd better find some way of our own to make it politically expedient for them to fight tooth and nail as you so quaintly put it."

Petrakis spent a day mulling over the Trioxsone situation before taking action. There was no need to do anything precipitously. And the case was too potentially dangerous to make any snap decisions. It was dangerous in ways that he preferred not to think about, dangerous in a personal sense because he had actually been general counsel to Lefcourte Laboratories at the time the Trioxsone deal was cooked up. That was years earlier, before Nixon, and before Watergate, in another world, run by another set of values. The Trioxsone deal would not bear scrutiny, not any kind of scrutiny. It was too dangerous.

That evening Petrakis had an appointment to have dinner with his daughter, Diana. She was eighteen, a sophomore at Vassar College. She was to take the train down from Poughkeepsie and he was to meet her at Grand Central Station. He had made reservations at Lutèce, and afterwards they would go to Petrakis' Fifth Avenue duplex to talk. In the morning she would return to school.

Petrakis' wife was dead. It had not been an especially good marriage. Diana was different. She was her father's girl. The one being who had always ruled his heart. The only person who could consistently bring him pleasure, and the one person around whom he could truly relax. She was sharp, witty, sophisticated, and pretty. He treated her as an equal, loved her. And she loved him. The Trioxsone business ruined the prospect of her visit.

He spotted her across the station at just the same moment that she saw him. She ran toward him, hugged him and kissed him.

"Hi, Dad, what's doing?" she asked.

"Nothing much," he said. "Everything's been pretty dull around here. How are things at school?"

She spent the next three hours bringing Petrakis up to date on the latest doings on campus. He learned about her decision to major in English and he approved the decision. She discussed the political agitation that some gay liberation groups had been raising at some of the schools and they discussed lesbianism in general. They both agreed that they were tolerant, and that sexual preferences were matters of taste and style, and shouldn't be considered questions of morality or law. They rambled over a dozen similar subjects, and in the process she managed to completely divert Petrakis. It was only when he had kissed her good night and gone into his bedroom to sleep that he realized that he had a knot in the back of his neck, that his head ached. Sleep came slowly, fitfully.

The next morning Petrakis put in a call to Ed Regis, the senior partner at Regis, McCormick, and Letterman. Transcontinental was the law firm's largest single client, and annually paid to the firm anywhere from five to seven million dollars in legal fees. Regis, McCormick, and Letterman were corporate counsel for the conglomerate, they handled its financing, its antitrust work, its labor problems, and most of its major litigation. Transcontinental's legal needs kept no less than twenty-nine of the firm's two hundred fifteen lawyers gainfully employed on a full- or part-time basis. As a practical matter, Petrakis knew that Regis would do almost anything that Petrakis wished.

"Ed, I want to know everything that there is to know about this new Trioxsone lawsuit filed against Lefcourte. Send me copies of all the pleadings as they come in. But I want you to do it discreetly, without covering letter, so that there is no record of my interest in the case."

"Sure, George," the lawyer replied. He had heard such requests before. And knew not to ask questions. He had not risen to the head of a Wall Street firm by being indiscreet.

"Also," Petrakis went on, "I do not want any major decisions made in the case without my being consulted first."

"Fine."

"And I also want you to oppose absolutely granting any pretrial discovery in the case. Tie the other side up with procedural motions, and any other motions you guys can think of in order to slow things down. Bury the plaintiff in paper, move to dismiss, ask for a change of venue, ask for summary judgment. Just do whatever you can to tie them up."

"That's pretty much what I intended anyway," the lawyer replied affably.

"Good. But there's one thing that I want crystal clear. I was general counsel at Lefcourte during part of the relevant time period. Under no circumstances is my name to appear in any pleadings. I don't want any documents to be produced on which my name appears, and I will not permit myself to be deposed in this lawsuit. At all costs you must do that."

"Do you want me to try to settle the case?" the lawyer asked. "You know that the insurance people are being a little sticky about coverage and you might have to use corporate funds if you want to close this case down quickly and quietly. Is that what you want?"

"Yes. If it has to be, I will authorize the use of corporate funds."

"How much?" the lawyer asked.

"Try a half million up front. If that doesn't do it you have authority to go as high as a million. Wait until you've hit them with your motion practice and then open settlement. They'll be glad to settle rather than have to get into a paper-flinging contest with your firm.

"By the way," Petrakis asked as an afterthought, "who is the plaintiff's lawyer anyway? Maybe if he's small enough we can get away for less than half a million. Who is he?"

"Phil Sabotnik of Sabotnik and Horowitz. They're a pretty good Jewish personal injury—"

"I know who he is," Petrakis cut in abruptly, "I went to law school with him. In fact we lived in the same dormitory at one time. He's a nice fella."

"He's also a good lawyer, George. His complaint is ingenious and it could really give us fits, especially in front of the judge he drew."

"And who's that?"

"Mary Ann Salisbury. She's bright and she's liberal, George. She's not going to be especially sympathetic to our cause in this case. In fact, she could be quite a problem."

"I know Mary Ann," Petrakis said quietly. "I know her quite well. And I don't think that she will be a problem at all."

And then he said no more. Petrakis knew enough not to share with the lawyer what he knew of Mary Ann Salisbury, or even of Phil Sabotnik.

"I think that you had better hold off on offering any settlement money to Sabotnik for the time being." That was his final instruction to the lawyer.

4

Ted Murcer learned of his opportunity during a phone call from a senior member of the Senate Judiciary Committee. The senator called on his private line to Murcer's office at the Justice Department.

"Ted," he said, not bothering to identify himself, knowing that the Deputy Attorney General would recognize his voice, "I've got some information that should be of real interest to you. I learned it this morning from John Ryan, the lawyer I hired last year to be chief counsel to my environmental affairs subcommittee. A few years ago Ryan used to be a law clerk to Justice Smith, and apparently over the years he has remained close to the justice, and has continued to see him socially. Anyway, what

Ryan just told me was that Smith just spent two days at Walter Reed Medical Center undergoing tests."

"I think I know that."

"Yes, of course, everyone knows that. But what nobody knows is that the results of those tests were very bad. The prostate cancer that Smith was operated on for last year, that was supposed to be caught in time, has spread. Now his colon and spleen are involved, and there's nothing they can do. It's only a matter of time."

"I'm sorry to hear that," Murcer said sincerely. "Smith has been a good justice. I've always respected him."

"Yes, he is. And I'm sorry too," the senator said. "But I'm concerned right now with who will replace him. I would like to see you on the Supreme Court, Ted."

Murcer would have liked to have seen that too. The senator knew that, and Murcer knew that the senator knew it. They were old friends and political allies. "Is the justice planning to submit his retirement papers immediately?" the lawyer asked.

"I doubt it," the senator replied. "He is a pretty stubborn guy, and from what Ryan tells me, his inclination is to continue to work as long as he is physically able. Apparently he feels that he will spend his remaining time better working than he would in retirement feeling sorry for himself."

"I think he's right. I don't blame him at all."

"Sure, I don't blame him either. And frankly, I think that this hiatus can be put to advantage. I think that it is time for us to mount a campaign on the President to persuade him to appoint you to the Court. It ought to be fairly easy to get him to decide that a prominent member of his administration ought to be on the Court. You're a moderate, from the East, and you've got a strong law enforcement background. You've got no real enemies, so no one in the Senate is likely to get his nose too out of joint by your appointment. You would be a safe and I think a popular selection. I think that the nation is ready for some new blood on the Court."

"Maybe so."

"And besides," the senator went on, "it's become almost a tradition for presidents to put their high Justice Department people on the Supreme Court. White and Rhenquist were both at Justice, right?"

"Yes. So were Marshall and Burger at points in their careers."

"Yes. So I think that we've got a pretty good shot at putting you over. How are you getting along with the Attorney General these days?"

"Fine."

"What about the President? Have you had anything much to do with him?"

"Not really. But I'm certainly on good terms with him."

"How about the Bar Association types. Are any of them likely to oppose your appointment?"

"No. I don't think so. Although I've pretty much ignored most of the Bar Association bullshit."

"Well maybe you ought to butter them up over the next few months. Generally, you should keep your nose clean and not do anything to antagonize anyone. With a little bit of luck, we should be able to put this thing together."

Murcer learned about the Trioxsone case in Nancy Revering's bedroom.

Nancy Revering was twenty-seven. She had graduated with honors from Yale Law School, clerked for a federal district court judge in New Jersey, then joined the Justice Department's special litigation honors program. She had been assigned to a small group of attorneys who drew their assignments directly from the Deputy Attorney General. That's where she met Ted Murcer.

The first case she drew was the air force pap test affair. It was a nasty business involving a cytology laboratory in Illinois whose medical director had contracted with the Air Force to interpret roughly 150,000 pap test slides per year obtained from air force personnel and dependents. At over two dollars per slide it was a tidy contract.

Only the laboratory wasn't reading the slides. Or at least not 95 percent of them. Instead it reported the unread slides as negative and then charged for the work as if it had been done.

The lab director knew, of course, that cervical cancer is an asymptomatic disease in its early stages, that by the time it produces symptoms it is usually too far advanced to be cured. By thus reporting hundreds of thousands of unscreened slides as negative, the lab director was effectively guaranteeing that hundreds, or possibly thousands, of easily curable early stage cancers would not be diagnosed, that dozens or possibly scores of women would die terrible and unnecessary deaths.

For almost seven years the Air Force had permitted this laboratory to continue this practice. Seven years without even the most primitive effort to determine the quality of the work done by the laboratory, without spot checks, without anything. The scandal broke when a disgruntled employee at the laboratory blew the whistle.

Murcer had assigned the case to Nancy Revering for the simple reason that she was a woman. It was a woman's case, a case that would look good being handled by a woman. Murcer smelled that there might be political capital to be made out of the case.

She had worked like a demon. Fourteen, fifteen, sixteen hours a day. Six, seven days a week. She had gone into federal court and obtained a search warrant. She had gotten the FBI to swoop down on the laboratory to execute the warrant, and had seized almost two hundred thousand slides that were sitting around unscreened. She had organized a massive emergency rescreening operation at a dozen university medical centers, which led within six weeks to the proper diagnoses of all existing slides. She had worked tirelessly to see that all the women who had developed cancer were notified, and then received the best possible treatment.

She worked with lawyers from the local United States Attorney's Office setting up a grand jury investigation, which led quickly to an indictment of the director, and then to a trial, conviction, and a well-deserved prison sentence. And she set up a group of attorneys from the Civil Division to defend the damage actions that would inevitably follow from the families that were injured. She even managed to settle a substantial number of those cases before they got to court.

It was nearly two years of her life that Nancy Revering

devoted to the case. And in those two years she reported directly to Ted Murcer, brought her problems directly to him, sought support, and guidance and solace, from him.

Murcer's job then was mostly that of an administrator, of policy setting, politics, speech making, public relations. There was little traditional lawyering. No courtroom work, no investigations, no human clients to deal with. There was none of the excitement he had known as a young prosecutor.

Then there was Nancy Revering. She was eager and idealistic and effective. Murcer spotted her as a winner. At first it was just one of a dozen sensitive cases that Murcer directly supervised the progress of. Nancy was just one of a dozen young lawyers handling them. But she infected him with her enthusiasm, drew him into the day-to-day world of the case, got him excited, got him to care about its outcome.

Strictly speaking he should not have become as involved with the case as he did. He didn't have the time. It wasn't his job to become involved. But he made the time, rationalizing that it was a good idea for him to keep his hand in the working details of at least one case, to keep in touch with the realities of practice.

So he traveled out to southern Illinois with Nancy Revering, spent parts of two weeks overseeing her investigation. Later they went off together to a number of the medical centers setting up the rescreening operation. After that he arranged for a journalist to write a major magazine article about the case, and spent a number of days and evenings with Nancy and the reporter, both on and off the record, making certain that the article would make Justice, and Murcer in particular, look good.

It was all innocent at first. She was pretty. He enjoyed her company. And they shared their own private universe that was the case. It absorbed them both, the problems, the villain, the sense of crisis and urgency.

The few times they were on the road together they had eaten dinner, gone to a cocktail lounge, both drank scotch and waters, and talked until past midnight. They talked round and round, drew each other out, revolved back to talking about the case, exchanged confidences. He learned about the professor of surgery at the University of Pittsburgh Medical School that she had been seeing, learned that he had spent six months in Washington at the National Institutes of Health, that they had fallen in love, moved in together. He learned that the professor had returned to Pittsburgh, that it turned out that he had a long-time girl friend there, that Nancy had been a temporary diversion for him. He learned a great deal.

And Nancy learned for her part that Murcer loved his wife and his two boys, that he managed to keep Sundays free to attend the younger boy's soccer league practice and games. She learned that Ted Murcer was, under his politician's veneer, a sensitive, thoughtful man who seemed to care about the people around him. She learned from him about years of high-powered and successful law practice, about war stories and philosophy. She also learned a great deal.

Then Murcer decided that he wanted to go to bed with her. It was a terrible idea. For many reasons. And he spent many weeks trying to talk himself out of it. She was an employee, many years his junior, his subordinate. She might say no. He was not experienced at these things. She might make a scandal, claim sexual harassment, destroy a good working relationship and maybe both of their careers.

Or she might say yes. And what then? A quick encounter, probably not very satisfactory, to be followed by a totally compromised working relationship, maybe guilt, maybe discovery and domestic scandal. For what?

And if it turned out to be good, then what? He wasn't about to leave his wife and children. Not at any cost. If he fell in love with her he would not be able to see her much. They would be forced to lie, and suffer, and cheapen themselves. It couldn't possibly be worth it.

Still he asked.

And she said no. Firmly. Not angrily. "I don't sleep with married men."

Three weeks later he asked again.

No again.

He did not ask anymore. Relieved, they went on with their work, maybe closer than before.

It was a Tuesday night in New York City. Murcer was giving a speech on proposed reforms in federal criminal procedure statutes to a prestigious Bar Association group. Nancy Revering was in town meeting with physicians collecting information about pap test cytology. They met for drinks after his speech. It was too late to catch the last shuttle back to Washington.

They both drank too much, enjoyed each other's company too much. She mentioned a draft of an appeals brief she was working on. He said he would be interested in seeing it. She said it was upstairs in her hotel room, would he like to come up? He said yes.

They made love through the night. Three times. Four times. He lost count. And it didn't matter. Except that he hadn't felt that way in ten or fifteen years. Maybe never.

In the morning he put on his reading glasses and carefully read through her brief. Then he carefully discussed it with her. And he did not so much as kiss her. They said nothing of what had happened, got dressed, ate breakfast, talked business, returned to Washington. In the office they were natural, as they had always been.

Murcer expected to feel guilty when he returned home to Chevy Chase that evening. He didn't. He expected to feel different toward his family, distant, or angry, or maybe overly loving and affectionate by way of compensation. He didn't. Years of marriage made for habits and feelings much too deep-seated to easily change. He was home from a business trip and glad to be home. Glad to discuss the boys' schoolwork, glad later that evening to make love to his wife. In the same comfortable, satisfying, routine way that they always did. He decided before he fell asleep that he would not see Nancy Revering again.

Two weeks later he asked if he could see her. Shyly. Unsure of himself. Unsure of what she would say. Unsure of what he wanted her to say.

"Yes," she said. Also shyly. And so it began.

Months went by. Months punctuated by an evening here, two days stolen there. And always the same passion in bed, the same more distant professional rapport in public.

And in those months the pap test litigation wound down, became routine and uninteresting. It became time for Nancy to either draw a new project to work on, or more likely, to begin to look for a new job, to use her job as a springboard to something lucrative in the private sector.

It was then that the Trioxsone case came along. It had been referred to Murcer by federal lawyers in New York, and Nancy had read the files when they arrived before Murcer did as part of the intake screening function she performed. She read the files, and read Sabotnik's complaint, and knew instantly that she had found her new case.

She waited though until the following night to raise the issue with Murcer, waited after they had made love, for a quiet moment.

"Ted," she said, "there's a new case referred to us by the Civil Division that really bothers me."

"Yes," he said, rolling onto his side, "go on."

"It concerns a Vietnam vet with cancer who claims that it was caused by some drugs that he and the other soldiers were given in Southeast Asia. The suit claims that the drug was experimental and that the soldiers were guinea pigs."

"So?"

"So it turns out, at least on the basis of one day's quick research, that the allegations are true. Or at least in a sense they are true. The drug was experimental. It was not licensed or tested by the FDA. And it does cause cancer. Or anyway it causes cancer in test animals. I've been reading through the Defense Department and the FDA files on this business, and it concerns me."

"What exactly is it that has you concerned?"

"Well, for starters, there's the way in which the drug got approved for military use in the first place."

"How was that?"

"By getting the Food and Drug Administration to surrender its administrative control over new drugs whenever the Army declared something called a National Defense Health Emergency."

"And what the hell is a National Defense Health Emergency?"

"It's whatever the Army said it was. Basically, anytime the Army wanted to use drugs on soldiers, it got to do so, without having to worry about complying with all the FDA regulations that are supposed to guarantee that the drug in question is safe and tested. I have a feeling that ever since this deal between the FDA and Defense Department was cooked up in 1964, that there's been nothing to prevent servicemen from being used as drug guinea pigs. I think that that's what happened with Trioxsone, and it scares the hell out of me to think about how many other situations like this may be buried in the Pentagon files waiting to explode."

She fell silent, and Murcer said nothing. She was seated upright now, and had put on her glasses. The sheet had slipped down to her waist and he stared at her breasts. They were small, the nipples small, and she was self-conscious about them. He thought them desirable.

"This lawsuit, what is the relief the claimant is seeking, the usual money damages, or something else?"

"It is both money, and something else. They're asking for equitable relief, for an injunction to force us to warn all Vietnam vets that they were exposed to a risk of cancer, to urge them to get medical checkups, and then to force us to provide or pay for their medical care."

"That's very shrewd," he said. "They're in effect asking us to try to save the lives that they claim we put in jeopardy."

"Exactly."

"And if we refuse, or try to fight them, we're going to look just awful."

"That's right. And I don't think that we ought to refuse. I'd like to consent to the equitable relief and send out the warning, and maybe tell them to all go to VA hospitals or military facilities for free checkups."

"But tell me, is the Pentagon or the FDA ready to go along with this? Are they ready to admit that they were screwing around with the health and safety of how many servicemen?"

"About a half million."

"Really?"

"That's what I'm told. And I can also tell you that the agencies are not ready to go along with it."

"And that's why you're telling me?"

"Yes."

"So that I can go to bat for you, and get the Pentagon to agree to do the right thing?"

"Yes."

He smiled. "Is there any other little thing that I can do for you? After all, taking on the United States Army and the Department of Health, Education and Welfare isn't really much of a sign of affection."

"Yes there is," she said earnestly.

"And what is that?"

"I'd like you to open up a criminal investigation into the circumstances under which the decision to use Trioxsone was made, and especially into the way that the contracts for supplying the drug to the government were let out."

"Why do you want me to do that?"

"Because even looking at the files superficially, which is all that I've done, the whole thing stinks. Lefcourte Labs made a fortune selling this poison to us, and the general who contracted with the lab for the Army is now the president of Lefcourte. That's a guy named MacCauley, and he's the same guy who cooked up this National Defense Health Emergency business. I don't have any proof, but I suspect that there had to be some bribery or something. An awful lot of money passed hands and the files on that are kind of funny. The whole thing just stinks, and I think that the Criminal Division should look at it."

"So you would like me to indict some former generals, and maybe some prominent businessmen, is that it?" he asked.

"If they did anything wrong."

"And if they didn't?"

"That just means that we weren't clever enough to catch them."

"Okay," he said at last, "why don't you draft a confidential memo on this case, and on your suspicions and recommendations, and get it over to me as soon as possible. I'll talk with the Attor-

ney General about it, and see what I can get started. Now," he
said slowly, "is there anything else I can do for you?"

She looked as serious as possible and then said, "Yes. I've got
an itch under my left shoulder blade that's driving me crazy. Do
you suppose you could scratch it?"

It was a week before she got her memorandum to him, and another week before he had read it and digested the accompanying
files. He felt it was as she described, a thoroughly bad situation,
and he passed the memorandum along to the Attorney General,
and to the White House. Yet another week later after the memo
had been again reviewed, a meeting was arranged between
Murcer, the Attorney General, the chief White House adviser
for domestic affairs, and the special counsel to the Secretary of
Defense. Government policy on the Trioxsone case was going to
be set from on high.

The representative of the Defense Department set the tone of
the meeting as soon as the preliminary amenities had been completed. It was clear from the outset that he was determined to
stop the whole thing right at the beginning, before it could get
started.

"Do you have any idea of what it will do to military morale if
this Trioxsone thing is allowed to become a *cause célèbre?* I
don't have to tell you that in the years since Vietnam we've had
a terrible morale problem. We can't keep experienced men and
officers in the services as it is. Not when the public, and even the
servicemen, perceive the military as a dirty and somehow dishon-
orable career. And now they want to dig up some ancient event
and make a fuss about it. I can tell you right now that if this case
goes forward in earnest, and if, God forbid, we ever reach a
point where we have to make admissions of misconduct or settle
the civil case on terms adverse to us, it will be a true injury to
the national security. It will hurt our morale severely. About this
crazy idea of a criminal investigation, I won't even talk. It is absolutely out of the question. There is no way we can possibly
permit high officers to be subject to criminal sanctions, or even
to the possibility of such sanctions for decisions that were made
in good faith, in wartime, to save lives from tropical diseases."

"But what if they weren't made in good faith?" Murcer inter-jected. "What if the allegations in this complaint are true?"

"They're not true," the special counsel went on undeterred. "The truth is that back in the late sixties we had a bad health problem in Vietnam with strains of tropical disease that were re-sistant to the usual drugs that were normally used to prevent them. We had soldiers dying of fevers and others who were effectively rendered useless. Units were often dangerously understrength and the safety of those who remained was jeopar-dized. It was a true health emergency, and the fact is that it was a good faith effort to deal with a major crisis."

"If that is the case," said Murcer, picking up the cudgels, "then the Pentagon certainly shouldn't mind a full-scale investi-gation. After all, it would just lead to a complete exoneration and a clean bill of health, wouldn't it?"

"You know," the Attorney General interjected, suavely seek-ing to cool things down, "that the military isn't the only depart-ment that has its morale problems. You had Vietnam, but that was a decade ago. We at Justice have lived through Watergate even more recently. Ted and I have a lot of young lawyers working for us who are hypersensitive to anything that they might characterize as a cover-up. The hard fact is that a bunch of these lawyers, including the young woman who wrote the memo you have all seen, are pretty agitated about this Trioxsone business. I simply don't think that it is realistic for us to do noth-ing but blindly oppose this lawsuit that has been filed. We might win in court, and I suppose that I can even live with the damage to morale, but frankly I would be worried about our inaction being leaked to the press. I'm not sure that any of us want to be put in the public posture of trying to deny half a million vet-erans their day in court, let alone trying to withhold from them medical care that might save lives. None of you would like to live with the political consequences of being perceived in that light, would you?"

There was a silence as the Attorney General's remarks sank in. He seemed to be backing Murcer and his staff, and the old man's political clout had to be reckoned with. He had the President's ear, and he had an independent power base back in his home state. He was a veteran of the political wars, a veteran and a survivor. What exactly his intentions were was carefully considered by the other men in the room.

"Who exactly are the outfits that sold this drug to the Army?" the White House adviser asked.

"Lefcourte Laboratories," Murcer answered, "a subsidiary of Transcontinental Communications."

"Is this one of the deals that George Petrakis put together?" the adviser asked, quickly calculating the political costs involved in taking on the conglomerate and its new chief executive.

"Yes," Murcer replied, "it is probably Petrakis' deal. He was general counsel to Lefcourte at the critical time. And yes," he went on, "I know that Petrakis is an important supporter of the President. He was also an important supporter of mine back in New York when I was running for office. I've known him well for many years."

"Is Petrakis a possible target of your investigation? Is that what you're saying?" the White House counsel asked unhappily.

"He might be."

"Is there any hard evidence against him?"

"No. Nothing that I would be willing to show to a grand jury, anyway."

"Still that doesn't mean that you won't come up with something if you look hard enough."

"That's right."

"Well maybe the thing to do," the Attorney General suggested, "is to look, but not to look so hard. We can start an investigation and appoint someone nice and slow, someone who's maybe a little lazy or a little incompetent to run the criminal investigation. Then, I think we can have the best of all worlds. No one will be able to accuse us of a cover-up. After all, we will have an active criminal investigation underway. On the other hand, we will be able to move deliberately, and hopefully we'll be able to prevent anyone from getting unnecessarily hurt. I would hate to do damage to military morale, let alone do anything to upset a valuable political supporter of the President."

There was a faint ironic smile on the Attorney General's face as he said this. It was only in part ironic. In part it was a smile of pleasure, a cynical smile of a devious politician who was satisfied at having found a satisfactory solution to a sticky problem.

Before they left, the group considered what approach to take to Cleveland Daniels' pending civil lawsuit. Without much debate they decided to fight it, including the request for warning and medical care. The consensus was that it would be a dangerous precedent to allow private litigants, or even the courts, to force the government into making policy decisions about the public welfare. They would hide behind the tried and true doctrine of sovereign immunity.

Later that evening the Attorney General walked into Murcer's office unannounced. The two men had an easy relationship, and the Attorney General often did this.

"You were skating on thin ice this afternoon," Murcer was told. "Both the Pentagon and the White House could get mighty upset if they felt that a major scandal was brewing over this Trioxsone business. And that wouldn't do you much good, Ted, not much good at all, if you know what I mean."

Murcer knew exactly what he meant. The old man was alluding to the soon to be vacant Supreme Court seat. He knew about Justice Smith is what he meant. Of course he knew. And he was warning Murcer to tread lightly, not to jeopardize his chances by antagonizing anyone; Murcer understood him perfectly. He would take care to jeopardize nothing.

5

Mary Ann Salisbury was in the middle of a two-week vacation on the day that the Daniels case was assigned to her. She and her daughter were in Maine, on an island in the Penobscot Bay, staying in a summer cottage that the judge had rented from an old friend of her former husband's. The idea of the vacation had been to bring mother and daughter closer together, to give them uninterrupted time to talk, and to try to recapture some of the warmth and closeness they had shared when Christine had been a little girl. But it was not working. The seventeen-year-old had resisted violently the idea of surrendering two weeks of her summer vacation, away from the group she hung out with. She had no interest in spending time with her mother, and had made it quite clear that she would rather be left alone. She had gone to Maine under duress, gone sulkily, not willing to be a good loser, intent upon punishing her mother for enforcing her will. She was withdrawn, moody, uncommunicative, and as best she could, she tried to avoid her mother. She went to bed early, slept late, and took long solitary walks along the shoreline. It all made Mary Ann Salisbury quite miserable. They were both quite miserable. The island was quite beautiful.

Three months earlier Mary had inadvertently discovered a prescription for birth control pills made out in Christine's name. It was being used as a bookmark in a textbook that Christine was using that semester. The book had been sitting on the dinette table, and the judge had been thumbing through it idly while eating her breakfast one morning. She had turned a page and there it was.

She was surprised at how upset she had become. Mary Ann had always assumed that she would somehow know when her daughter was no longer a virgin. She didn't like to think that she was that out of touch. Or was she? It occurred to her that maybe her daughter wasn't on the pill, that maybe the prescription was something that girls nowadays got and carried around, but didn't fill and didn't use, pretty much the same way that boys back in Indiana used to carry prophylactics in their wallets for years on end when she was a girl. Maybe it meant a lot of things.

Mary Ann Salisbury did not like birth control pills. She did not like the idea of pouring artificial hormones into anyone's body, certainly not into her daughter's. She didn't like the uncertainties about the pills, the stories about high blood pressure, and cancer, and God knew what else that the pill might cause. She had once presided over a DES trial. She remembered the twenty-one-year-old girl forced to have a hysterectomy six months before her marriage because of cervical cancer caused by a drug that her mother had taken while pregnant twenty-two years earlier. She wanted to tell Christine about these things, to warn her, to make sure that she didn't hurt herself. She also wanted to know what was going on with her daughter. To share vicariously the beauty and wonder of it all, if that was the case; to ease the pain and provide comfort if it was the other way. She wanted to be able to talk to her daughter. And she found that she couldn't. The idea of the vacation had been to provide a setting that would encourage them to talk. At least at first, it didn't.

It was her first real vacation in five years, the first time in all those years that she had forced herself not to take work with her, the first time she had not tried to catch up on her case load by drafting overdue opinions. This time she was determined to leave it all behind her, to sleep a lot, to laze around, to recharge her batteries. The prospect had seemed pleasant. The reality wasn't. She dreamed bad dreams, slept poorly. Her mind raced unfocused, and she had excess energy to burn.

Mary Ann Salisbury had been a federal district court judge for exactly five years, and the accumulated pressures of those years had been extraordinary. She had not been at all prepared to take the bench, not after a career mostly devoted to promoting the day care movement, to women's rights and social welfare law. She had never really been a trial lawyer, had had virtually no experience inside a courtroom, could barely remember from law school the rules of evidence. She had not really appreciated the scope of the demands that are imposed upon a federal judge, the range and the intensity of the pressures. If she had understood what it meant, if she had appreciated the costs of the job, she would have chickened out.

Instead, she had taken the appointment, honored by the opportunity, determined to make good, ambitious to advance, to show that a woman might be every bit as good a jurist as any man.

It had been an ordeal. There was a whole universe of law to learn and relearn, subjects that she hadn't thought about in decades, others that she had not even known to exist. She was assigned hypertechnical admiralty and patent law cases. There were tax cases and complex commercial class actions, personal injury or wrongful death cases, and labor law actions about unfair labor practices, secondary boycotts, and union busting. There were criminal cases, white collar crimes, frauds, drug cases, conspiracies, and bank robberies. Each case had its own special rule of law to be mastered, each case came complete with its own set of lawyers who specialized in the particular field of law involved.

Mary Ann had been determined not to be taken advantage of by any of these specialists. She was even more determined not to make a fool of herself. She was determined to make good. Which meant that she had had to spend an enormous amount of time studying the law. From nine to five, five days a week, she had to be on the bench, presiding over trials, conducting hearings, taking testimony. Nights and weekends she worked in her chambers or at home, reading the lawyers' papers, studying the basic cases that they cited, reaching decisions and drafting opinions.

She learned very early to hide her ignorance of what was going on around her, to ask intelligent questions, to be a very quick study. She learned to preside over trials, to control her courtroom, and to keep even the most fractious or difficult lawyers well in line. She learned to be firm without raising her voice. She learned to project a presence that was at the same time authoritative and feminine. She became well liked around the courthouse, and in time she became well respected. It was said of her by the lawyers who appeared before her, by both plaintiffs' and defendants' lawyers, by prosecutors and legal aid attorneys, that she gave them and their clients a fair trial. And there was no higher praise than that. As a jurist she was a great success.

But there were costs to be paid, and they were exorbitant. Her personal life, or what was left of it after the divorce, shrank away to almost nothing. After a year of the tensions of the job, and the first year had been the worst, she had come down with a series of sharp stomach pains that had frightened her half to death. The doctors had diagnosed an incipient ulcer, and put her on a bland diet and medication. Four years later she was still living on cottage cheese, fruit, and yogurt. She had given up cigarettes and coffee, and had gained and then fought to lose fifteen pounds. At fifty she was still attractive. Honey blond hair just going gray, her figure still good, but it was all work. It was important, to remain attractive.

She had virtually given up men too, and that was also a possible cost of the judgeship. She had felt sharply the need to be discreet and that had cramped her style considerably. Remarriage was out of the question. She just couldn't imagine wanting to do that. There was one man she had been seeing on and off for years, a sixty-five-year-old news executive, a widower. He was comfortable, easy, and unchallenging. But a year earlier he had suffered a heart attack. He had become frightened and withdrawn, and their sex life had shrunk away to almost nothing. She had been seeing much less of him. There was no opportunity to develop new relationships.

But the worst cost was her relationship with Christine and the preoccupation with her career that had led to its deterioration. The cost was paid in a sense of estrangement.

She was glad to be back at the courthouse. Suddenly it was familiar, a good place to be. There was a sense of being home about it, of belonging.

The Daniels case had been filed while Mary Ann had been in Maine, so she had missed the small burst of publicity that had attended its commencement. In fact the newspaper articles and radio broadcasts that reported the case had not even mentioned the name of the judge to whom it had been assigned, and no one in Mary Ann's chambers, neither her secretary nor her two young law clerks, had any awareness of the case, let alone of its significance. It was three or four weeks before any of them really appreciated what they had gotten.

But there was plenty of legal business on hand to occupy Judge Salisbury's mind once she was back in harness. The worst of it was the criminal sentencings, and the worst of those was the Markowitz case.

Harry Markowitz had been the treasurer and chief financial officer for a chain of old-age nursing homes that had been run in the New York metropolitan area by a group of vicious businessmen. About two years earlier the scandal had broken when an investigative reporter had succeeded in revealing the horrors of mismanagement that plagued the industry. Old, senile men and women were left unattended to lie in their own excrement. Others died slowly while incompetent attendants neglected to give them life-preserving medications. There were people who were sustained on diets of near rancid meat and stale vegetables. The whole thing had been sickening—and doubly so because huge and fraudulent profits had been made by the nursing home operators, who had pocketed public and private funds, dummying up records, and then supplying grossly inadequate goods and services.

It had become a hot political issue and the prosecutors had swooped in to divide up the cases for indictment and trial. The big shots had gone to the New York State Authorities because it had been an election year and the state officials had needed the publicity. A number of the smaller fraud cases had been handled by the U. S. Attorney, partly as a training exercise for his young assistants, and partly so that it could not be said that he had ignored the nursing home scandal. The Markowitz case was one of these small ones. It had been assigned to Mary Ann for trial.

The conviction had been a foregone conclusion. The evidence had been overwhelming, the fraud obvious, and the attempts to hide it had been naïve, and even pitiful. The prosecutor had even been able to produce the double set of books in Markowitz's cramped handwriting—one showing the real receipts and expenditures, while the other contained the doctored records prepared for tax purposes, and for the federal and state auditors. There was a wealth of incriminating evidence and not a prayer for the defense.

At trial, Markowitz had seemed more pitiful than evil. He was overweight and sweaty, nearing fifty, with a series of double chins. He had been unable to provide reasonable answers to the prosecutor's sharp, incessant questioning. At one point he was brought near the point of tears, fought to control himself, lost his fight, and began to sob silently, his face in his hands. Everyone in the courtroom had been embarrassed, everyone but the young prosecutor. He seemed to be smiling at what he wrongly thought to be a forensic success.

The conviction had been unavoidable, and the jury had barely bothered to deliberate before returning its verdict. Now, Mary Ann was faced with the miserable task of sentencing the man. Her discretion was enormous. She could give him anything from ten years in federal prison and a ten-thousand-dollar fine down to an unconditional discharge with no penalty altogether. Before her vacation she had ordered a lengthy pre-sentence, and postponed the day of sentencing until after she got back.

The report that came back was hostile and had recommended incarceration. It focused upon the horror of the crime, the pain and suffering of the elderly, and would not see beyond it.

"This man," the report concluded, "knowingly stole federal money. These funds were supposed to be used to provide proper food and decent services to indigent old people. Instead of doing this, the defendant Markowitz wrongfully enriched himself knowing as a result that others would go cold and hungry, knowing that the ill would be uncared for, knowing that some would get worse or even die for this lack of care. This was no ordinary theft, but rather an extraordinarily vicious, and in a sense even a violent crime. It was committed cold-bloodedly with a full appreciation of the injury that was being inflicted. Rarely is there a case that calls more strongly for incarceration than this one. Although it is true that others, not before this court, profited more from these crimes than Markowitz, and that others were more culpable in the sense that they masterminded these outrages, nevertheless, Markowitz was a major and conscious participant in these crimes. He did not act out of duress, and he should be severely punished."

That was one side of the story; but as Mary Ann well knew, there was another. A letter from Markowitz's rabbi, a prominent Bronx clergyman, had eloquently pleaded the defendant's case.

"I do not condone Harry's conduct," the letter read, "and I do not pretend that it is not worthy of the most severe punishment. Indeed, members of my own congregation have lived in some of the nursing homes that Harry worked for, and I know from my own experience the suffering that was inflicted.

"However, I believe that to do proper justice, your honor must know something of Harry Markowitz the man. You must know something of the tragedies he has suffered, and of the good deeds he has done. You must know these things so that when the time comes to pass sentence you will be able to act justly with a full knowledge of all the facts. It is for this reason that I write.

"You should know, your honor, that ten years ago Harry lost his wife. Rhonda Markowitz, may she rest in peace, was a severely disturbed woman. From the early years of their marriage she suffered from a manic-depressive state, and she was twice institutionalized as a result of her mental illness. It was during the second illness that she succeeded in taking a razor, slashing her wrists, and committing suicide. Harry was left then with two children, Karen, who was five, and Stephen, who was a baby eleven months old.

"All these years Harry has raised these children alone, and he has raised them well. They are always at services on Saturday morning, all three of them; and both children have attended our congregation's Hebrew school. Many times I have seen Harry with his children, and I can report that he has always been a patient, loving, and concerned parent. Karen is today an honor student at the Bronx High School of Science, and Stephen seems certain to follow in her path.

"Harry himself worked honorably for many years with a firm of certified public accountants. He earned a modest but decent salary. However, five years ago, upon the death of its senior partner, the firm broke up and Harry first took his position with the nursing homes.

"You must understand, your honor, that Harry is a product of the Great Depression. For him, job security was everything, and the experience of seeing the firm he worked for dissolve was terrifying. He clutched at the nursing home opportunity like a safe port in a storm. He would never do anything to jeopardize this job.

"I am sure the evidence at the trial made it clear that Harry did not conceive of the terrible schemes that were committed. Instead, he was put up to it by his bosses. And out of weakness and fear, he went along. Once he became involved, he was, of course, much too frightened to correct his conduct. He has lived all these years with the shame and guilt of what he did.

"I have been assured, and I deeply believe, that Harry Markowitz did not profit personally from the wrongs that were done.
Others, far worse than he, pocketed the millions that were stolen.
Harry took virtually nothing. He is, in spite of it all, not a bad
man. I know that he is deeply ashamed of his crimes, that he is
truly contrite.

"Your honor, this man has suffered great and terrible tragedy
in his life. He has been, and he is, a loving and a devoted parent.
He is a weak and a confused man who is, as much as anything
else, a victim of circumstance.

"It would be a pity and a shame to now send him to prison. It
would deprive two lovely and wonderful children of their only
remaining parent. It would not undo the wrongs that were done,
and it would not make society any safer. Harry Markowitz is
certainly now no menace to anyone. Prison for him would serve
no useful purpose. Such a sentence should not be imposed."

Mary Ann did not disagree with what the rabbi had written.
She did not disagree with the pre-sentence report calling for
imprisonment either. Each view had validity, and it would be her
job to mediate between the demands of social justice, which
required harsh punishment as a deterrence, as a warning to
others, and frankly as retribution for a horrible crime, and the
demands of individual justice, of doing the right thing to the
person of Harry Markowitz. She was inclined to send him to jail.
But she knew from experience that both children would be in
the courtroom on the day of sentence. They were old enough to
understand what was happening and she would have to face
them as she pronounced sentence. That's why they would be
there, to intimidate her with their innocence. It was wrong that
they should suffer. Still . . .

She brought the dilemma of the Markowitz sentencing home
with her three successive nights. Then she finally went to speak
to Homer Anderson, who at ninety-two years of age was still an
active senior judge on the United States Court of Appeals for the
Second Circuit. Anderson was almost a legendary figure in the
law, having been first appointed to the bench by Franklin Delano
Roosevelt during the height of the New Deal. In over forty

years on the bench he had not lost his liberal reformer's passion, nor his political acumen. At ninety-two he still put in a full day in his chambers, serving among other things as a kind of legal godfather to younger judges of similar philosophical persuasion. Mary Ann Salisbury had long been one of his protégés. She was one judge he always had time for.

"Mary Ann," he said, after listening patiently to her description of the Markowitz sentencing dilemma, "you know that no one can really give you advice on something like that. I certainly cannot. I've been a circuit judge all these years, so it's been a long time since I've had to worry about passing sentences upon individuals. I just get the appeals. You're just going to have to do what you think is right. Do it and then forget about it. Move on to the next case. That's the only way to maintain your sanity."

The old judge paused for a minute, waiting for Mary Ann to reply. When she didn't he went on.

"There is one thing that I do want to caution you about though. There's probably going to be some publicity about this sentence, and while I don't think that usually a judge should give a damn about publicity one way or the other, your situation right now is a little different."

"Why," she asked.

"Because I just spent the weekend down in Washington where I was supposed to visit my old friend, Justice Smith. I was unable to though, because he is quite ill."

"I did not know that," Mary Ann said.

"Well it's true. And he will be forced to retire within the next six months at the outside. Which means . . ."

"That the President will have a Supreme Court appointment to make," she interrupted him, suddenly understanding.

"Yes," the judge replied, "and both Justice Smith and I would like to see you replace him. It's time for a woman to be appointed to the Court and there is no woman jurist in the country better qualified than you are. You are a New Yorker, and you are progressive. You're also young and you are attractive. You would be a popular appointment with the media, which would be politically useful to the Administration just now. But it is important, right now, that you don't do anything too controversial.

Tell me, aside from this little Markowitz sentencing, is there anything controversial that you've got coming up? Any school desegregation cases or anything like that?"

"No, not really." Then she paused reflectively. "There may be one though. A new case that involves a Vietnam vet who claims that he got cancer because of drugs that he was given in the service. It was just assigned to me this past month."

SECTION TWO

6

That summer Cleveland Daniels spent a lot of time figuring out how to raise the money it cost to buy bleacher seats at Yankee Stadium. He ran errands for Fat Dominick, who took most of the numbers action on the block. Going down to the corner deli to pick up a hero sandwich and a beer might be worth a nickel tip, or if business was really good, a dime. He was also very accomplished at finding empty soda bottles and returning them to stores to collect the two cents per bottle deposit. Later he learned how to steal empty bottles from behind the Grand Union supermarket where they were stored, and to return them to the A&P. Then he would steal from the A&P and return to Food Fair. Food Fair's bottles he would return to Grand Union. One way or another, when the Yankees were in town, he managed to make it to the stadium at least once a week.

Mickey Mantle was young that year. He was at the height of his powers. His knees were still sound, and the injuries would come later. He would win the triple crown that summer, and for a while, it even looked as if he might break the Babe's record. It didn't happen. Not that year. Still, it was a great summer to spend in the bleachers, one of the best summers of Daniels' life.

Back at home, Cleveland took a lot of verbal abuse from Ralph about going to the stadium. Ralph worked for the Transit Authority and was his mother's most recent boyfriend. He was a good and patient and basically kind man. Cleveland did not like him.

"Why you spending so much time watchin' them Yankees for, boy?" Ralph would ask him. "They're just a bunch of damned crackers. It's just beyond me why you bother to go see them."

Cleveland wasn't about to enlighten him about his love for the Yankees. He sat there tight-lipped while Ralph went on.

"Boy, you want to see baseball like it's supposed to be played, you come down with me to the Polo Grounds some weekend.

Then we'll see Willie play the game the right way. Your white boy can hit. He can run and he's got power. But he can't field like Willie. His arm ain't nothin' to write home about neither. He's not a complete ballplayer, no way. Willie can do it all, son," he continued. "Ain't no one gonna go from first to third on that man's arm. And there's nothin' hit in his direction he ain't gonna reach. An' you know that whatever he reaches he's gonna catch. An' he can hit as good as that white boy. Better if you ask me. Willie's got power. He's got speed. And he's smart. He doesn't strike out much like that white boy does. He's got discipline. An' he's black, boy. He's a nigger, boy. Jus' like you an' me. We're niggers too."

It was the same debate that was being repeated all over New York, maybe all over America, that summer. Who was the best? Was it Mickey? Or Willie? Or maybe the folks in Brooklyn were right when they said it was the Duke. In bars, on street corners, in school yards, it went on endlessly. Even at his young age, Cleveland could not escape the debate. In truth, he did not want to.

Nighttime, in the modified studio apartment, Cleveland would sleep in an alcove, on a cot. His mother would pull a curtain across the alcove so that she might have some privacy. He would stare out from behind the curtain and watch his mother in her housedress, reading the *Amsterdam News* or watching the tiny fuzzy television that she had scrimped and saved to buy. Then he usually fell asleep. Sometimes he didn't. He would be lying quietly, pretending to be asleep, and then sometimes Ralph would come by. He would let himself in quietly, with his own key, big and bulky in his motorman's uniform, just off his shift's work.

He would watch as Ralph unbuckled his belt, unzipped his fly, took off his trousers. He would watch as Ralph sat down on the easy chair, would watch as his mother would kneel between his outstretched legs, as she seemed to bury her head in his crotch. Later he would watch as she struggled excitedly out of her housedress, would watch her loose pendulous breasts with their large brown nipples. Sometimes he would fall asleep.

7

The lecture hall was well lighted, but dark and gloomy in comparison with the warm Indian summer September day outside.

It was a polished set-piece speech they listened to, a speech delivered every September to the incoming first-year law students. It was meant to awe, to intimidate, and also, in some measure, to excite them with a vision of what might lay ahead. It was the beginning of a rite of initiation, the start of a process that would, for many of them, lead inevitably to Wall Street law practices, to wealth, to power, to prestige. That was a near universal, almost unquestioned expectation and goal for the incoming class. Without exception, they listened attentively. It was only an orientation speech, part of no course, nothing they would ever be tested on. Nevertheless, a good half of the class sat taking notes, some in shorthand, straining to get down every word. They were a group that knew from the start that competition was the name of the game, that only 5 percent, one in twenty, would make law review. And to those very few, more talented, or more determined or luckier than the rest, would go the sweetest prizes, the best jobs, the most money. That was understood at the outset. And there were few in the audience that September day who were not ready to give making law review their very best shot.

"You will learn here," the professor told them, "to think like a lawyer. You will learn to think analytically. You will learn to write precisely, to write without ambiguity. You will learn to speak in public, to speak clearly, to persuade hostile or skeptical audiences that your clients' cases have merit, that they and you should prevail. . . ."

Mary Ann Salisbury listened to this speech with mixed emotions, sat in the lecture hall with mixed emotions. She sat in the back of the hall not knowing whether she was conspicuous or invisible, not knowing how she would fit in or if she would fit in at all. She looked around the hall. Out of roughly two hundred

fifty incoming students in the incoming class, she could see four
other women. There were five or six students who appeared to
be black, and two or three who were oriental. What she
saw was a sea of very earnest, somewhat frightened, highly competitive young white masculinity. She felt very alone, close to
overwhelmed, and had to stifle the desire to get up and walk out.

The professor droned on, speaking of the virtues of equality at
the law school. "No man in this room," he said, totally unaware
of having made any gaffe, "starts with any advantage over anyone else. Race, religion, wealth, or social position means nothing
here. Here only talent counts. Talent and dedication to the law.
Any man in this room," he repeated himself, emphasizing his
point, "can become editor-in-chief of the law review. Any of
you can succeed. Here you must make it solely on merit, on
talent and determination. . . ."

Mary Ann listened to the speech with a growing sense of dis-
satisfaction. Nowhere in the professor's remarks had a word been
spoken about justice, of the need to use the law as a tool to effect
social reform, of legal ethics, or of the need to provide legal aid
to the poor or the oppressed. He said nothing of the reasons
Mary Ann had decided to be a lawyer, nothing to give her comfort. Lincoln had been a lawyer she thought. And Lenin. And
Gandhi. She did not want to be a partner at Cravath, Swaine,
and Moore. She did not want to represent the Standard Oil Company of New Jersey. She did not want to go to work for the
highest bidder. She felt out of place.

The message that filtered through to Mary Ann, and the message that the professor incidentally wished to filter through, was
that mastery of the law, mastery of its techniques and its disci-
plines, was everything. Mastery equaled morality. Being a good
lawyer was the main thing. Winning was the main thing. And it
mattered not at all on whose behalf one won. "Anglo-Saxon law
is adversary," he told them. "And even Hitler," he said, "had he
been brought before an American court, would have been entitled to the representation of a good lawyer. It is our job to make
you into good lawyers. . . ."

"Your law school application and your college transcript both
indicate that you were divorced, and that you took a year off be-

tween your sophomore and junior years at college?" the assistant
dean had asked her when she was interviewed as part of the law
school admissions process. The dean was an elderly, kindly-look-
ing man, and Mary Ann got the sense that he was not offended
by her divorce, just curious. She answered the unstated question
frankly.

"I was a sophomore at the University of Indiana when I got
married. I was nineteen years old and he was a graduate student,
an economist, and I thought he was brilliant. He was a socialist,
he said, and he idealized Eugene Debs and Norman Thomas, and
I suppose I idealized him. Anyway he would talk on and on, and
I would listen. He seemed to me incredibly full of ideas, persuasive and self-confident, and unlike anyone I had ever met
growing up in Fort Wayne. He talked about redistributing
wealth, and providing free medical and health care for everyone,
and he dreamed about establishing a left of center, new political
party, based upon socialist principles, kind of like the Labor
party in England. It was all pretty exciting stuff to me back then.
I was in a sorority at Indiana that year, one of the better ones,
and in retrospect, I think I was bored by it, by the pledging and
the rushing and all the silliness that seemed to go with it."

"So you got married?" the dean asked.

"Yes. It was getting to be summertime and he was planning
to go down to Texas, to Corpus Christi, to go to work for the
International Ladies Garment Workers Union as an organizer.
The idea was that he was supposed to help set up locals among
the Mexican women who were working in the sweatshops down
there. That June he was supposed to have finished all his course
work towards his Ph.D., and the plan was for him to spend a
year working on his thesis while he was doing the labor union
work down in Texas.

"Anyway, I couldn't bear the idea of being away from him
for a year, so we decided to get married. It was all pretty impul-
sive. We decided late one Wednesday night, I guess it was in the
beginning of May, and we eloped that Friday. I was able to ar-
range to get a leave of absence from the university. I remember
that even then, when I was telling the administrators at Indiana
that I was getting married and would be moving to Texas, that I

knew somewhere deep down that I was making a mistake and that I would be back to finish up. It wasn't anything that I could admit, or think about consciously, but in retrospect, I'm sure that that was why I took a leave of absence and didn't burn my bridges behind me by just dropping out."

"And did you make a mistake?" the dean asked, his voice free of irony.

"Yes and no. The time in Texas turned out to be just awful. I thought that it would be romantic and exciting trying to organize immigrant workers, but it wasn't. Most of the women were illegal immigrants, wetbacks they're called down there, and they were all so afraid of getting caught and deported that they wouldn't even talk to us. Besides, compared to what was available to them in Mexico, the horrible conditions in the Texas factories seemed like paradise. They were happy to work for less than the minimum wage, let alone for union wages."

"So you got nowhere?"

"It was worse than that, it wasn't just that we failed. We were a joke. First of all, we didn't either speak a word of Spanish, so we couldn't even communicate with most of the people we were trying to reach. Secondly, we didn't really have the faintest idea really of what we were trying to do, of what the local grievances really were or of what local conditions were like. We had a lot of high-sounding philosophy when we should really have been agitating about cleaner toilets for the ladies. We were so ineffectual and so out of it that I think we became a joke. The local company men, the bosses, who we figured would hate us and maybe even try to run us out of town, didn't even take us seriously. They were polite and one of them even invited us to dinner, which we refused to do. Mostly they ignored us, which was really the most clever thing for them to do."

"So what did you do?"

"Nothing, really. We lived in a cheap motel room that the union paid for, and I think that after the first month or so my husband even stopped trying. You know what we used to do? We used to go bowling. Every day we used to go bowling in this old beat-up bowling alley with pinboys instead of machines. It was just across the highway from our motel. We used to go bowling and have these violent arguments about whether or not the United States was going to end up being a right-wing fascist-type dictatorship. It was just ridiculous. After a while he even stopped working on his thesis altogether. We were doing nothing at all."

"So you went back to school?"

"Yes. I left him in June, exactly thirteen months after we were married. The next September I returned to Indiana to start my junior year."

"And you did very well, extremely well, judging from your record. And now you want to go to law school?"

"Yes."

"Why? Do you still want to promote social upheaval or revolution?"

The question was not a hostile one, and the dean was still smiling.

"I'm not sure," Mary Ann answered. "And I really can't give you a simple answer. I knew lawyers back in Fort Wayne, like Ed Bradley, my dad's lawyer. You know, the kind who write wills, and draw simple contracts, and take care of speeding tickets and drunk driving charges, things like that. Anyway, I certainly don't want to practice that kind of law, and I don't want to become a Wall Street-type lawyer either. I don't want to become a government lawyer, I don't think, and to be honest, I'm not exactly sure what type of lawyer I do want to be. I don't know enough about it. But I do know this, if there's one thing that I did learn down in Texas, it's that you can't do one thing in this country if you don't have skills and training. And I figure that the best kind of skills and training you can get in this society today are legal skills. So I don't know right now exactly what I will do with a law degree. But I will use it, and use it well. You can count on that."

The assistant dean did count on that. He was taken with Mary Ann, liked her spirit and her candor. She was soft-spoken, smiling, polite, and pretty, looking almost like a teenager, the sort of girl I would like to have met, dated, and married, the dean, a lifelong bachelor, thought to himself. He strongly recommended her admission, and the rest of the admissions committee went along. They had been looking for more qualified women students, felt that it would be good for the law school if ten, maybe fifteen, women would be members of each class. The law school had a reputation for being liberal.

8

Sabotnik found law school a strange, almost eventless experience. Day after day he went to class, listened to lectures, took notes, tried to respond to the professors' questions. Night after night he sat in his dormitory room, reading his casebooks, taking more notes, trying to be prepared for the next day's lectures. He felt keenly the growing pressure of the competition, and even more keenly the anxiety of not knowing how well he was doing. There were no term papers to submit, no periodic quizzes or midterm exams to give any guidance or measurements of where he stood relative to his classmates. It was just a steady diet of lectures—lectures and what passed for the Socratic method, questions from the professors, answers from the students. He thought that he was learning, hoped that he was learning well, worried that he was missing something essential.

Then came the time for the moot court competition. It was mandatory for the first-year class, the one time that they would get the chance to act like lawyers, to write a real appellate brief, and then to argue the case before a court made up of a third-year student, a practicing lawyer, and either a law school professor or a judge. But, moot court didn't count on your grade point average and doing well in it did not help a student make law review. Still, it was something different, a break in the tedium, and a chance to make a little noise in public, maybe even to excel. At a minimum, there would be winners and losers, overt competition, with measurements and comparisons openly made. Sabotnik wanted that. He was also afraid of it. They all were.

Moot court divided the entire first-year class into two-person teams, and then pitted each team against another team, one assigned to represent the appellant, or the party that had lost in the lower courts, the other to represent the respondent, or the party that had prevailed below. The teams themselves were formed arbitrarily and were simply posted on a long list on the law school bulletin board.

Sabotnik studied the list, looking for his name. He was assigned to a team representing an appellant, a Dr. Albert Pasteur, in a lawsuit against the state of Erehwon. Some sort of criminal appeal, Sabotnik thought. He looked for the name of the teammate he had been assigned to work with. Petrakis the list read. He looked across the sheet to read the names of his opponents. Ted Murcer and Mary Ann Salisbury were going to be representing the state of Erehwon. Sabotnik went upstairs to get the packet of materials that would tell him what *Pasteur* v. *Erehwon* was all about. He knew Petrakis slightly from class and hoped that they would work well together. Murcer he knew better. They lived on the same floor in the same dorm, both worked out and played pickup basketball in the university gym. Murcer was a much better athlete. But the two men were friendly. They had eaten dinner together a few times. Everyone knew Mary Ann Salisbury as the only woman in class who was physically attractive enough to be worth looking at. In five months Sabotnik had not had occasion to say a word to her. He envied Murcer the opportunity to work with her.

Pasteur v. *Erehwon* was a hypothetical case set in a nonexistent jurisdiction drafted by the law school faculty. As the background for the case, the students were presented the following statement.

Dr. Albert Pasteur, age seventy-five, is a distinguished obstetrician-gynecologist who has practiced medicine for forty-five years in Erehwon's leading city. In addition to his practice he has been a full professor of medicine at a leading university medical school, has published many articles in learned medical journals, co-authored a leading obstetrical text, and is credited with having done some groundbreaking work in the area of pre-natal monitoring of fetal heart rates. In recent years, Dr. Pasteur has become an increasingly outspoken critic of certain provisions of the Erehwon Penal Code that make it a felony for a physician to perform an abortion unless such action is "necessary to preserve the life of the pregnant woman." He has lectured, written articles, and even lobbied the Erehwon legislature in an effort to have these statutes repealed or liberalized to expand the gambit of permissible therapeutic abortions. To date his efforts have not met with success. Accordingly, in the fall of 1953, Dr. Pasteur, accompanied by a young woman named Cheryl Andrews, and a substantial number of journalists, arrived at the offices of the local Erehwon District Attorney, where he confessed to the startled prosecutor that he had, two weeks earlier, performed a therapeutic abortion on Mrs. Andrews. When asked whether he had done so in order to preserve the woman's life, the doctor refused to answer, other than to state that Mrs. Andrews, her husband, and their four children were living in poverty, and that Mrs. Andrews had stated that she "could not cope with another child."

Mrs. Andrews confirmed the doctor's story. He was duly indicted and charged with felonious abortion in the first degree. The prosecutor, mindful of all the circumstances, had offered a plea bargain which would have given the doctor a suspended sentence, and a relief from civil disabilities in order to ensure his continued ability to practice medicine. The doctor refused.

At trial, the doctor repeated his confession, and offered no additional proof or defense other than a statement of his belief that the Erehwon antiabortion statute was an illegal and unconstitutional violation of his own professional and his patient's personal rights. At the completion of the testimony, the jury, having been properly instructed under the Erehwon Penal Code, returned a verdict of guilty. In due course, Dr. Pasteur was sentenced to three months in Erehwon State Prison, had his sentence suspended. Under applicable provisions of Erehwon law, he lost his license to practice medicine.

On appeal, Pasteur's sole contention was that the penal statutes under which he had been convicted were unconstitutionally vague, and violated a woman's right under the Bill of Rights to determine what should happen to her own body. His arguments were met with success in the court of appeals, Erehwon's intermediate appellate court, which held that these Penal Code sections were unconstitutional, and vacated his conviction. The supreme court of Erehwon, however, disagreed, reversed the court of appeals judgment, and reinstated the original conviction in a closely split five to four vote. The doctor's writ of certiorari to the Supreme Court of the United States was granted. Now, in this moot court exercise, each team is to write a brief addressed to the Supreme Court, supporting their client's position. Afterwards oral argument will be held at which each student will be called upon to defend his position, and to reply to points raised in his opponent's brief.

Sabotnik loved the case, from the moment he read it. It was a case you could love, an important social issue, something you could feel strongly about, and he had the good fortune to be assigned to what he believed to be the right side. Defending the doctor, and forcing the courts to liberalize abortion law, that was what law school was supposed to be about Sabotnik thought to himself. It was in the courts that racial segregation was being struck down, and the Supreme Court under Earl Warren was bound to strike down so much more of the old conservative repressive past. Sabotnik could daydream about being a part of all that. The Pasteur case was an invitation to such a daydream, a chance to pretend that he was at the cutting edge of the law, briefing and arguing a case of national importance. For Sabotnik it was an important dream.

Phil Sabotnik knew that he was bright. He had run almost a straight A average at City College, and you didn't do that if you weren't bright. Still, he was worried that he wasn't quite as bright as many of his classmates. In the discussions in class there were plenty of students who seemed to see things in the cases that escaped Sabotnik altogether, students who were much quicker on the uptake. There were others, like Ted Murcer, who were polished and sophisticated in ways Sabotnik could never hope to emulate. At the bottom, Sabotnik suffered from a growing sense of inferiority, a fear that he would never be able to compete with those around him. In his heart he knew that he would never be a brilliant or famous constitutional lawyer. He would be a competent practitioner, he thought. He would earn a living. But moot court would be an opportunity to pretend that he might be something more. It might also be a cruel experience, he realized, a hard exposure to the fact that he could not compete. It was a challenge, at a minimum, a challenge to make certain that he did not embarrass himself.

9

From the very outset, Ted Murcer was effectively able to resist the dominant ethos of the law school. He had no interest in being number one in his class, did not particularly care whether or not he made law review. He refused to become obsessed with his work, refused to sit up half the night, hunched over a desk, going half blind reading, analyzing, and taking notes on every last case and footnote in the casebooks. He was bright. He had always done reasonably well with his schoolwork. He would do reasonably well in law school. Not brilliantly, but reasonably well. That was enough.

Murcer had come to law school in part to mark time. He had started his senior year at Amherst without any specific idea of what type of career he wanted to make for himself. He was ambitious, sought success, money, maybe politics, public service, public acclaim. But he could not see anything concrete that he wanted, no job opportunity that captured his interest. And he certainly didn't wish to go on to do graduate work in any discipline, to become an academic, to retreat into an ivory tower. Law school was a way of putting off the decision. Whatever he did end up doing, Murcer figured, a law degree wouldn't hurt. The credentials would be useful and he expected that with three years of study he was bound to pick up some useful skills. At a minimum it would be three more years in which he might leave his options open. He liked that idea.

Murcer's problem had always been his skepticism. He saw too readily, or thought he saw too readily through façades, and was quick to imagine hypocrisy or bad motives behind the behavior of those around him. He was almost congenitally incapable of committing himself to causes. He was self-contained, an observer, a critic, and he saw the law school in a harsh uncompromising light. Murcer saw his law professors by and large as petty tyrants who were great at running the world on paper. He watched them terrify his classmates, watched them posture as ultimate sources of wisdom, and he wondered how many of them had ever successfully managed a business, or run successfully for public office, or founded a successful law practice for that matter. Very few of them, he thought. He wondered how many of them were capable of making a hard decision, how many of them had good judgment or common sense to go with their academic expertise. For himself, he wanted no part of it. He kept his distance.

As a child, Ted Murcer had been terribly shy. Shy to the point of refusing to answer a telephone, the kind of kid who always knew the answer to the teacher's question but never raised his hand for fear that he might possibly be wrong. He was a reader, history mostly, and a daydreamer. He imagined himself a hero, winning the World Series in the bottom of the ninth of the seventh game with a two-out home run, the usual daydreams. Forced back to reality he was quiet and withdrawn.

When he got to prep school an insightful teacher turned it all around for Murcer. He prevailed upon the student, forced him really, to go out for the school debating team. The results were a revelation. Murcer had been nervous, almost petrified, before his first debate. He had to run into the school bathroom, sick to his stomach just before the debate began. But once he began, once he staggered up to the podium, he was completely transformed. It was an unexpected talent. He had a rapid, almost passionate delivery, an agile mind that was quick on the uptake. Astonishingly, he even discovered a measure of wit, was able to crack a joke, to be sarcastic. Resolved, that the electoral college should be abolished and presidents be elected by direct nationwide popular vote. Resolved, that off-track gambling on horse racing should be legalized. Resolved, that a national right-to-work law should be enacted. Murcer ended up debating all these issues, pro and con. He learned to do his research and he learned to do it well. By the time he graduated, he had won two state championships for debating. More importantly, it had taken him out of his shell, given him self-confidence, a sense of worth. He had run and lost a race for class vice-president, lost to the co-captain of the hockey team. But it hadn't been a bad loss. He had given a campaign speech to the whole class and he almost won when by rights it should not have been close at all.

From a distance, over the course of the year, everything Mary Ann Salisbury saw of Ted Murcer put her on her guard. He seemed to her everything she disliked about law school. He was, she thought, a typical New England aristocrat, a preppie, well groomed, self-assured, complacent, probably superficial. He was the type, she thought, who was bound to do well. He would join the right clubs, marry the right wife, have all the right prejudices, and make out like a bandit practicing corporate law. Mary Ann was a Midwesterner. She thought of herself as a rebel, a populist or a radical. She was a product of public school from grade school through college. Everything that she was, or thought she was, made her distrustful.

He invited her out to dinner. It was a Friday night and his altogether logical pretext was that she had to meet with him anyway to map out their moot court strategy, so why not do it over dinner? He knew a terrific Greek restaurant, he told her. It was small, occupied the ground floor of a brownstone off Columbus Avenue on 113th Street, had a terrific, fat old man who played Greek songs on the accordion. There was a good shish kebab, pitchers of resinated wine, and baklava, drenched in honey. He urged her to accept, promised her a good time and a good meal. She almost said no. They could meet in the law school lounge, she thought, or in one of the conference rooms adjacent to the library. It irritated her to have Murcer use the accident of their moot court pairing as an excuse to take her out, to try his hand no doubt at seduction, to cheapen her status as a law student, to fail to take her seriously. It irritated her, and she almost said no. But she didn't. They would have to work together, she reasoned, and there was no point in being antagonistic or rude. Besides, the restaurant sounded like it might be fun. Mary Ann had never been to a Greek restaurant.

"Christ, we sure were stuck with the rotten end of the case to defend weren't we?" Murcer started the conversation as he poured out some wine. Mary Ann nodded her head in agreement, surprised at his opening.

"We're going to come off as Neanderthals, trying to throw a venerable, courageous doctor in jail for acting on his conscience. And if that were not enough, we can be portrayed as being responsible for every woman who tries to abort herself in some back alley with a coat hanger and manages to kill herself in the process. God, I sure am glad that this is all make-believe. Politically, it would be suicide to ever be publicly identified with either side of this case."

"I feel the same way," Mary Ann said. "But I guess we have no choice. We can't very well go back to the moot court committee and ask for a different case, can we? They would laugh at us and give us that little speech about a lawyer's responsibility to represent any client to the best of his ability, regardless of the lawyer's personal opinion of that client."

"You mean the one about even Hitler being entitled to an able defense?" Murcer asked, smiling.

"Yes."

"The funny thing is," Murcer continued, "that when you think about it, there really are a lot of good arguments that we can make on behalf of Erehwon. I thumbed through the Constitutional Law text this afternoon, and I've got some ideas about how we can even win this thing."

"How in the world are we going to do that?" Mary Ann asked, more interested by far than hostile. They were on their second glass of wine, working their way through a large Greek salad, tearing off chunks of freshly baked bread, and mopping up two dips, one made from fish roe, the other a yogurt, cucumber, and garlic combination, both delicious. She gave in to the food and to his charm, dropped her guard, and decided to begin to enjoy herself.

"I think we can win because the Erehwon antiabortion statute is over a hundred years old and because courts are usually pretty reluctant to strike down laws passed by democratically elected legislatures and signed by democratically elected governors. All we have to do is show that there is some rational basis for the statute, some plausible reason why Erehwon should outlaw abortion, and we'd be home free. Because then we would only have to argue that it is not the function of the court to substitute its own policy judgment for that of the legislature, which better reflects, at least in theory, the will of the people. The courts would have to stand back, no matter how the judges might feel, and leave questions of reform to the political process. We can win on that argument."

"But what reasonable or even rational basis can we find for the statute?" Mary Ann asked. "As far as I'm concerned it just stinks."

"Of course it does. But there are reasons we can advance just the same. Maybe reasons you and I don't like, but reasons just the same. For instance, how about justifying the statute as a means of protecting the lives of Erehwon's conceived, unborn, and defenseless future citizens. Maybe the statute is designed to protect women from the medical risks of the abortion itself, or maybe it is supposed to promote population growth. Erehwon might be an underpopulated western state and for all we know, it might be reasonable for them to want to see their population grow by eliminating abortions."

"You don't honestly think any of those are reasonable justifications for a statute that discriminates against the poor and the uneducated. Rich people go to Sweden or to Puerto Rico to get their abortions nice and neat. In the meantime, poor women are forced to endure their unwanted pregnancies and raise kids that they cannot afford, or more likely they end up in a back alley somewhere getting cut up by some butcher with dirty fingernails. I know a guy who's a second-year resident up at Presbyterian Hospital and he once told me that they see two, maybe three women a month who come in bleeding heavily from what he calls self-inflicted incomplete abortions. Some of the women are so desperate that they deliberately cut themselves up just to force the doctors to finish the job. Some of them end up inadvertently sterilizing themselves, or with really nasty infections. One or two even manage to kill themselves. How the hell are we going to justify a statute that permits that kind of suffering?"

He looked at her squarely, listening carefully to what she said, waiting, making sure that she had said everything she had to say. He answered her quietly, making her listen by seeming not to argue. He had the gift of never seeming to argue, the gift of the born diplomat, of the politician building a coalition.

"I can't justify that kind of suffering. No one can. And if I were a legislator, I would vote to repeal that statute. And when I go to vote, I vote for candidates who want to liberalize the abortion statutes. But we don't have to justify the statute, or to measure it against the suffering it permits. That kind of cost-benefit analysis, or even call it a moral judgment if you like, is not what we have to do as lawyers in order to win this moot court. All we have to do is show some rationale, even a lousy one, that supports the legislature's action.

"The way I see it, the Erehwon legislature, and every legislature for that matter, has to choose between difficult competing values on the abortion question. After all, whether you agree or not, it isn't unreasonable to consider a fetus as a human being, a particularly helpless human being. And if you do that, then abortion is murder, and obviously it is rational to prevent and deter murder. Besides, you've got to remember that it isn't the legislature that makes them injure themselves. Those injuries are self-inflicted. Maybe it is more reasonable, or at least somewhat reasonable, to protect defenseless beings, rather than to protect women from their own folly."

"What you're saying," Mary Ann said, not giving in, "is that a fetus has rights that are superior to those of the woman who must carry it. Do you think that it is legitimate to call a fertilized egg, at the moment of conception, a human being? Do you want to give this tiny bit of protoplasm a human being's full legal rights, especially when giving such rights works such hardships and causes such injury? Abortions are usually done in the early weeks or months of pregnancy and I don't think that a fetus at that stage is human, that it has any thoughts or feelings, or anything that would entitle it to legal protection."

"Well, what do you think it is?" Murcer asked. "Is a fetus like tonsils or an appendix or something? Is it just tissue that belongs to the mother, something that she can get rid of without thought? Maybe it is. Maybe I think it is. But an awful lot of people are going to disagree with us. And I'm not sure that they're unreasonable, or even that they are wrong. I don't think that you can be so sure either."

And deep down she wasn't sure. Not about herself. And not about Ted Murcer. He was not what she had imagined him to be. He was bright, skeptical, uncertain, willing to listen, and altogether more attractive than she had expected. She sensed the residual shyness hidden under eight years of polishing at Amherst and at prep school. He took her out to dinner, filled her with wine, looked her in the eye, spoke well, listened well, and he didn't make a move on her. When dinner was over he took her back to her dormitory. He didn't take her arm, made no effort to kiss her good night, just stood in the entranceway, nodded his head, and left. Mary Ann watched him walk down Broadway.

10

Petrakis and Sabotnik had each decided to do some preliminary research before meeting to plot their moot court strategy. It had been a wise approach. It had given them the opportunity to learn a little of what the courts had already written on the subject, what the law professors and scholars writing in the law reviews had to state. It was a more professional approach, less ideological, more pragmatic. It had been Petrakis' idea to work that way.

When they met, Sabotnik was awed by the power of Petrakis' analysis of the problem. Sabotnik had worked hard and had thought a great deal about the abortion issues involved in the appeal. He had framed in his mind what he thought might be a strong argument about how the Erehwon statute was a violation of a woman's right to unlimited control over her body and her health, and how her physician's right to practice his profession was also violated. He had found a few cases and also a few articles that seemed to support these ideas.

Petrakis quickly demonstrated to Sabotnik how shallow, naïve, and unimaginative his research had been. Petrakis had filled an entire pad of foolscap with notes and a detailed outline of points that he thought needed to be dealt with in their brief. Sabotnik listened almost in awe as his partner ticked them off.

"First of all," Petrakis said, "I think that we can win this appeal on a technicality without even forcing the court to face the abortion issue."

"How is that?"

"By arguing that the statute is defective on its face and should be struck down for bad draftsmanship. Just read the damned thing. It says that abortions can be performed in order to preserve a woman's life. The statute doesn't say what that means. Does it mean only to prevent a woman's death? Or does it mean to protect her health? And if it means that, does it mean physical health only, or emotional health as well? Or does it mean to protect health only from serious threats that might be life-threatening? Or what about protection from injuries that might be serious but not life-threatening?

"You see what I mean? This statute is arguably so vague and imprecise that old Dr. Pasteur really could not know whether he was violating the law when he performed that abortion. Remember, he refused to answer when asked whether he had acted in order to preserve his patient's life. I think we can argue that he did not know what that statutory language meant."

"But what is the good of that?" Sabotnik asked. "Ignorance of the law is no defense."

"Yes," Petrakis agreed patiently, "but I've found a whole flock of Supreme Court cases that hold that when a criminal statute is so poorly drafted that you cannot reasonably determine what behavior it is forbidding and what it is permitting, then the statute must be struck down as vague. Here's one, for instance, which holds that you cannot force an individual to try to guess about what he can or cannot do, if the cost of guessing wrong is that he goes to jail. The statute must be clear on its face."

Sabotnik saw the point. "You mean that Dr. Pasteur maybe didn't violate the statute in the first place? Maybe he isn't guilty and was wrongly convicted?"

"More or less," Petrakis answered. "Of course, Pasteur really thought he was breaking the law. He was trying to do a Thoreau- or a Gandhi-type civil disobedience number, and if there were such a real person, he would probably want to go to jail to publicize his cause. Still I think that we can beat this charge on the technicality of vagueness. And I think that we should."

"But do you think that the court would duck the real issue? After all if they throw out the statute as vague, then the legislature could always just pass a new one that wasn't vague. Then the whole case would just come back again."

"Maybe it would. But so what. Courts like to duck tough and controversial issues like abortion on technicalities, if they can. And maybe it's not a bad idea if they do. Besides, who knows what the legislature might do if they had to pass a new statute. Who knows, they might not pass one, or they might pass one that Pasteur found acceptable."

"Okay," Sabotnik answered, "I'll buy it. I suppose that we should make it the first point of our brief."

"That's the way I saw it."

They went on for another two hours, and at each point Petrakis seemed to have come up with some new insight or angle. He had done research into the old common law, even into the early English case law, and had developed arguments based on those cases. Anglo-American law, he said, had never really afforded any personal rights to the unborn, and had always drawn a sharp distinction, allowing only those who were born alive, for instance, to own property or to sue for personal injury. He had found a dozen arguments, some of them subtle, some quite elegant, to support their own position. Most of them had not occurred to Sabotnik at all.

"What do you really think about abortion?" Sabotnik asked after they finished their meeting. "I'm in favor of abortion on demand," he added quickly, not wanting it to seem that he was holding back on his own views.

"I'm against it," Petrakis said quietly.

"Is it a matter of religion?" Sabotnik asked.

"No. Hardly that," Petrakis answered. "Back home in Philadelphia, a lot of people are against abortion, but when the chips are down, nobody really pays attention to that. I know lots of good religious people who, when their daughters get pregnant, suddenly lose their religion and find a way to get an abortion for them. In the end, I think that most people who want abortions get them one way or another and in the final analysis the church and the law don't make a whole hell of a lot of difference in what happens."

"Then why do you oppose abortion on demand? If people are going to do it anyway, why make it illegal? Isn't that going to foster disrespect for the law, just like prohibition?"

"Maybe. But that's no argument. Everyone cheats on taxes, but that doesn't mean there shouldn't be taxes. There are places where there are blood feuds and vendettas, where people burn each other's barns and kill one another for revenge. Does that mean that there shouldn't be laws against arson and murder in those places? I just don't like abortion. I think it's wrong, and I don't think the law should sanction it."

There was almost a vehemence in Petrakis' manner, and Sabotnik decided to tread lightly, to change the subject, but Petrakis went on, an uncharacteristic break in his self-composure.

"My sister had an abortion once," he told Sabotnik. "She's two years older than me and I was a sophomore in college at the time. She had been going out with this guy and he had jilted her. She wouldn't tell the guy and she couldn't tell my folks, so she told me."

"What did you do?"

"I talked around the college, and I eventually got the name of a doctor in Harrisburg who was supposed to be safe. He charged two hundred fifty dollars, in cash, and he would only do his work at night, on Sunday nights, in his office, where there wouldn't be any witnesses."

"So you raised the money."

"Yes. And I drove her to Harrisburg. I remember she didn't talk all the way down there, and we got lost and she got a little hysterical. It was a little tense, because if we didn't get there on time, the doctor would just leave his office and that would be that. We had already paid him a hundred fifty dollars in advance, and that was a lot of money."

"Did you make it?"

"Yes. I dropped her at the doctor's office and I waited a minute until she stuck her head out and told me that the doctor was in. I wasn't allowed to go in because the doctor insisted that she go in by herself, you know, no witnesses. Anyway I sat in that car for about thirty minutes imagining that she was dying in there for God knows what. Then she came out and walked kind of weak-kneed toward the car."

"How was she?"

"She looked all right at first. A little pale but all right. I thought that it was all over and I drove fast to get out of there like I was doing a getaway from a bank robbery. What I didn't realize was that that bastard hadn't finished the abortion. He had done something to make her uterus contract and she ended up having the damned abortion right in the back seat of my dad's car. She had cramps first and then she started to bleed, and we were too scared to go to a hospital. I was driving on the highway and I tried not to look in the rearview mirror. When it was over, we stopped at a gas station and I waited while she got rid of whatever she had to get rid of."

Petrakis never spoke to Sabotnik in such personal terms again. He never spoke to anyone in the law school in such terms. Still, Sabotnik remembered. Twenty years later he would remember. Somehow from that moment he considered Petrakis a friend.

11

The brief writing process proved equally arduous for each team. They were given a twenty-five-page maximum length in which to work, which at first seemed like plenty. But as they did their research, there was more and more that needed to be included. The twenty-five-page limit started to get smaller and smaller.

Murcer and Sabotnik played basketball together at the university gym. They took to teasing each other, promising to beat each other's brains in when the moot court argument came around.

Sabotnik was tall and gangly, played basketball with more enthusiasm than talent. He loved going up for rebounds, played a tight, clinging, pressing defense, and couldn't score to save his life. He just didn't have a soft touch. Murcer on the other hand was fast and graceful. He could drive toward the basket beautifully, dribbling with either hand, accelerating suddenly and laying the ball in, or pulling up short to sink a jump shot. He had a beautiful touch and when he was on he could score flocks of baskets from all over the court. He didn't play defense though, not really. And he did best in free-wheeling, high-scoring, wide-open games.

Murcer and Sabotnik complemented each other, and they did well together in the two-man pickup half-court games. It was a release for both men, a chance to get rid of the built-up tensions of law school. When they finished playing, after they had showered and dressed, they usually went together for cups of coffee and slices of pie at an off-campus diner. They got on easily, the two of them, had a rapport that grew from the fact that neither one felt threatened by the other. They weren't competing with one another.

"You're living in the dorm now, aren't you?" Sabotnik asked Murcer one evening.

"Yes."

"I've got an apartment. Or I should say that I'm going to get an apartment," Sabotnik stated. "It's a two-bedroom place that belongs to Morty Ackerman, a third-year student who's a college friend of my brother's. I'm going to be taking over the lease for next year. Would you like to share the apartment with me?"

"Sure," Murcer answered instantly. "What's it going to cost?"

"Ninety a month, gas and electricity included. We'll split it down the middle, forty-five each. But I better warn you though, it's a fifth-floor walk-up."

Murcer offered Sabotnik a hand. "You've got yourself a room-mate."

Their moot court oral argument was held on a Wednesday evening. The chief judge they had drawn was Professor Charles Madison, former law clerk to Justice Oliver Wendell Holmes, a nationally known expert on labor law, and, by reputation, an acid-tongued, thoroughgoing son of a bitch. The second judge on the three-judge panel, Oscar Wedermeyer, was a senior partner at Standish, Boynton, and Linville, a large and prestigious old downtown firm, specializing in the representation of investment bankers. The third judge, Terence McCarthy, a third-year law student, was no less than the Notes Editor of the law review. McCarthy at that moment was reputed to have the highest grade-point average in his class. They had drawn a heavy panel, a panel to be afraid of.

Mary Ann was sick to her stomach that evening. There hadn't been a ghost of a prayer of keeping down dinner. She studied her note cards, trying to prepare herself, trying to commit to memory the important facts of all the cases she had cited in her brief. She could just imagine one of the judges asking her what was the holding of *Smith* v. *Jones*, and why had she put it in the brief—and her standing there like a moron, unable for the life of her to remember *Smith* v. *Jones* or why she had cited it. She could imagine standing there unable to say a word and wishing for the floor to open up and swallow her.

She had prepared a list of points that she would try to make. But she knew that the judges would never let her. They would ask her questions, try to pin her down or trap her. There was no way she could match wits with that group. None of them could. She showered, used the toilet, started to dress, decided to use the toilet again. Her stomach was a mess. Finally she dressed in her best gray woolen dress. She put on the string of pearls that she had inherited from her grandmother, looked in the mirror, and decided not to wear them. She fussed with makeup and washed it off. Then, a full half hour earlier than she needed to, she left her room and walked across the campus to the law school. She felt like a lamb being led to the slaughter.

Murcer, Sabotnik, and Petrakis were all there when she arrived at the mock courtroom. Sabotnik, whom she thought was sweet, looked excited. He kept glancing at a pad of foolscap that he held in his hand, and he was pacing back and forth across the back of the courtroom muttering to himself. He looked excited, nervous, but prepared. Mary Ann knew he would do well.

Petrakis, on the other hand, looked as sick as Mary Ann felt. He was wearing a black pin-striped three-piece suit, and his naturally dark complexion appeared unnaturally pale. There were beads of sweat on his forehead. Twice during the half hour before the argument was scheduled to begin, he had left for the bathroom.

Ted Murcer was nervous too. She knew that he was nervous. But it didn't even begin to show. He was the only one with a smile, the only one who looked relaxed. Once he had stepped into the hall to smoke a cigarette. Mary Ann had stepped out to join him. He had reached for her hand and gave it a quick squeeze.

"Oyez! Oyez! Oyez! All rise!" said the second-year student posing as the court clerk. "All those having business before this the Supreme Court of the United States, draw near and ye shall be heard! God save the United States and this Honorable Court!"

And the three "judges," looking grim and serious, each holding copies of the briefs that had been submitted, each even wearing black judges' robes, marched in and took their seats. Professor Madison, seated in the center, turned toward them. Mary Ann and Ted Murcer, as respondents, were seated on the left.

Petrakis and Sabotnik were on the right. The chief judge turned to the right and looked at Petrakis.

"You may begin, sir," he said in a dry and peculiarly high-pitched voice.

Petrakis picked up his notes and walked to the podium like a condemned man on his way to the gallows.

"May it please the court," he began in an unsteady voice. "My name is George Petrakis and I am an attorney for Dr. Albert Pasteur, the appellant. This case involves . . ."

"We know what this case involves," Professor Madison cut in sharply. "What I'd like to know is what it is that makes you think a one-hundred-year-old statute written in nice simple one- and two-syllable words is vague and confusing? Do you really think that a brilliant and learned fellow like Dr. Pasteur did not understand that he was breaking the law?"

"Yes, I do," Petrakis answered lamely, too cowed to take the initiative, as he was supposed to, and begin to explain why that statute was vague.

"If he had no idea that he was breaking the law," Madison went on relentlessly, "may I ask why he walked into a police station to turn himself in? Isn't that very odd behavior? It seems to me that the good doctor was well aware that elective abortions were prohibited, that he had committed a crime. What is it about his conduct that seems to you confused or uncertain?"

Petrakis had no satisfactory answer. Had he been sitting in a living room with the professor he would have instantly replied with a dozen answers. He could have explained that the court should not speculate about Pasteur's own purposes in walking into the police station. Nor should it speculate about the doctor's personal belief of what the words of the statute might mean. Rather, he would have told the professor that the court should look at the statute itself and realize that it applied to everyone, and not only to learned men or political activisits like Dr. Pasteur. Average men, he would have argued, can be sent to jail for violating this statute. And so the court should check and see if the average man can make sense of the statute.

Petrakis knew all these things, but he couldn't say them. There seemed to be a block between his mind and his mouth. He heard

himself uttering banal or stupid answers to the judges' questions
and knew that he was embarrassing himself. He stumbled
through his twenty minutes blindly, desperately hoping for it to
be over. He was no performer, and he would never be a litigator,
subjected to the cruelties of the courtroom. He hadn't needed
moot court to tell him that. He was almost weak with relief
when Professor Madison finally said, "Thank you," and asked to
hear from his partner.

Sabotnik turned out to be surprisingly good. He had listened
to Petrakis' argument, they all had the advantage of seeing
Petrakis go first, and he understood that he had to be more aggressive and persuasive.

"Your honors," he said, going to the heart of the matter, "we
feel that you should strike this statute as vague. But frankly we
feel that any statute, no matter how well worded, if it indis-
criminately prohibits therapeutic abortions, is an unconstitutional
and unjustifiable governmental intrusion and violation of both a
woman's right to control what happens to her body, as well as a
doctor's right to practice his profession."

"What constitutional right are you talking about?" Wedermeyer, the Wall Street lawyer, cut in sharply. "I am unaware of
any constitutional amendment in the Bill of Rights which gives a
woman or her doctor freedom to abort at will."

"There doesn't have to be a specific, articulated amendment
dealing with abortion for constitutional protection to exist,"
Sabotnik answered quickly, hurrying to explain before he could
be interrupted by another question. "The First Amendment,
when it mentions freedom of assembly; the Fourth Amendment
talking about freedom from unreasonable search and seizure; the
Fifth and Fourteenth Amendments guaranteeing due process and
equal protection of the law; the Eighth Amendment outlawing
cruel and unusual punishment—these are not just narrow phrases
that this court should look at with blinders. They are guarantees
of personal liberty and self-determination. Nowhere in the Constitution does it say that race discrimination is unconstitutional.
But that hasn't stopped the Supreme Court from stating not long
ago, in *Brown* v. *Board of Education*, that segregaion violated
the Constitution. I think that the same thing applies here. This

criminal statute represents an impermissible and intolerable governmental intrusion into the most private and personal part of a woman's life . . ."

Sabotnik ran a little too long, but he had the right idea. Mary Ann was very impressed listening to him. She had thought of Sabotnik as a tall, awkward, not especially brilliant, not especially effective person. She had liked him because there was nothing about him not to like, because he was Ted Murcer's friend. But now he was in his element. There was an intensity about him as he argued, a determination to do well, almost a passion. She would never have guessed it to be there.

Sabotnik and McCarthy, the judge from the law review, had gotten themselves tangled up in a dispute over some cases in which courts had compelled parents to submit their children to necessary medical treatment even though the parents' Christian Science beliefs forbade such treatment. "Aren't the courts violating their First Amendment rights by compelling these children to have appendectomies?" McCarthy asked.

"That case is distinguishable from this one," Sabotnik answered, too canny to say yes or no and submit to cross-examination. "In the Christian Science case, the treatment is for the child, while the belief is that of the parent. The courts certainly can protect a child's welfare even from the child's parents. But in this case we are talking about a woman's beliefs about her own body. The courts cannot force a person to have an operation he needs if he doesn't want it. If he dies because of his stupidity, well so be it. It's the same thing here. The law must not meddle with personal self-determination."

"What about the fetus then?" McCarthy went on. "If, as you concede, courts can protect children from their parents, why cannot they protect unborn children in the same way?"

Before Sabotnik could answer, the red light on the podium went on, indicating his time was up. Professor Madison then interrupted, and thanked Sabotnik. It was like breaking a trance. The student was reluctant to sit down, and no one really wanted him to. Sabotnik stood at the podium a minute, looking lost. Then he grabbed his paper and sat down.

It was Mary Ann's turn. As she approached the podium, before she could even open her mouth, the professor had a question for her.

"As a woman, Miss Salisbury," he asked, "how can you personally argue that women do not have the right to protect and control their own reproductive destiny?"

It was a nasty and unfair question, and it hit Mary Ann where she lived. She answered without thinking, falling right into the trap.

"Personally I do believe that women do have those rights, and I would be much happier arguing the other side, your honor."

"What does your happiness have to do with this?" the professor thundered, appearing furious. "How dare you stand in front of this court and state that you personally believe that your opponents should prevail. Your responsibility is to your client, the people of Erehwon. Your obligation is to do everything in your power to persuade this court that your client's position is correct and should prevail."

It degenerated from there. It was almost as if the judges weren't interested in hearing Mary Ann's arguments on the merits. Rather they threw one trick question after another at her, keeping her on the defensive, interrupting her answers with new questions, changing the subject abruptly, sometimes arguing with one another and ignoring her completely.

"What is your function here as a prosecutor?" Professor Madison asked toward the end of the twenty-minute period.

"To get a conviction, I imagine," Mary Ann answered.

"That is wrong and highly improper," the professor shot back, again raising his voice. "Your task is to see that justice was and is done—not merely to get convictions. A single-minded concern with convicting Dr. Pasteur would be a disgrace."

Mary Ann flushed a deep red. She was furious. She knew that once she sat down she would think of things to say but now she was too angry to speak. They were picking on her because she was a woman. None of the others had been subjected to this kind of abuse. They had been given a chance to make their arguments, but these three would not even listen to her. She sat down, suppressing a desire to cry. She would not give them the satisfaction.

Ted Murcer got up, having figured out the judges and having figured out how to handle them. He realized that the trick was to provoke them, or to intrigue them, or to surprise them, but above all to keep them off-balance. He alone, of the four students, approached the podium with a sense of assurance. He stood up there as if he had been born there, waited a moment before starting, looked at each of the judges squarely (he was the only one to have done so), and flashed a smile at them.

"Your honors," he said, "I see this as a case of civil disobedience. Dr. Pasteur is an admirable and I believe a courageous man. But I also believe that the record clearly demonstrates that he very much wants to be punished for violating and deliberately violating laws that he dislikes. I can respect and admire Dr. Pasteur. You can respect and admire him. But that doesn't mean that he shouldn't serve his sentence.

"Justice Madison," he said, looking at the professor, "if I may say so, your suggestion that Dr. Pasteur obviously understood the meaning of the statute, and knew that he was breaking the law, is clearly correct."

The professor shook his head but did not interrupt. Murcer was permitted to go on, launching into a brief, but very effective oration about the importance of having the courts not meddle with the democratic process and the voice of the people as expressed by the legislature. Then, turning to McCarthy, the student judge, he reminded him of his earlier question concerning the state's interest in protecting unborn children from their parents, and then he hammered home the idea that it was reasonable for Erehwon to provide such protection. The judges asked him one or two questions along the way. But they were easy questions, and he handled them easily. He ended on a gracious note, thanking the court for its attention, and suddenly it was over.

The three judges rose and exited to begin their deliberations. The students stood up in respect and watched them exit. Suddenly they were alone in the classroom.

Murcer and Sabotnik walked across the aisle, grinning at one another, shook hands, clapped each other on the back. Then Mary

Ann came up to the two of them and gave them each a kiss. Petrakis walked over and shook both men's hands.

"You guys were just terrific," he told them. "I don't know which one of you was better. Those judges are certainly going to have a tough time selecting a best speaker."

In their elation at being finished with the ordeal of oral argument, the other three had forgotten that there would be winners and losers, that one of them would be designated best speaker and eligible to enter the prestigious second-year moot court honors competition. There would be a grade given to the briefs they had written, with a cash award given to the best brief submitted in the entire class.

"Your brief was fantastic," Mary Ann said to Petrakis. "It made ours look sick by comparison."

"Yeah, but I sure blew it in oral argument," Petrakis answered ruefully. "I might as well have stayed home for all I accomplished in front of those judges. One thing's for sure. I'm never going to make it as a courtroom lawyer."

They all sat down and began to do a post-mortem of the argument. The four of them felt comfortable with one another, commiserated with one another over their errors, relived the good moments, which were mostly Murcer's or Sabotnik's. The men agreed that Mary Ann had been treated unfairly and did what they could to make her feel better.

The student clerk reentered the classroom. "All rise," he announced, and the three judges trooped in. The four students remained standing, while Professor Madison rendered the decision.

"First of all," he told them, "considering that this was your first attempt at this sort of thing, you all did quite acceptably. If the three of us were to decide the case on the merits, I believe that we would split two to one in favor of the state of Erehwon. However, we are here really to judge the quality of your work and not the merits of the case.

"Turning first to the briefs, on a scale of one to a hundred we have awarded Mr. Petrakis and Mr. Sabotnik a grade of ninety-two, which I might add is the highest grade awarded to date this year. Your brief was outstanding, easily as good as some that we have seen submitted to the Supreme Court itself.

"Mr. Petrakis," he went on, "your oral argument did not live up to the expectation of the brief and we award you a seventy-three. You need more experience in oral advocacy.

"Mr. Sabotnik, you did quite well. We award you a grade of eighty-six.

"Miss Salisbury, your grade, like Mr. Petrakis', is seventy-three, and, Mr. Murcer, your grade is eighty-nine, and we designate you best speaker."

12

Even Murcer got swept up in the May madness that set in at the end of that first year of law school. At the beginning of June they would all be sitting down to their final exams. Five of them, Contracts, Torts, Criminal Law, Civil Procedure, Property, each exam would run three and one-half hours. There would be an hour or an hour and a half of short-answer questions. They would be multiple choice for the most part, trick questions that had to be carefully read and reread, questions where you couldn't trust your instincts, where the obvious answer was usually wrong, except that sometimes it wasn't and then you could kick yourself for being too damned clever. Then there were the essay questions, impossibly convoluted hypothetical fact patterns were given, all to be untangled and analyzed in sharp, crisp prose under the tightest of time constraints. There might be four or five such essays in each exam, each essay to be answered in roughly twenty or thirty minutes. They called for an instant and powerful command of extremely complicated subject matter. There was little margin for error. On top of it all, the five exams would come one after another in rapid succession. They would literally walk out of a grueling Civil Procedure exam at five-thirty on a Tuesday afternoon for instance, and sit down to take their Property exam at nine the following morning.

As May wore on, the level of tension and anxiety at the law school rose sharply. The intense competitive spirit that had pervaded the class when the year began degenerated into a fear of failure, of the disgrace of not making the grade. Everything, making law review, entire professional futures, seemed to ride on the outcome of those tests. They would be taken and then graded anonymously, the professors unable to know the name of the student who wrote any particular exam. Everything depended upon what was put down in the exam blue book during those seventeen and a half hours of testing.

Murcer and Mary Ann had taken to studying together from the time they had first begun working on their moot court brief. Mary Ann had found a small seminar room which was deserted in the late afternoons and evenings. They would retire there, loaded down with their casebooks, class notes, course outlines and synopses, and work well into the night. They worked old exams together, asked each other questions, debated the answers. They read each other's class notes, trying to catch important points that they had missed themselves. They ate dinner together virtually every night, hurriedly wolfing down hamburgers and Cokes, always talking their way through their courses, never letting up on the pressure. Sometimes they studied alone, each in a separate corner of the seminar room, neither talking, each busy trying to extract and distill the essence of every major case in each course. They shared, but they never expressed their fears. Murcer too proud to admit his concern that he might somehow fail; Mary Ann unwilling or unable to acknowledge an anxiety that Murcer would not also admit. Neither fooled the other. It was all around them, everyone in the same boat. And between them they built a rapport, a sense of being subjected to the same ordeal, of being fired and tempered in the same crucible. It was unspoken, but they drew very close, became colleagues and equals, chain-smoking cigarettes and drinking endless cans of soda, purchased from a machine in the building's lobby. They worked until roughly midnight each night, gathered up their books, trudged back to their respective dorms, and collapsed into sleep. Come morning there was more of the same.

The exams when they came were an ordeal to be endured. Mary Ann found them endless. She knew the answers to many of the multiple-choice questions, and didn't have a clue on a number of others, just guessed wildly and didn't worry about them. Then there were those ten or fifteen short-answer questions that she would agonize over, questions where two possible answers would look equally good, where she would scrutinize the wording of the question, looking for a trick or a clue. There were always two or three questions that she kept returning to, where she might change her answer three or four times. Then there were the essays where she didn't have enough to write, and the ones where she had too much to write. Once or twice she even wasted ten or more precious minutes on an essay, realized that she was making some serious error, and had to rip up her answer and start over. Then she would go nuts over the rest of the exam, trying to make up for lost time.

And when each exam ended, when the bell rang and the proctors picked up their booklets, when they all staggered out into the hallways drained and exhausted, faced with the ordeal of four or three or two more exams, there began the separate ordeal of the collective post-mortems. "Did you catch the statute of limitations problem in the breach of warranty essay?" one student would ask. Or, "How about the choice of law issue in that wrongful death essay? Was it New York or Massachusetts law that should apply?" The post-mortems drove her crazy. She had no idea how she had done. None of them did. And she didn't want to begin worrying about particular questions that she might have missed. There was no time to worry about what was over, especially with new exams looming one or two days away. Still she couldn't tear herself away from the post-mortems. None of them could.

One test after another, night after night of cramming, none of them had ever experienced anything like it. Then suddenly at five-thirty on the Thursday night of the second week of the

exam period it was all over. Civil Procedure was the last, and for
Mary Ann the worst, of the exams. Then it was over. The exam
was over and the first year in law school was over. Mary Ann
found herself shaking as she handed in her paper.

They had promised themselves that they would celebrate the end
of exams. They would go out and stuff themselves full of good
food, drink lots of wine, maybe get drunk, release tensions, forget.

"Promise me one thing," Mary Ann said when he arrived to
pick her up.

"What?" Murcer asked.

"No matter what, I don't want to speak a single word about
law school tonight, nothing about the exams, nothing about the
professors, and nothing about next year. I've had it."

Murcer agreed. But it was impossible. For both of them. They
went down to Little Italy, to a run-down restaurant with lino-
leum floors and tables without tablecloths, to a restaurant that
served oversized portions of pasta and large bottles of chilled
deep purple, homemade wine. And they talked of law school,
talked as if they had been emptied out of everything else, talked
as if there was nothing else.

They walked downtown. Past Chinatown to Foley Square,
past the courthouses—100 Centre Street, the criminal courts; 60
Centre Street, the State Supreme Court; the United States District Court, the Second Circuit Court of Appeals. They walked
downtown, aimlessly, past City Hall, past Trinity Church, past
Wall Street. He took her arm. At long last he took her arm.
They held hands, and they reached the Battery, Battery Park,
the southern tip of Manhattan, row on row of monuments, me-
morials to war dead. They turned to face each other. He kissed
her. They kissed each other. Strained against one another.

They began to walk again. Towards the ferry. He paid the
two nickels and they walked up the concrete and steel ramp. A
horn sounded and the engines began to churn. They climbed up
to the upper deck, went to the outside. It was starting to rain
lightly. They looked back at the skyscrapers receding in the distance, a million lights reaching up into the sky, looked up the

East River to the bridges, the Brooklyn Bridge, Manhattan
Bridge, Williamsburg Bridge. They kissed again, his hands
roamed over her body and she pressed close to him.

They stood holding hands in the rain. Heading toward Staten
Island, they passed the Statue of Liberty.

It was a time of beginnings.

13

That summer was for working, or for loving. But it was not for
the law. They were shell-shocked and they needed a release.
There were very few of them who had been foolish enough to
take a summer legal job between their first and second years of
law school. There would be enough time for that between their
second and third years. And then after graduation there would
be a lifetime.

Sabotnik spent that summer working for his uncle's accounting
firm. It was a small firm that had started out representing textile
manufacturers, suit and cloakers, dressmakers, the *shmatte* trade
as it was known in Yiddish. The clients were growing though;
they were leaving New York, or at least they were opening
plants down south in North Carolina or South Carolina, anywhere where labor was cheaper. The clients were growing that
year so his uncle's accounting firm had to grow too in order to
service them. There was no choice. If you didn't grow you lost
your clients. You lost your clients and then you starved. So firms
grew and they made more money. There was no choice and as a
result there was plenty of part-time summer work available for a
willing nephew. They paid Sabotnik fifty dollars a week.

Some of the time they sent Sabotnik out of town on audits.
He went with the junior accountants to places like Wilkes Barre,
Pennsylvania, or Camden, South Carolina, or West Upton, Mas-
sachusetts, where he got to count hundreds of thousands of

broom handles, or hundreds of miles of fabrics on thousands of dozens of little girls' dresses, always verifying that inventories were as stated, that financial statements were accurate.

It was the first traveling he had ever done, working that summer. He lived in motels while they were on the road, sharing a room with one of the "juniors," Tony Mazzerelli. They ate dinner in sad little restaurants and they went to bed early. Mazzerelli, Sabotnik discovered, suffered from a deviated septum and snored like a buzz saw. Sabotnik never had the heart to wake the man up. He just suffered.

That was the summer when Sabotnik first met Marilyn. It began on a Friday night. He had just returned from Wilkes Barre, and he was eating dinner at his uncle and aunt's.

"Philip," his aunt told him, smiling ironically, "I know a girl you would just hate. She's very pretty so you won't feel comfortable when you're around her. She's an intellectual snob just like you and she's always got her nose buried in a book. Of course she's Jewish and that's no good, because God forbid you should make me or your mother happy by going out with a nice Jewish girl. And worst of all, I'm the one who's giving you her name, which I know is worse than the kiss of death, because who in this day and age would ever go out with a girl whose name they got from their aunt. So here, I'll write her name and phone number on a piece of paper. Her name is Marilyn Dragutsky and she lives on the Grand Concourse. Her mother works at the Board of Elections with me. Anyway, here's the paper. I know that you won't use it, but at least I can tell her mother that I tried."

Sabotnik put the piece of paper in his pocket and promptly managed to forget about it. It sat for four days in his pants pocket until he rediscovered it, was about to throw the paper in the trash can, thought better of it, and stuffed it back in his pocket. It took him three more days to muster the courage to make the call.

"Hello," he said. "I'm Phil Sabotnik and my aunt thought that maybe you would like to go out with me. She gave me your phone number and I thought that I would call to see if you would like to go out Saturday night."

He felt like a jackass blurting out his invitation.

They dated all through the summer. The concerts at Lewisohn Stadium. Sunny Sunday afternoons at Jones Beach. Baseball games at Yankee Stadium. But not in the bleachers. He bought general admission tickets and they sat in the third deck, right over home plate, the best seats in the house, he thought. Better than the reserved seats or even the boxes down the first and third base lines. Saturday nights, sometimes, they went to Sheepshead Bay in Brooklyn, to Lundy's Restaurant on the waterfront to eat gargantuan shore dinners. They ate shrimp cocktail and endless numbers of hot buns, steamers, and clam chowder, and whole Maine lobsters, corn on the cob, coleslaw, and blueberry pie with vanilla ice cream. Sometimes they went to Coney Island and ate hot dogs, french fries, and Cokes. Wherever they went though, and whatever else they did, they never stopped talking.

She was not as beautiful as his aunt had promised. But she was near enough. Lean, animated, dark-haired, she was someone Sabotnik was happy to be with. It was not a summer for thinking or talking about law. She was an English major at Hunter College, minoring in education, doing some student teaching, expecting to teach junior high school when she graduated.

"I don't really want to teach," she told him. "I'd rather go on for a Ph.D. in English and maybe teach at the college level. I'd like to write a thesis on modern American literature, maybe something about the American writers in Paris in the twenties, the lost generation. But it's not in the cards. There's no future in college teaching for a woman. Except maybe teaching at a women's college like one of the seven sisters. But there's no way that a Jewish girl from the Bronx, especially one with only a degree from Hunter, is going to get a job teaching at Vassar or Wellesley. So I'll get my teaching license and teach junior high or high school. That's safe. You can't get in trouble with a teaching license. That way, if you get married and have children, you can quit. And then later, when the kids get older, you can go back to work first as a sub, then later go back full time. Besides, when you teach, the hours aren't too bad. You're out by three or three-thirty and you can get home to make dinner and take care of the house. There are also lots of vacations and the long summer break, so there is plenty of time to spend with your family."

She sounded to Sabotnik like someone trying to persuade herself that she was not selling out. But somehow it didn't bother him. He felt comfortable with her, as if he belonged at her side, had always been there. The cadence of her speech, its accent, its idiom, all were natural to his ear. He understood her, understood her expectations, understood her fears, understood what she wanted. And he had the sense that she understood him too. It was unstated, but they saw one another as the type of person they were bound to marry.

They did not make love that summer. On living room couches and back porches and park benches, they did what they could to feed and then relieve each other's desire. But they did not make love. Again it was unstated but understood that they would wait for the right time and for the right place, not for something quick or sleazy in the back seat of a parked car or in some roadside motel with a Gideon Bible next to the bed and a leering clerk at check-out time. Sabotnik was living with his parents that summer, he would not take over his student apartment until September. Marilyn lived with her parents, to whom Sabotnik dutifully returned her at the end of each evening. They sat and whispered into the small hours of the morning in the living room of the small two-bedroom apartment, conscious, constrained, and somehow protected by the fact that her parents were not too soundly asleep, or maybe not asleep at all, less than twenty feet away. Occasionally they would hear her father discreetly walk out to the bathroom, hear the door close quietly, and after what seemed like a long time, hear the toilet flush. Then he would return quietly to his bedroom, never once disturbing them.

14

Grades were posted by mail late in July. In early August George Petrakis and Mary Ann Salisbury learned that they had made law review. Ted Murcer and Phil Sabotnik didn't make it. With grade-point averages somewhere between B+ and A— Murcer and Sabotnik were both in good shape, good enough, they felt, to be reasonably sure of graduating near the top of the class, good enough to command excellent jobs upon graduation. Good enough so that for them the pressure was off.

Having missed law review, by even a small margin, Murcer and Sabotnik knew they were out of the running for the Supreme Court judicial clerkships and the two or three other plum positions that would only go to those who had law review on their resumés. For Murcer and Sabotnik and the others in the ninety-five percent of the class who didn't make review, the material incentive to excel was gone. It was possible to relax, to do enough work to maintain decent grades, to lead some sort of normal existence.

Not so for those who made review. For them the pressure increased. Not everyone who made review would end up clerking for a Supreme Court justice. Far from it. Not everyone would be invited to join the law school faculty. Only one or maybe two would get that honor. The pressure was on to maintain their high grades, to graduate first or second or certainly no lower than fourth or fifth in their class. A single B— or C+ might be fatal. Even a B or a B+ could ruin your chances in a world where straight A's were a norm, and A+'s not uncommon.

And that was just regular classwork. Then there was the work on the review itself. Twenty or thirty hours a week had to be spent in scholarly research, double- and triple-checking citations, editing and revising articles and columns, drafting endless footnotes, trying to cover every possible angle of what were often narrow and technical legal issues in the first place. It was dry and tedious and demanding work; dues paid more toward a future reward rather than tasks undertaken for either the pleasure of the experience or the growth in skill or insight to be derived.

For Mary Ann and Petrakis and the others who made law review it was just beginning.

Over the summer Murcer and Mary Ann had traveled together. Neither needed to work, and Murcer had been able to borrow a car from his parents. They had purchased sleeping bags, a pup tent, and had driven south, living cheaply, camping and hiking their way down the Shenandoah Valley, down the Skyline Drive, into the Smoky Mountains of eastern Tennessee and western North Carolina, finally pushing into Alabama and reaching the Gulf of Mexico. They had an easy, relaxed time of mutual discovery, a kind of unmarried honeymoon, a time divorced from responsibilites, divorced from reality. They found quiet back-country ponds where they went skinny-dipping, found streams where Murcer fished for trout while Mary Ann perched peacefully on a rock, read a book, wrote letters, daydreamed. At night they lit campfires, pan-roasted the trout Murcer caught; sometimes they sat back to back, staring into space, talking intimately.

Murcer was shy at first, the façade of his preppie sophistication pierced, he was slower to become comfortable with what they had. He had made love before, with Smith girls in the back seats of convertibles, rented a motel room or two; he had gone to Springfield once or twice with a group of fraternity brothers, to a whorehouse that a lot of the college guys had patronized. But he had never lived with a woman, never really shared an intimacy, never had to think about let alone cope with a woman as a sexual equal. It left him shy and tongue-tied, and to Mary Ann, in an odd sense, all the more boyish and charming. She drew him out of himself, watched his inhibitions drop, his self-confidence grow. She felt older than Murcer, more in control, could listen to him talk, listen to him posture without feeling threatened. She also knew better than to talk to him of her own past. He knew she was divorced, but she was careful never to speak of her husband, feeling that he couldn't handle it. And that was her first mistake. Murcer sensed her reticence. He misinterpreted it, decided that Mary Ann still loved her husband, that he was playing a poor second fiddle.

They were in Pensacola, Florida, on the day they learned that Mary Ann had made law review, that Ted hadn't. They were calling home from a pay phone booth on a highway on the outskirts of town. There were two billboards on either side of the highway near the phone booth. One billboard sign said in bold black letters, IMPEACH EARL WARREN. The other read, THIS IS KLAN KOUNTRY, SUPPORT THE UNITED KU KLUX KLANS OF AMERICA.

The next morning they headed north.

15

In September Murcer and Sabotnik moved into their apartment. They hit it off well. Neither of them had the slightest interest in their furnishings and even less concern with housekeeping. They lived in a kind of friendly, disorganized clutter, making do with cast-off furniture, building bookshelves out of unfinished lumber and cinderblocks. They cleaned or dusted once every two or three weeks, and did their laundry on the day that one or the other ran out of clean socks or underwear. Cooking, when they attempted it at all, was rarely a more elaborate effort than heating up a TV dinner or a can of ravioli. More often they just sent out for pizza or sandwiches.

It was to be an easy, relaxing year for them academically, with the traumas and pressures of the first year mercifully forgotten, and the anxieties of job hunting far off in the future. They had both done well. Not law review, but well enough to be in the top quarter of their class. It was a year to ease up, to live a little, to enjoy life.

Murcer gave Mary Ann a key to the apartment. He asked Sabotnik and there was no objection. She didn't move in though. She maintained her dormitory room as an escape hatch, a token of independence, and she visited the apartment, spending a night or two nights with Murcer, then staying away a few nights, sometimes spending an evening and then returning to her dorm room to go to bed. It was all unstructured.

Three weeks into the new semester they stopped studying together.

"I don't think it makes sense for us to cram together all year the way we did for finals," he told her.

"Why?" she asked, knowing the reasons.

"Because for one thing, this year we're not taking an indentical course load like we did last year. We're both taking Constitutional Law and Trusts and Estates, but I'm taking Evidence and Criminal Procedure and Federal Income Taxation while you're taking Labor Law, Family Law, and that Philosophy of Jurisprudence course. There isn't enough overlap."

Murcer wasn't telling the truth. Mary Ann knew, they both knew, that the real reason he didn't want to study with her was that her commitment to her courses, to making really top grades, was much too intense, while his was nonexistent. She was swept up in the law review things, in the obsession of being number one, and he wasn't. She was worried that he might be jealous of her making review, put off that her grades were higher than his, and in truth he was, at least a little. But there was something else, a subtle shift in their relationship that was also operating on them, a shift that was both unstated but very real. In the spring and into the summer when they had first gone to bed, had first traveled, it had been Murcer who had been shy, tentative, and dependent, Mary Ann who had been the more confident, more experienced, and the more giving. As summer changed to fall this changed. Murcer became confident of Mary Ann and more important, confident of himself. In a way he grew up sexually over the summer, grew up emotionally, learned to share, to be intimate, to shed the last vestiges of his hard-dying childhood shyness. And come the fall, back in school, back in the eastern, elitist, academic milieu that was his element, he felt the strength of this new maturity, felt a harmony and a balance. He had mastered law school he felt. He had a woman. And he began to expand. He played more basketball, kept his body in shape, and on Thursday nights he joined a friendly poker game with a couple of guys from the law school and two more from the business school. He also joined a university chapter of the Young Republicans and became politically active, supporting the nascent candidacy of Nelson Rockefeller for what would ultimately become his first term as governor of New York State. In short he built a busy, active, well-balanced life.

And Mary Ann was out of balance. Everything remained focused on law school. Friends, social life, recreation were all sacrificed to academics, and gradually she found herself dependent upon Murcer for her only release from the pressures of law school. Increasingly, he was the one who was relaxed and she the one who was tense and hesitant. Suddenly she was the one whose needs were greater. It was unstated. But it was there.

There were plenty of good times that year though, tender times, fun times. There were Saturday nights when they made love and Sunday mornings when Mary Ann made breakfast. Murcer and Sabotnik would sit around in their living room reading the newspapers while Mary Ann prepared bacon and eggs, pancakes, biscuits, squeezed fresh orange juice, and brewed fresh coffee. They would eat too much those mornings; it added to the lazy warm nature of the day.

Sabotnik and Mary Ann shared a passion for the big crossword puzzle in the magazine section of the *Times*. They would work together side by side, sprawled on the living room carpet, hip to hip, propped up on their elbows working the puzzle. Mary Ann dressed in a nightgown, wrapped in Murcer's old blue terry cloth bathrobe, Sabotnik in blue jeans and a sweatshirt, they grew close those Sunday mornings, friendly close. It would take thirty minutes, sometimes longer, for them to finish the puzzle. Between them, they were rarely stumped.

In the beginning the four of them had tried double dating. Disastrously. Marilyn was the odd one out, isolated, forced to sit mute while the others chattered on about law school personalities, about their courses and about their careers. She was bright and she was articulate, and they made her feel stupid and tongue-tied. And while she could tolerate Murcer, relate to him on superficial levels, Mary Ann she detested. It was a visceral, immediate thing, a mixture of defensiveness and jealousy, made worse by the fact that Mary Ann tried to go out of her way to be friendly and unthreatening. In the end, the chemistry between the two women was just plain bad.

Marilyn struggled to suppress her dislike. She was not a prude, she thought. Still she was uncomfortable sitting with Sabotnik in his living room, trying to ignore the sounds of Murcer and Mary Ann making love in the adjacent bedroom. She heard it all through the thin walls, listened to them get up when they were done and pad down the hallway toward the bathroom. She listened to them shower and had to smile thinly when they emerged from the bathroom wrapped in bathrobes. She would watch Mary Ann drying her long hair with a towel, as Mary Ann walked into the living room, sat down, and started to talk to them.

It was not the way she wanted it to be for Phil and herself. It was either too sophisticated or too sleazy and she rebelled against it. The summer was over and Phil had his own apartment now, a place where he could take her, a place where, if Mary Ann Salisbury and Ted Murcer were any example, they were expected to make love. She resisted it. Marilyn found herself thrown on the defensive, suddenly unsure of herself intellectually, unsure of herself sexually, unsure of her surroundings. She was twenty years old, almost twenty-one, and in June she would be graduating from college. She was unsure of herself, but she had the character to make a decision.

"I don't belong here," she told Sabotnik one night as he was getting ready to take her home. "It's not right and I'm not comfortable and I don't think we should see each other anymore."

Sabotnik said nothing. He wasn't surprised. And he was surprised. He had no ready answer.

"Ever since September, since you moved in here and went back to law school, it's been no good. You're all wrapped up in law and in your law school friends and I'm left out of that. It's as if you have no time for us and instead all you talk about is law and politics and your professors as if that is all there is in the world. Well there are other things too, and when I'm at my school, or with my friends, we talk about them. Why is it that whenever I'm with you and Ted and Mary Ann, I feel so stupid?"

She was near tears and he reached for her. "You're not stupid," he said softly.

"I know," she said, beginning to cry, pulling away from him. "It's you who are stupid. You're so hung up on law, and on this Ivy League world, and on being just like Ted Murcer and Mary Ann Salisbury that I think you've forgotten who you are and what the world's like.

"But I know who I am, Phil. And I know who you are. You're Phil Sabotnik from the Bronx. You're a nice Jewish guy, with a good heart, who's probably going to be a hell of a good lawyer. You're dazzled by Ted and Mary Ann just because she looks like a cheerleader and he looks like a toothpaste commercial, and I think you'd like to be like them. But you know something, I don't think either of them know who they are themselves, especially Mary Ann. She isn't a cheerleader and she isn't an intellectual and she isn't going to be a lawyer either, not really. She's not going to be anything, Phil, and she isn't happy, and she isn't going to make anyone happy, and you shouldn't be in love with her."

There was more silence. Again he had nothing to say. Marilyn caught her breath, fought back tears, continued.

"Maybe you think you can be like Ted Murcer, have casual affairs, sleep around, get married, get divorced. Maybe you can do that, Phil. But not with this girl. Not with me."

She got up to leave, put on her coat, began to button it up, started to cry. He realized that she had made up her mind, that he had these last few moments to try to change it, knew deep down that he should try.

"Can I take you home?" he asked quietly, paralyzed.

"No," she said. "I'll take a cab."

She walked out of the apartment, closing the door behind her quietly.

16

"My mother's not at all well," Murcer told Mary Ann that spring. "So I think that this summer I'm going to look for work up in Boston so that I can be near my folks. My father has contacts with a number of law firms up there, so I should get a position even though I'm not going to Harvard."

He did not ask Mary Ann to come to Boston with him. Nor did he ask her what she thought of their being apart for three months. It was true that his mother was ill with Hodgkin's disease, that it was advancing inexorably, that she would not survive. It was also true that he would have felt compelled to spend that summer in Boston even if he had wished to remain in New York with Mary Ann. In a sense he was not lying.

But the unstated truth was that he wanted out. And so did she. It was not in the nature of either of them to fight. They parted for the summer without discussion or rancor. It just happened.

Palmer, Fredrickson & Joyce was an old-line Boston gentleman's firm doing a considerable amount of trust and estate work, tax counseling, some simple corporate work. It bored Murcer half to death. Within a week he knew that he would not want to return there to work permanently. So he took it easy, working short hours, trying to impress no one. It looked to be a bad summer. He spent a number of evenings with his parents, sitting, talking, trying to be cheerful.

They were open about the Hodgkin's disease, acknowledged that it was terminal, then tried to ignore it. Murcer worried about his father. His parents had been married over thirty years, and in all that time his father had never ironed a shirt or cooked a meal or vacuumed a carpet. Murcer felt that he was watching his father shrink and age before his eyes that summer.

Then he began seeing Karen Clark and things turned around.

Karen was the daughter of old, old friends of his parents. Murcer had known her since they were small children, had known her well from the time when the two families had spent summer vacations together at adjacent rented cottages on the Maine coast.

She had just graduated from Wellesley and was at loose ends, looking for a job as an editorial assistant at one of the Boston publishing houses, thinking about possibly going to graduate school for a master's degree in English.

He had not seen her for a few years on the evening that Karen and her parents came to pay a courtesy visit to the Murcers. After an hour of sitting around, Ted asked her out for a drive.

They saw each other the next night, and the night after that, reminisced about long-ago summers, and talked about Ted's mother. She seemed sensitive and concerned and Ted found himself comfortable with her. They continued to date and in the process gave their parents more than a little bit of pleasure.

He wrote Mary Ann once or twice and received one or two letters in response. But neither was much for correspondence. And in the meanwhile Karen was present. He had not planned to get involved with his old friend, expected to return to New York and Mary Ann in the fall to finish up his third year of law school. And in any event, he was not that sexually attracted to Karen, not really, just comfortable.

They decided to go for a weekend in New Hampshire though, drove up to Franconia Notch, rented motel rooms, and spent the days hiking in the mountains. And at night, after dinner, and a bottle of wine, he knew that she wanted to make love with him. And he found that he wanted to too.

It wasn't the best night he had ever spent in bed with a woman. But it was far from the worst. And again, his dominant emotion was a sense of comfort, of an easy rapport.

For the rest of the summer they continued to sleep together. And in the weeks that remained he never once mentioned to Karen the existence of Mary Ann. He planned to deal with that in the fall.

Mary Ann for her part ended up spending the summer in Mississippi as a law student volunteer helping the Southern Christian

Leadership Conference with a voter registration drive. She worked without pay, receiving a minimum stipend that didn't really cover her expenses.

She traveled through three rural counties with an elderly black man, a retired Atlantan who was an emeritus professor of botany at one of the black colleges. They held meetings in run-down Baptist churches attempting to collect affidavits that would document the historic pattern of abuse and discrimination in voting registration.

"I went down to the courthouse and told them I wanted to vote," one woman told them. "That was back in 1948. I told them I could read an' write and I brought my high school diploma with me as proof. Then they took me up to see old Judge McCaferty and he asked me, 'Hattie, what you want to vote for?' He said I shouldn't worry myself about voting because how could a poor colored lady like me possibly know how to vote. But I said that I wanted to vote anyhow, and he said I should come back the next week, and I said okay.

"But by the time I was to come back, Tommie Lee, that's my husband, got told by the foreman over at the lumber mill that he might get laid off on account of my wanting to vote. Tommie Lee and his daddy worked that mill going on twenty-five years. So I never went back to the courthouse, and that was that."

It was the same story over and over. One affidavit after another. Different details and the same result.

Then toward the end of the summer, Mary Ann became involved in working up an appeal from a death penalty conviction. A black boy accused of murdering a white gas station attendant during a robbery. Convicted principally on the basis of a confession to the sheriff made on the second day of his detention. There were many aspects to the case and Mary Ann was given a relatively modest issue to work up—the question of the fairness of the grand jury that had indicted the boy. Or more specifically the fairness of its composition from a racial point of view. Toward this end, Mary Ann pulled five and then ten years of records from the county courthouse to look at the pattern of grand jury selection. She eventually was able to demonstrate that in over ten years there had been only one black grand juror, es-

tablishing conclusively a statistical pattern of racial discrimination.

It was an absorbing summer for Mary Ann and it went by too
quickly. In the nine weeks she spent in Mississippi, she not once
thought seriously about Ted Murcer.

17

Murcer made a muddle out of the fall. He and Mary Ann got
back together and he made the mistake of not telling her about
Karen. Mary Ann for her part was glad to be back in New York,
and quickly forgot that she had spent the summer quite happily
without Ted Murcer. They were taking completely different
courses now, barely saw one another at the law school, didn't
crowd one another, and seemed all the better for it. What
remained, and what endured between them, was a strong physical attraction. It went a long way toward papering over their
differences.

Alternating weekends he went up to Boston, ostensibly to visit
his mother, in fact to see Karen. It was she that he loved and it
was she with whom he began to speak of marriage. Not propos-
ing. Nothing that serious. Just a type of speculative chatter.
Wondering what it would be like, talking about what kind of
home they would buy, the vacations they would take, how many
children they would have, their sexes, names, and where they
would go to college. They were trying each other on for size.
Hypothetically. But he never spoke to Karen of the reality of
Mary Ann.

Inevitably it was Sabotnik who first discovered that Murcer
was seeing two women. He paid the apartment's phone bills and
could not miss the long-distance Boston calls, or fail to overhear
snatches of the conversations themselves. He held his peace for a
while, then broached the subject.

"You've got a girl in Boston," he began.

"Yes."

"And Mary Ann doesn't know?"

"I don't think so."

"What about the girl in Boston?"

"Karen doesn't know either."

"Aren't you going to tell them?"

"I'm not sure. I planned to talk to Mary Ann when the summer was over. But somehow I couldn't. And I've also wanted to tell Karen and I probably should have when I first started seeing her this summer. But I didn't want to complicate things. Besides I didn't really plan on getting involved with Karen. It just happened."

Sabotnik just looked at his friend. He didn't have to say it.

"I know the situation stinks," Murcer went on. "And I certainly didn't want to create it. But now I don't know what to do. I care for Mary Ann. And I don't want to hurt her. Maybe I even love her. But my relationship with her is not going anywhere. We're going more on inertia and habit than anything else. And I'm certain that we'll never make it after we graduate. Even if I wanted to, Mary Ann will break it off because I just won't fit into the life she has to lead."

"And the other girl, Karen, where are you going with her?"

"I'm going to marry her," Murcer replied. And as he said it he knew for the first time that it was true.

"Then don't you owe her the truth?" Sabotnik pressed. "Can you start a marriage with a lie?"

"There's a difference between owing the truth and telling a lie," Murcer answered. "I've never lied to Mary Ann or Karen."

"Because neither one ever asked about the other?"

"Yes. And I'm not sure that volunteering the truth at this point is going to do anybody any good. It will end things with Mary Ann, which has to happen anyway. But it will end on a worse note than maybe it has to.

"And Karen is not going to get any benefit out of the truth. Knowing about Mary Ann might destroy what Karen and I have. And if it doesn't destroy it, it sure as hell will hurt."

"So what are you going to do?"

"I don't know."

"And until you figure it out?"

"I'll do nothing."

"And continue to sleep with both of them?"

"Yes."

"And hope you don't get caught?"

"Yes."

"And what am I supposed to do?"

"If you're my friend . . ."

"Yes."

". . . nothing."

"And if I'm Mary Ann's friend?"

"Still nothing."

And Sabotnik did nothing. And for him things were never the same with Murcer.

Sabotnik for his own part found himself feeling guilty about his silence. Guilty and dirty. And he wasn't sleeping with either woman. He wasn't sleeping with anyone.

18

It should have been a simple uneventful chore. Mary Ann Salisbury and George Petrakis were starting their third year in the law school, and the time had come for them and the other editors of the law review to meet and elect the incoming second-year students who would join and then succeed them on the review.

The term "elect" was a technicality. For years, for as long as anyone could remember, the election was actually nothing more than the editors meeting and automatically designating those students with the highest grade-point averages as the new members of the review. So Petrakis and Mary Ann had been "elected" the year before although they were virtually unknown to the third-year students who had elected them. So they expected it to be in late August when they met with the other editors to select their successors.

They first read about the problem in the newspapers that July. The *Daily News* headlines screamed it out. HOUSE SUBCOMMITTEE FINDS COMMUNIST ORGANIZER AT UNIVERSITY LAW SCHOOL. The article said that a subcommittee of the House Un-American Activities Committee, investigating communist infiltration into higher education, had announced through its counsel that it had uncovered no less than five active communist organizers at the law school. One of these students, the article went on, Martin Drabkin, was about to be elected to the prestigious university law review where he would assume an important leadership position with the student body. Drabkin, according to the subcommittee's counsel, had been a prominent member of the Young Communist League while he was an undergraduate at the College of the City of New York. He had been active on a number of committees and organizations that had demonstrated against and actively opposed the American involvement in the Korean War. The article quoted an excerpt of a speech Drabkin had once delivered at City College denouncing Presidents Truman and Eisenhower as imperialistic adventurers who were perpetrating a racial war upon a weak and defenseless Asian people.

More banner headlines in early August reflected that Drabkin had been subpoenaed to give testimony before the committee. He had appeared, represented by a well-known left-wing counsel, and he had taken the Fifth Amendment eighty-four times in the course of two hours. He had been dismissed by the chairman of the subcommittee with the threat that he would be cited for contempt of Congress. To date the threat had not materialized.

Unwillingly they found themselves dead in the center of the Drabkin controversy. Along with a group of other editors Mary Ann and Petrakis had gone for guidance to several of the prominent faculty members. They had effectively received no guidance at all. One had spoken movingly of preserving the prestige and the intellectual and scholarly purity of the review. Another had spent an hour analyzing the review's charter and bylaws, ultimately reaching the conclusion, well known to the editors before they began, that technically they had the power to decide who would work with them on this "student publication." A third professor declined to discuss the matter with them altogether, suggesting that the faculty should not "meddle" in such affairs. Petrakis, listening to that professor, knowing that he was rumored to be in line for a prominent appointment with the administration in Washington, understood that the professor was ducking the question, would not go on record one way or the other, and would not share in the blame or anger that would be inevitably heaped on those who had to decide. He had the impression that the Drabkin decision was one that everyone would rather pass on. And everyone was passing, everyone but Petrakis and his fellow editors. They had no choice.

"I say we must elect Drabkin," Mary Ann announced as they met in conference. "The review is not and never has been a political organization. It is devoted to scholarly excellence and Drabkin has demonstrated the excellence. I don't care if a man is a Democrat, a Republican, or a vegetarian, and I don't care if he is a communist; if he can cut the mustard as a legal scholar we must take him. If we don't take him, then we are guilty of playing politics with the review. We would be saying that a man's political views might disqualify him as a scholar. That would be a hideous precedent for us to make, one that in the long run could only hurt the review and everything it has stood for."

"That's a lot of shit," another editor shot back hotly. "We live in the real world and we had all better face up to the fact that in this society, and probably in any society, there are people and political positions that are beyond the pale. For better or worse, in this year of grace, being a commie is beyond the pale. Is there anyone in this room who is so naïve that he thinks that electing an avowed or even a widely suspected communist to this review would not be a political statement. It would be the most political thing most of us will ever do in our life. And it would also be one of the most ill-advised. In today's climate it would bring terrible criticism and probably do lasting damage to the review, the

law school, and even to the university. I don't think that what
the House subcommittee did was just. I don't think, in the abstract, that Drabkin should be excluded from the review whatever his political beliefs. But we live in the real world. And I say
that electing this man is just not worth it."

The conversation seesawed back and forth. Petrakis sat silently, listening to the rationales, sensing an almost equal division,
a third strongly, almost violently, opposed to Drabkin's election,
a third just as strongly in favor, and a third, like Petrakis, silent
and uncommitted. As the debate moved into its third hour, as the
speakers began to get more and more repetitious, as well as more
and more acrimonious, Petrakis finally decided to speak. As a
new voice in the dialogue he was listened to closely.

"First off," he said, "I think that we would be and maybe we
are being just a little bit hypocritical in arguing this Drabkin
business as if it were just a matter of abstract political or social
interest in which we are trying to solve the problems of the
world, of the university, or the law school. There is no one here
who doesn't know damn well that each and every one of us is
personally on a spot and will have to pay a price for our decision.

"Let me be blunt. Each of us has worked his ass off to make
law review. And each of us has continued to work his ass off
since he made review. I must spend thirty or forty hours a week
working on review and I spend at least that much time again on
my classwork. I have sacrificed vacations and I have sacrificed
my social life and I have sometimes sacrificed my sleep in order
to do well here. And there's no man here who's any different.

"Now this Drabkin thing comes up. And each of you knows
full well that however it goes our decision is going to be controversial. I don't want, fairly or unfairly, to be labeled as a communist sympathizer or as a pinko or anything like that. But on
the other hand, five or ten years from now, when maybe the
pendulum has changed, I don't want to be remembered by the
civil libertarians as a person who changed the rules in mid-game
and kept a man off the review because of his political views. Let
me be honest, and let's all of us be honest. I would like to win a
clerkship next year with one of the justices of the Supreme

Court. I've worked hard to win that and so have a number of you. It's going to be hard enough to win that appointment as it is, and I sure as hell don't need to be saddled with having to explain or justify whatever we do here about Drabkin. There are going to be lots of guys from Harvard or Yale or Virginia who won't have to justify or explain a thing. I'd like to face them on an equal footing."

There was silence in the room. Petrakis' remarks had hit home. He had, at least for the moment, put an end to a debate about principles. After a time, one of the editors rose to the bait and asked Petrakis whether he had any suggestions.

"I do," he answered promptly. "I think that there is one party not present at this meeting whose views are awfully important, and that's Drabkin himself. I think that before we decide anything we should first start a dialogue with Drabkin to see where he stands. I don't know, maybe we can get him to withdraw his name from consideration. Maybe he will make some kind of statement about his past behavior and his future intentions that will make his election relatively palatable and uncontroversial. Maybe he won't, and maybe we'll be faced with the same hard decision we've been facing all night. But first, shouldn't we explore all the possibilities?"

Within fifteen minutes, Petrakis had been elected as the law review's emissary to Martin Drabkin. Mary Ann Salisbury, the only one of the editors who knew Drabkin, if only slightly, was selected to go along. It was unstated, but she was selected to represent the liberals who wanted to make sure that Drabkin made it. She was there to check up on Petrakis, to keep him honest. With that, the meeting broke up.

Drabkin lived in a tiny studio apartment on Claremont Avenue and 123rd Street. Its only window was small and dirt-stained, and stared out on a dreary alleyway and towards the backs of adjacent apartment buildings. An alcove with a hot plate, a tiny refrigerator, a sink, and a small cabinet served as a kitchen. The whole apartment was littered with books and magazines of every possible description, and had a dusty uncleaned look. His bed, more a cot really, was unmade, its sheets appearing crumpled and soiled. The room was stuffy and smelled of stale cigarette smoke.

Drabkin himself, when he opened the apartment door to let them in was a thin, intense young man with unkempt curly red hair and watery rather pale blue eyes, which peered out from behind wire-rimmed glasses with an expression that seemed at once both frightened and pugnacious. Petrakis had the impression that Drabkin was the kind of individual who would be completely harmless, so long as he was not backed into a corner. He tried to set the man at his ease.

"We're here as representatives of the editors of the law review," Petrakis began slowly, feeling his way. It was agreed beforehand that Petrakis would do the talking. Mary Ann kept quiet. "We thought that before this business got any further along, it would make sense for us, at least informally, to make contact with you. We've all read the newspaper, and all of that, but certainly we want to hear everything that you want to tell us, your side of the story so to speak."

"My side of the story is very simple," Drabkin answered bitterly. "I worked hard last year, I made almost a straight A average, my grades make me eligible for election to law review, and you have to elect me. For the last fifty years grades have been the sole determinant of who makes the review. Well, I've got the grades so you have no choice. If you change the rules to keep me out, then you will be exposed as hypocrites, frauds, and cowards."

Drabkin was chain-smoking as he spoke to them. His features were animated and his manner self-righteous. He was an easy man to dislike, Petrakis thought. Absolutely without tact or common sense, unyielding and probably humorless. Petrakis tried to lower the temperature.

"Most human beings," he said, smiling, "are in some measure hypocrites, frauds, and cowards. Why do you suppose the editors of law review should be any different?"

"I don't," Drabkin answered seriously, missing the irony. "I know that you are here to tell me that I haven't been elected. I've been expecting it."

"Well you're wrong then," Petrakis answered.

"I was elected, then?"

"No, not that either. We really haven't acted yet, and we really haven't made up our minds. The whole purpose of our coming here is not to debate with you or anything like that. And it certainly isn't to tell you that you're elected or not. We have no power alone to do that, and we're really here to sound out your views, to find out how things stand, and to see if we can assist the review in making a decision. What I'm saying is that we want your help."

"In what way?"

"Well, I'd like to be candid with you and I would hope that you would be candid with us."

"What do you want to know," Drabkin answered bitterly, "whether I really was a communist or not?"

"No," Petrakis shot back. "Frankly I don't give a shit whether you were a communist or a Martian. I know damned well that whatever you may believe politically, at least so far as the last year is concerned, you were much too busy studying law to do anything more political than going to the bathroom. Nobody, and I don't care how brilliant they are, makes the kind of grades you made last year and has time left over to seriously devote to politics, let alone to the violent overthrow of the American government. And if you agree that's true of last year, I can promise you that if you make review, next year and the year after you'll be too busy to even go to the toilet. Your politics isn't the question."

"Well what is then?"

"What we or at least some of the editors want to know is whether you really want to make the review in the first place. I don't have to tell you that the review is basically a scholarly journal. It requires virtually a total dedication, and frankly the intrinsic rewards of the work are not necessarily that great unless you are looking for a scholarly legal career, say in teaching or something like that.

"Let me be frank. The other benefit of making review is that it has prestige, and that that prestige opens doors, creates career opportunities and things like that. Honestly, I think you know that with all the publicity about you, those doors will be closed to you regardless of whether you make review or not. That's not right, but it's so. The point is, that for you, the only reasons we can see for you to go on review are either because you want the intrinsic research experience or because you want to make some political statement by being elected in the face of the controversy. Some editors want assurances that you really want the review for its own sake and that you will not involve the publication in politics."

Drabkin thought a minute. "I don't understand," he said. "Do you want me to promise to be a good boy and give up my politics while I'm on review? Do you require that of anyone else who is being asked to join review? Do Republicans or Democrats or southern racists get asked to be apolitical when they join review? Why should I have to do what they don't? Or are you asking me to withdraw my name from consideration, to say that I really don't want it anyway, and to take you guys off the hook?"

"I'm not asking you to do either, although to be perfectly honest, I would be delighted if you withdrew your name, and I would be equally happy if you made a statement that your politics would not affect or be a part of your serving on the review. What I am looking for is your cooperation. Tell me what you want. If you want to join the review, let's figure out a way to make it happen. Surely we can work out some statement you can make that won't compromise any principle you hold but that will make it clear that the review will remain nonpolitical."

"I won't do it," Drabkin answered. "I will not make a statement, I won't apologize, and I don't have to explain myself. All I want is to be treated like everybody else. That's what I want."

"Well do you want to be on the review?" Mary Ann finally interjected. "There are many of us who would like you to be on the review, who feel that you've been treated unfairly and who would be proud to stand up and say that you've earned review and that you deserve to be among us. And frankly those of us who feel that way are going to be awfully upset if, for any reason, you don't make it.

"But not everyone feels that way and if you want to make it

you've got to realize that. I don't think that it's any great renun-
ciation of principle for you to sign a statement saying that you
hope to join the review to promote your career as a legal scholar
and to try to make a contribution to legal scholarship. No one
would be asking you to renounce your political beliefs, whatever
they are, and in the long run the prestige of making review will
give weight to whatever political or legal statements you make in
the future. So for Christ's sake, you'll do your causes and beliefs
better service in the long run if you give a little now, sign an in-
nocuous statement that we can sell to our fellow editors, and
then you'll be elected. Isn't that the best way to fight back at the
bastards who are trying to crucify you? Can you really afford to
be so simon pure if you're going to even be effective in promoting reform or revolution or whatever. After all, even Lenin
wasn't above dealing with the German general staff in order to
get himself back to St. Petersburg in 1917. Surely you can deal
with the editors of the law review?"

"I won't do it," Drabkin answered immediately. And it was
clear to Mary Ann and Petrakis that he hadn't been listening to a
word she had said. Within a few minutes they left his apartment,
left without shaking his hand.

"Well, no one can say I didn't try," Petrakis said, after they left.
"And you certainly tried. But I think I knew from the minute
we walked in there that he wasn't going to cooperate. And now
I don't think that there is a prayer in the world that he'll be
elected to review."

"No," Mary Ann answered, "he won't make review, not after
your report on his attitude. Too many of the editors will be
scared of him, so he won't be elected.

"I'm going to vote for him though. He's a jackass, and I don't
like him, but I think that he's right."

She waited a moment, then went on. "And if he's not elected,
George, I'm going to resign from the board of editors and end
my relationship with the review. I don't think that in the years
to come I will want to be identified with a publication that
caved in to right-wing red-baiting scare tactics. So I'm going to
resign."

Petrakis turned to her, alarmed, about to speak, worried about the prospect of Mary Ann's compounding the scandal. She cut him off, reading his mind.

"Don't worry," she said, "I plan to resign quietly and privately, and I will make no public statement about my reasons. All I will do will be to write a private confidential letter addressed to the new editor-in-chief, who I hope will be you, stating my reasons for resignation, in the most respectful terms possible. I have too high a regard for the review, and for all of you, to do anything to hurt any of you. It's just that I couldn't in conscience stay on review."

Petrakis said nothing.

A week later Drabkin was denied election to law review. Mary Ann Salisbury did resign, and George Petrakis was selected editor-in-chief.

19

It was a kind of autumn ritual. There would be two hundred fifty, maybe three hundred third-year law students, most of whom had been attending one school or another nonstop since they were five years old. Four years as an undergraduate, three more in law school, many with additional post-graduate work in one academic discipline or another, few, precious few, with any type of true full-time, year-round work experience. They were overripe, overanxious, past masters at writing research papers, at taking short-answer multiple-choice exams, in sounding clever across seminar tables. And utterly inexperienced and possibly useless at the practice of their chosen profession. Not one of them had ever interviewed a client, cross-examined a hostile witness, or negotiated a settlement with an adverse party. Most of them did not know where the local courthouse was located. Still, in eight months or so they would be law graduates, admitted to

the bar, theoretically capable of practicing law. It was time to
get a job, time for them to get nice short haircuts, to buy new
three-piece suits, to put on starched white shirts with tight col-
lars, to laboriously type up almost but not quite dishonest
resumés that made each trivial academic citation or honor seem
akin to an award of the Nobel peace prize, time to be interviewed, to receive job offers, to make important decisions about
the future.

The law school placement office kept files and catalogues filled
with the letters and brochures the big law firms sent describing
each firm and explaining why it was a great place to work. Phil
Sabotnik read through them all carefully, feeling the expensive
linen bond paper on which the letters were typed, reading the
engraved letterheads, scanning the list of partners' names printed
in small rows on the left- and right-hand sides of the stationery,
trying to decide which one would be likely to offer him a job,
which one he would like to work for. If he wished to, he could
interview with virtually all of them. There were sign-up sheets
available for interviews broken down into fifteen-minute time
slots. All he had to do was to sign his name in a slot and submit
his resumé, and then on the designated day show up at the placement office in his three-piece suit and be ushered into a little cubicle where a shell-shocked hiring partner who had interviewed
four students an hour steadily from 9 A.M. onward would try to
look interested while he asked the same questions and received
more or less the same answers he had heard twenty or thirty
times before that day alone. The point of the exercise was to be
one of the students who was asked down to the firm itself for
extended further interviews. Once invited down, the prospects
of receiving a job offer were pretty decent.

It was almost impossible for Sabotnik to distinguish between
the firms. He wasn't sure in his own mind precisely what type of
law he wanted to practice except that he had a vague idea that
he wanted to be a litigator or more precisely a courtroom lawyer. None of this was any help in selecting one firm over another. Reading the letters was depressing to Sabotnik, and in the
end he selected ten firms virtually at random.

Regis, McCormick, and Letterman was one of the firms Sabotnik signed up to interview with. Its self-descriptive letter was no different from twenty others.

The firm of Regis, McCormick, and Letterman has proudly been practicing law in the City of New York since 1839. Today Regis, McCormick, and Letterman is a firm of one hundred and forty lawyers providing legal services to an impressive list of important corporate clients in virtually every important field of law. Partners in the firm are nationally recognized leaders in such areas as security law, trusts and estates, antitrust litigation, tax law, and real estate law. Past partners have sat on the United States Court of Appeals for the Second Circuit, as well as the New York State Court of Appeals, and one partner, now on leave, is currently serving as the United States Ambassador to Ireland. . . . No associate is hired at Regis, McCormick, and Letterman unless, in the opinion of the partnership, he stands a reasonable chance of ultimately making partner and becoming a member of the firm. All associates, after an initial orientation period, are assigned to work in one of the firm's major areas, corporate litigation, trusts and estates, antitrust, real estate, or securities. Associates are reviewed on an annual basis, and salary increases and bonuses are awarded on a merit basis. Starting salaries for first-year associates are competitive with the going rate paid to associates at other firms of comparable size and prestige.

Arthur Carrington, the hiring partner who initially interviewed Sabotnik, seemed to hit it off well with him.

"I see that you entered the moot court honors competition in your second year," the partner asked.

"Yes."

"How did you make out?"

"I won second place for the best speaker and my team won second place for the best brief."

"Tell me what the case was about."

"It was a civil rights case, sir. It involved a park in a southern city that had been owned by a wealthy family. When the patri-

arch of the family died, he had willed the park to the city with
the provision that the city should only permit the park to be
used by whites. A lawsuit had been brought by the NAACP to
force the integration of the park, and both the city and the heirs
of the dead patriarch had resisted, claiming that the courts
should not interfere with a private person's right to dispose of
his property."

The discussion proceeded well from there. Carrington was interested in the case, turned out to be a contributor to the
NAACP Legal Defense Fund. The interview became animated
and Sabotnik and the partner seemed to be on the same wave
length. They both seemed unhappy when the fifteen minutes
ended, and Sabotnik was not at all surprised when he received an
invitation to come down to Regis, McCormick, and Letterman for
further interviews. What did surprise and upset him was that he
received no similar invitations from any of the other large firms.

The law firm was located on the forty-fifth, -sixth, and -seventh
floors of an enormous office building on the lower tip of Manhattan. The walls were all wood paneled, polished, subdued wal-
nut. The floors were plushly carpeted. When Sabotnik arrived
for his day of interviews, an attractive, perfectly dressed receptionist ushered him into a comfortable living room-like waiting
room. He sat in an overstuffed armchair and stared out through
large double windows at an absolutely stunning view of New
York Harbor. He could see Brooklyn stretched to his left, Staten
Island and New Jersey on his right. The Statue of Liberty was
down there, green, tiny, yet still inspiring. He could see the harbor traffic, vessels great and small, tugs and tankers, moving in
one direction or another. The idea of going to work, of spending
each day, in an office that provided such a view was appealing.

The interviews began well. A junior partner in the litigation
department sat down with Sabotnik and they talked for almost
an hour. "Most of the litigation we do here is complex com-
merical stuff in the federal courts," he explained. "One case that
I'm working on for instance, involves a dispute between Republic Steel, who we represent, and the Kansas Pacific Railroad.
Republic was supposed to fabricate some rolling stock for the
railroad, about ten million dollars' worth, but when they began

delivery on the product, the railroad refused to accept delivery, claiming that they did not meet specifications. The lawsuit followed. We've been running around the country taking depositions to show that we didn't breach any warranty or fail to meet specifications. We're moving for summary judgment, filing motions left and right, and generally having a terrific time."

"Will the case ever be tried or will you get summary judgment?" Sabotnik asked.

"Neither," the partner answered. "We'll settle, of course. The whole lawsuit is really about the railroad's trying to renegotiate the terms of the purchase. The prime rate has gone up quite a bit lately, and I guess the railroad didn't want to borrow the money that they were obligated to pay under the contract. So they refused to accept the stock, and let the lawyers diddle around with litigation, waiting for the prime rate to drop or to negotiate new terms. It's all a wonderful game, and in the end our clients will settle one way or another. There isn't much chance that we'll ever go to trial. Most of our cases don't go to trial."

They continued to talk. Sabotnik liked this partner, was attracted to his ironical, irreverent manner, was oddly unoffended by the underlying cynicism of the practice. It was almost as if it was unthinkable for anything improper or questionable to occur in such an elegant and understated office. With each passing minute Sabotnik found himself increasingly desirous of getting the job. He liked the idea of working in such a place, and it made him eager and agreeable. The interview went well.

The day progressed and there were more interviews. He met with senior associates and with senior partners, and if each interview did not go as perfectly as the first two, none of them seemed to go poorly. An aging partner in the trusts and estates division, Harlan VanVleck had been a bit short, maybe curt, with him, but not hostile, Sabotnik thought. When the day was through he was hopeful. There would be one more interview he knew, with Edward Regis, the senior partner of the firm. If he passed muster there, the job would be his.

Regis kept him waiting five days before calling him back for an interview. Sabotnik was early for their eleven o'clock appointment, but was kept waiting almost until noon before he was ushered into Regis' office.

Ed Regis appeared to be in his mid-to-late-forties, an impressively young age to be the senior partner at one of the most prestigious firms in the city. He was a short, solidly built, dynamic man, a brilliant corporate lawyer, who sat on the board of directors of half a dozen major corporations, had served as special adviser to the President of the United States. Sabotnik was awed to be in his presence.

"Sit down, please, Mr. Sabotnik," Regis began, striding across the room to shake the student's hand, directing him to a couch in a corner of his large office, seating himself on a facing easy chair.

"Tell me," he continued, "seriously, do you think that you will be comfortable and fit in at Regis, McCormick, and Letterman?"

"Why not?" Sabotnik asked, slow on the uptake.

"Well, most of the lawyers here, and most of our clients, have backgrounds very different from yours. We are a national law firm, and our clientele and our case load are nationwide and international in scope. We represent Arab oil interests from the Middle East for instance, as well as doing a great deal of the American legal work for a number of the larger West German banks and industrial concerns. Often our lawyers have to travel over to those countries or to entertain clients from those countries when they visit here. Do you think that would pose a problem to you?"

"No," Sabotnik answered reflectively, thinking that the answer was yes, realizing that Regis also thought that the answer was yes, and further realizing that whatever Sabotnik might think or feel, these clients would probably object to being represented by a Bronx-born Russian-Jewish lawyer. Or maybe it was Regis who would object. The firm had to have other cases and other clients who wouldn't care, Sabotnik thought in the next instant, and he realized that he would not be hired because he was a Jew. There were no Jewish names on the letterhead he recalled, or maybe one or two names that might have been German and might have been Jewish. He felt like a jackass, hopelessly naïve for not expecting this, for not understanding that the chances of being hired at Regis, McCormick, and Letterman were some-where between slim and none. He felt angry but not at Ed Regis. That would come later. He felt angry at himself. There was an uncomfortable silence while Regis watched Sabotnik fight with his conflicting emotions. The older man understood what was going on and watched with a detached, somewhat amused pa-tience. The interview did not last long. After it was over, both of them wondered why it had happened at all.

20

Friday night. Early December. Murcer was away in Boston. Sabotnik at home. It was the day the letter arrived formally ad-vising that there would be no job for him at Regis, McCormick, and Letterman. Sabotnik was reading. Drinking rum and Coke. Uncharacteristically. Feeling sorry for himself. Thinking of Marilyn. Worrying about not having a job, about it being De-cember already and all the good jobs gone, about having aimed too high. Feeling bitter about other guys, less bright, with lower averages, who had good jobs, some of them with Regis, McCor-mick, and Letterman. Feeling jealous of Murcer, who, he imag-ined, was off somewhere getting laid, off somewhere, unzipping a dress, unhooking a brassiere, watching some young, beautiful woman whom Sabotnik had never met climb out of her panties. It was a bad night. He was trying, pretending really, to read a novel. He had the phonograph on when Mary Ann came in. A key in the door. Her presence. Suddenly. The evening was changed. It had possibilities. She sat down. Gave him a smile. A sad smile. It made him feel better.

She poured herself a drink, several fingers of rum, an ice cube, not too much Coke. They sat awhile listening to the music.

"I heard about Regis, McCormick, and Letterman," she said.

He did not answer.

"You're better off, lucky really that you didn't go to work for those bastards," she continued. "It's just as well that you found out how rotten they were before you went to work for them rather than after wasting five or six years slaving in their sweatshops. They're anti-Semites, they don't hire women, and I don't even think that they hire Catholics, at least not Polish or Italian or even Irish Catholics. Just look at their letterhead. I think that they'd sooner drop dead than hire a Negro.

"Besides look at who they represent and look at the kind of work they do. Do you really want to spend your time representing oil companies, or the tobacco industry, or the drug manufacturers? Do you want to help defend price-fixing schemes, or antitrust violators, or maybe sit around figuring out schemes to help rich folks avoid paying their income taxes? You would spend the next ten years at the Regis firm doing menial scut work and carrying some senior guy's briefcase and watching other people argue and try cases. They'll work your ass off and ruin your social or family life, because they would be billing your time by the hour, so the more hours you worked, the more money they would make. And at the end of those ten years, they wouldn't make you a partner anyway. They'd get rid of you like an old shoe and hire some new idiot out of law school with good grades and no common sense. The worst part of all would be that in those ten years they would grind out of you all the initiative and motivation that you might have to make the world a better place or yourself a better lawyer. I'm glad that you didn't get the job, Phil. You're just better than that."

Sabotnik smiled, and took another drink of his rum and Coke. "You're probably right," he said. "Still, it hurts to be turned down. And the truth is that I would have taken the job, even though I probably knew deep down everything you just said. And if you want me to be really honest, if I got a call right now, telling me that the letter was a mistake and they want me to go to work for them, I'd probably still say yes. Or at least I don't know what I would do. They pay their associates a lot of money and there's a lot of prestige to it, and I guess I was taken in by it all. That's part of why I feel so cruddy."

"Why don't you come to work with me at the Legal Aid Society?" Mary Ann asked. "I'll be starting next September, working in their Civil Division, representing poor people in landlord-tenant cases, or helping them get divorces, things like that. I'll be overworked and underpaid. But at least we'll be doing something worthwhile, and we'll get a lot of experience and a lot of responsibility very quickly. We'll really learn how to be lawyers from the bottom up and we'll probably feel pretty good about what we're doing."

Sabotnik thought a minute, then said that he would think about it, which was the most polite way he could find to say no. He didn't want to tell Mary Ann that he wanted to make a good living for himself, that he wasn't too concerned about making the world a better place, that he wanted more and less for himself than being a savior of the poor. He had cost his parents many thousands of dollars in support and tuition putting him through college and law school and he felt keenly the need to succeed at being a lawyer, and to succeed in his parents' terms, which meant making money. None of this was he willing to discuss with Mary Ann.

They continued to drink rum and Coke, to talk of more trivial, gossipy subjects, to become high and mellow. It began to rain, a hard, driving, insistent rain and it became cold inside the apartment. It grew late, ten-thirty, eleven o'clock, and Mary Ann made no move to leave. The rain continued. She had brought no raincoat or umbrella. Sabotnik wondered whether Mary Ann knew that Murcer was in Boston, or whether she was waiting for him to return, waiting to go to bed with a guy who didn't really love her, a guy with lower grades and less on the ball than either Sabotnik or Mary Ann. He wondered whether Mary Ann had any idea about the girl in Boston. He wondered if she would be sitting and drinking, talking with him, if she knew that Murcer would not be back. He wondered why she hadn't bothered to ask where Murcer was. And he poured himself another drink, finishing the bottle. It had been almost full when they began.

"Why did you break up with Marilyn?" Mary Ann asked at one point.

"She broke up with me," he answered.

"Really?"

"Yes."

"That's strange, because if I'm any judge of it, she certainly was in love with you."

Sabotnik shrugged. "She certainly had a strange way of showing it," he said. "Or I guess I should say, she had a way of not showing it."

They were silent a minute.

"I'm not being fair," he said. "She broke up with me because she was jealous. She felt shut out of the law school milieu and probably felt inferior intellectually, which was ridiculous, but was the way she felt. But I think mostly she felt jealous and inadequate around you. You see, Mary Ann, she always believed that I had a thing for you, a crush or something, and that really bothered her. She didn't understand you, and she felt threatened by you, and she knew that she couldn't compete. And it didn't really matter that you were going out with Ted. In her mind you were competing with her, or she was competing with you. And in a way I think maybe she was right."

"What do you mean?"

"I mean that I think that she knew that I did love you."

He would never have said it, not ever, if he wasn't drunk. The words hung heavy in the air. He said nothing and did nothing, his will sapped. Their eyes locked. And she said nothing. She just got up ever so slowly, and as if in slow motion, walked from the easy chair where she had been sitting to the couch where he was. She sat down beside him, continued to look into his eyes, and still he did not touch her. She reached then and took his hand and held it gently in hers.

Then it was beyond words. She was in his arms. Struggling out of their clothes. He picked her up and carried her to his bed. They made love. Once quickly. Then slowly. And they came together and lay sweating in each other's arms. Shaken.

He looked at Mary Ann, her breasts, her belly, her long blond hair, her thighs. And he felt a return of desire. The pale light from the living room reflected into the bedroom, casting shadows. Outside, the cold driving rain continued to fall.

He lightly ran his hands over her body. And she responded. Kissing him on the mouth, then on the neck, the chest, the belly, taking him in her mouth, making him surrender to the feelings. Going beyond anything he had ever imagined.

All without words. He never remembered falling asleep.

In the morning he told her about the girl in Boston.

"I know, Phil," Mary Ann said.

"Ted told you?"

"No. And I didn't know her name, or who she was, or how serious it is. But I've just known. You do somehow."

"And that's why you went to bed with me last night?" Sabotnik shot back, immediately ready to be unhappy.

She looked at him. Hurt.

"No," she said. And it was the truth. And he looked at her and knew it to be truth. It was also a lie. They let the subject drop. Mary Ann began to talk about herself then.

"I don't really think that I know what I'm doing at this point," Mary Ann went on. "You know it was funny when you said before that Marilyn was afraid of me, or envied me or something, because I really felt the same way about her. She really seemed to know what she wanted from life, and she really seemed to know who she was. She's going to get her degree, and she's going to teach. Then she's going to get married and have kids, and probably after a couple of years, go back to teaching. Her career and her family life won't especially conflict with each other. It will all work for her. I also envied you and Marilyn being New Yorkers. You belong here, you were raised here, and you can be comfortable here. You've got your people in New York, your neighborhoods and your memories. It all makes sense to you, the Yiddish and the Italian and the Spanish slang expressions, everything. I'm a Wasp from Indiana, for Christ's sake, and I don't belong anywhere. I'm not comfortable back in Fort Wayne and I'm not comfortable in New York and would not be comfortable up in Boston with Ted's family either. They were too aristocratic for me, too—I don't know, too something for me to really identify with them.

"I'd like a family I think. Just like Marilyn, but I just can't imagine anyone I might marry. Ted would never marry me, because I think I was threatening to him. I fight with him, and I compete with him, and he would never want a wife who is a professional or a political equal. I'd be a threat to his ambitions. He would never be sure of what I might say or do. You would never be happy married to me either, Phil. I wouldn't make you the kind of comfortable home that you probably want, and I wouldn't stay home to raise your children, which you would want, and I wouldn't fit in where you would want to live, and we would end up miserable. We're better off as friends."

He sat up in bed, listening to her, staring out his bedroom window, looking through the morning gray across 112th Street to the apartment houses on the north side of the street. He heard what she was saying, understood it, but found his mind wandering. It all seemed unfair, hopelessly tangled in his mind. For months he might have imagined nothing better than to be in bed with Mary Ann, to have made love to her, to be sitting afterwards talking seriously about how they felt. He began to feel cold.

Mary Ann went on. She was also staring out the window, also alone with her thoughts. She was talking but not really to Sabotnik. To herself maybe.

Mary Ann left finally, and left behind her the key to the apartment. She never returned there again.

21

On Memorial Day, only two weeks before graduation, Ted Murcer's mother died. Suddenly. Without warning. Murcer was in New York.

Sabotnik went to Boston to the funeral. And so did Petrakis and a number of their classmates from the law school.

And so did Mary Ann. Impulsively. On her own. She arrived at the funeral services a few minutes late, sat quietly. She and Murcer had not spoken really since Sabotnik had told him about the night she had spent with his roommate—since the morning she had learned about the girl in Boston. But she could not stay away.

The clergyman who officiated seemed to have really known Murcer's mother. He spoke of her with feeling.

Later, at the graveside, Karen Clark took her place beside Murcer and his father, held Ted's hand as the casket was lowered slowly into the ground.

Afterwards there was a receiving line, people taking leave of the family, paying their last respects. Petrakis fell in beside Mary Ann and Sabotnik, and together, the three of them approached Murcer. The men shook hands. Murcer and Mary Ann embraced. Mary Ann and Karen looked at each other, understood who the other was, moved on.

It would be the last time that they would all be together in the same place.

22

Karen Clark surprised Murcer when he asked her to marry him. She said no.

"Ted, I love you," she told him. "And probably I have always loved you since we were kids but I'm not sure that I'm in love with you. And I'm pretty sure that you're not in love with me."

Then she told him about the boy she had been in love with. "It was in my junior year. He was a graduate student from South Africa, doing a year's study at Harvard in molecular biology. He was studying viruses and proteins and genetics. And he was going to discover how viruses cause cancer. Anyway his family was very wealthy, and he'd done his undergraduate degree at Cambridge and he had this beautiful accent and he drove around in an Austin-Healey and I would go weak at the knees whenever I saw him."

"So why didn't you marry him?" Murcer asked.

"Because he never asked," she answered simply. "I certainly would have."

"But he went back to South Africa?"

"Yes. And about a year later I got word that he had married a girl in Durban, which is where he came from. I sent him a note of congratulations."

"What was his name?"

"Paul. Paul Ashmead. He's a professor now. And he'll become rather well known someday, I think."

"And you still love him better than you love me?"

"No. In some ways, no, in most ways, I never loved him like I love you. It's just that he made me crazy sometimes and you don't. With you I feel comfortable, like I could love you and take care of you, and have your children, and share your life. And I would like to marry you very much. But I'm not sure that it's fair for me to marry you if I don't feel at least a little crazy or weak at the knees. And I think that I would like you to feel a little bit that way about me too. And I know you don't."

So he told her about Mary Ann then. And she took it very well. They both took it well.

And for the next six months they talked about getting married.

And then, one day, she said yes.

SECTION THREE

23

Cleveland Daniels began to grow up. He lost interest in baseball. The Yankees had become losers and the Dodgers and Giants had gone west. The new Mets were a joke.

Basketball was his game now. Not to watch though. To play. He was five foot nine and he would get no taller. But he was fast, more reflex fast than raw speed, with good anticipation and a good nose for the ball. And he could jump, often stealing rebounds from players three or four inches taller than himself. He had an instinctive sense of the game, knew without thinking where to position himself, drove to the basket nicely, played a pestering harassing defense, forced mistakes, stole the ball, was not afraid of mixing it up. He had his nose broken three times before his sophomore year in high school. It didn't faze him, and it was that sophomore year that he made it as the number-three guard, the first substitute on the varsity basketball team.

Varsity ball became his life then. Drugs were an epidemic at that point. Marijuana, hash, cocaine, heroin, methadone, uppers, downers, no end to it. Kids he had grown up with OD'd on bad shit, were found wasted or nodding out in public toilets. Others learned to deal, or to hustle, or to pimp. Girls learned to sell their bodies in order to feed a habit. It got very desperate very fast, and Cleveland wanted no part of it. He had basketball practice two hours each day after classes. And he had to make sure that he didn't flunk any courses, because that meant automatic suspension from the team. He couldn't even play hooky or cut classes often, because they kept track, and any day you missed a class you were also forced to miss practice. If you missed too many practice sessions you were bounced off the team.

There was status and it felt good to be playing varsity ball. There was a jacket with a letter sewn on the back, and there were cheerleaders and other girls who would put out for guys

who were on the team, the good feeling of being able to swagger
down the halls of the school or the streets of the neighborhood
with a pretty girl on your arm. But mostly there was the thrill of
the competition, the cheers from the crowd, the cheerleaders, the
pompoms, the satisfaction from playing well, from winning.
There were the daydreams of winning the division, of making it
to the Public School Athletic League finals, of playing in
Madison Square Garden, of winning a city championship. It
never happened. But there was the day he came off the bench
and got hot, the day he scored twenty-seven points, and almost
single-handedly beat the hated rivals from Theodore Roosevelt
High School. They even mentioned his name in the *Daily News*
schoolboy basketball roundup after that game. He cut out the article and brought it home to his mother and she saved it for
years afterwards.

Basketball and self-esteem, one related to the other, and both
kept him from messing with the stuff that was going down on
the streets. Even summertimes, there were the school yards from
early morning until sunset. He played three-man pickup half-
court games mostly. Twenty-one points to win, the winners re-
taining possession of the court, the losers sitting down while a
new three-man team challenged. You played until you lost. Then
you sat down, drank a soda, and waited your turn to challenge
again. Seven, eight, nine hours a day of basketball, played on
concrete surfaces and against metal backboards. He worked hard
at it, practicing alone sometimes, dribbling right hand only and
then left hand only, shooting right and shooting left. It was important to be able to work in both directions, to drive and shoot
right or left. Otherwise the defensive man would cheat and shade
a step or two in the direction you always drove or shot. Then
the ball got stolen or your shot got blocked, life became difficult.

By the end of the summer before his junior year, he had it
down. He made it as a starting guard that year, averaged 9.7
points a game. Senior year he was elected co-captain of the team.

He even got the knack of getting by with his schoolwork after a
while. He had always read well, testing at or above his grade
level, which made English and social studies pretty easy. Math

and science were problems, but with tutoring he managed to scrape by. There were always girls around who were willing to tutor a guy on the team.

Senior year he even began to enjoy some of the schoolwork. There was one course really, one teacher who got through to him, stretched his mind, made him think. Senior English. She was kind of skinny, white, pretty, with dark hair, and she wore tight skirts, cut short, sometimes sitting on the front edge of her big desk, her feet dangling, talking to the class. Cleveland would sit up front in that class, drop his pen on the floor, lean over and try to stare up her skirt. Miss Dragutsky. Marilyn Dragutsky. At night he fantasized about her, lay in bed and masturbated thinking about her.

Her focus was on literature. She made them read and whether her choices inspired, or her timing was right, or whether Cleveland was just ready, the books reached him. *Cry the Beloved Country* by Alan Paton. South Africa. Apartheid. An old black man. The father Cleveland did not have. His son, a murderer. The old-time religion, like his mother. The big city. People leaving the farm and the countryside and coming to the big city to get ripped off and fucked up. The despair and the heartbreak and the poetry of it. *Cry the Beloved Country.* It made sense to him. It was his story, his people's story, even if it was written by a white man, even if it was written about South Africa where he had never been and where he would never be. *Cry the Beloved Country.* He read the book twice, three times, and he cried himself. She was one fine teacher.

24

It was a year when many young lawyers went to Washington to begin their careers. It was a time of new beginnings, of opportunities, a naïve uncomplicated time. Anything seemed possible.

George Petrakis arrived in Washington that year. He was to

clerk for a justice of the Supreme Court of the United States. He was a winner. Starting at the top, at the right place at the right time. There would be opportunities. Anything would be possible.

But it was not Petrakis' time. He was not happy. Washington was not his kind of place, law clerking was not his kind of work. He was a nascent cynic surrounded by idealists, an establishment Republican surrounded by liberal Democrats; he was out of place. Washington was a town of talk. There was a premium on appearances, on rhetoric. It was not for him. From almost the start, he knew that when his term was up he would return to New York.

He worked hard. It was a habit. He drafted opinions and memoranda for internal distribution, wrote comments on the drafts of the other clerks. He made no friends. And no enemies. He was respected. His work product was good. He stepped on no toes.

The Warren Court was at the flood tide of its career just then. *Brown* v. *Board of Education* was several years old and Petrakis watched the Court work its way through a mass of desegregation cases. It struck down a local ordinance redistricting Tuskegee, Alabama, to deny Negroes municipal services, upheld a federal law requiring the desegregation of bus station restaurants and public toilets in the Deep South. He didn't care much about those cases though. They were correctly decided, he thought. But it wasn't his thing, those cases.

Other cases weren't either. The Court struck down an Arkansas practice of requiring public school teachers to file annual affidavits listing all political organizations to which they belonged. It upheld the right of the city of Chicago to censor films shown within its boundaries.

A case that Petrakis became particularly involved with called upon the Court to resolve a dispute between the federal government and the Gulf Coast states concerning the exercise of control over rich oil-bearing offshore lands on the continental shelf within three marine leagues of the coastline. It was a case that turned largely on a historical analysis of the terms under which those states, Texas, Louisiana, Mississippi, Alabama, and Florida, joined the Union, and particularly on what the boundaries of those states were thought to be at the time of their entry. Petrakis found himself delving into the background of the Louisiana Purchase, the Mexican War, and the negotiations between the United States and the Republic of Texas prior to annexation. He thought about the Civil War and the reentry of those states into the Union during Reconstruction and tried to decide if those events mattered.

It was dry, cloistered work and on a certain level he loved it. But on another, more fundamental level he resented it. The oil rights case was about power, the power to regulate and tax billions and billions of dollars of natural resources. It struck him as absurd to let the settlement of such an issue turn on nine old men's casting about in the entrails of obscure eighteenth and early nineteenth century diplomatic agreements to resolve the question. All too often his work at the Court seemed irrelevant to things that should matter in the real world.

Nights and weekends were hardest on Petrakis that year. There came a time when the pace had to slacken, a time when he had to return to his Georgetown studio apartment. Nights and weekends were dreary. He read books, periodicals, watched television, drank beer, ate pretzels. Often he fell asleep in an easy chair, fully dressed, lights on, television going. Waking up later in the small hours, groggy, disoriented, a bad taste in his mouth, he struggled out of his clothes, went to bed, felt prematurely old.

He met his wife in a restaurant, a kind of fancy Greek diner where he sometimes went to eat dinner. She was sitting in an adjacent booth, eating alone, reading, really engrossed in a copy of *The Brothers Karamazov*. Petrakis could not take his eyes off her, he couldn't open his own book, didn't read.

She left before he could muster the courage to speak to her. The next evening she was back, apparently a creature of habit. Petrakis was back too, hoping she would be there as well, pleased when she came. There were no rings on her fingers, no makeup on her face, no earrings, nothing but beauty. He wouldn't let her go. Not twice.

"Do you mind if I join you?" he asked, catching her eye. She hesitated a moment, looked at him, and in a sense their future hung in the balance. She closed the book, smiled. "Sure, sit down."

Her name was Emma Carrington. She had been born and raised in southern Virginia, and she was a teacher at a Montessori nursery school in one of the suburban Maryland counties. She was divorced, having been married for a year after she had graduated college. There had been no children and she had come to Washington after the divorce to start fresh.

She had majored in Romance languages at Sweet Briar College and her ambition was to become a published author of children's books. She was a fair artist and did her own pen and ink illustrations, but at the time he met her, all her submissions had been rejected.

He met her at the right time, at a time when they were both at low points, filled with self-doubts, lonely, unsure. They were both fundamentally aloof, self-sufficient, self-motivated personalities who met at a moment when each needed support. She was intelligent, as intelligent as he, better read and better bred. They met as equals and they fell in love. Six months later they were married. A year later their daughter Diana was born. And a year after that her first book, *Little Zebra*, was published. It was a modest success. And so was the marriage. Then they were living in New York.

Diana's birth was the greatest moment Petrakis would ever experience. It was the greatest, in part, because it was so unexpected in its intensity. He had resisted the novel idea of "natural" childbirth; gave in when Emma insisted. They had taken the Lamaze course, but nothing in the course, nothing in any course, could have prepared him for Diana's arrival. She was small, barely six pounds, with a headful of fine dark hair and big blue piercing eyes. The nurse handed her to Petrakis while they were removing the placenta and were stitching Emma up from her episiotomy. She handed Diana to him and he held her and he started to cry. He was and always would be in love with her from that moment onward. He didn't hear when they called him, told him that Emma was ready to hold the baby. He didn't hear and they had to call him twice.

25

It took Ted Murcer three years at the Manhattan District Attorney's Office to win an assignment to the Homicide Bureau. That was fast, but he seemed to be born to the courtroom. There was something boyish, something slightly vulnerable that he managed to convey to his juries, an intangible, priceless something that made them believe him, made them trust him. He was making an impression, gaining a reputation, attracting attention.

Murcer was a registered Republican and he was working hard at that too. It had seemed natural. His parents had been Republicans. And his grandparents. His great-grandfather had been an abolitionist and had been one of the founders of the Republican party in the state of New Hampshire. So it became natural for him to fall into the orbit of brilliant progressive Republicans that dominated New York politics—candidates like Jacob Javits, Louis Lefkowitz, and John Lindsay. And above all there was Nelson Rockefeller, the governor. Murcer liked him best. He watched him campaign, watched him press the flesh, work the crowd, smiling, enjoying himself, shouting "Hiya, fella!" and winning votes. He watched him spend money, watched him wheel and deal, watched him make promises, watched him keep them. He watched Rocky win elections. He watched them all win elections. And he caught the fever. He worked toward the day when he would run himself. He paid his dues.

"I got a nice murder two for you to try, Ted," his new bureau chief told Murcer, pointing at him for emphasis with two stubby fingers and a not-yet lit cigar. "It's technically circumstantial. We've got no eyewitness to the shooting itself, but it's still a good strong case, provided we don't fuck it up."

"What's it about?" Murcer asked.

"An Italian numbers runner, small time strictly, got himself shot up on a Harlem rooftop, got himself robbed of all his policy play and whatever cash he had on him."

"No eyewitness?"

"No. But we got a lady who lives on the top floor of the apartment, a middle-aged nigger lady on welfare with about a dozen kids and no husband, who heard the shots and who saw the killer come running down the stairs from the roof with a gun in one hand and a brown paper bag in the other. Anyway, this lady made the killer, picked him right out of a fucking lineup, a good clean lineup with a legal aid lawyer present and everything. She picked him right out and the detective tells me she was so fucking scared she practically crapped in her pants. That means she's telling the truth."

"But how did the cops know to pick the guy up in the first place? Did our witness know him?"

"No—all she gave at first was a description. The guy got picked up on account of his being a friend of the super of the building where the killing happened. The super is the other defendant in the case."

"Two defendants?"

"Yeah. An informant told the cops that he heard this super talking about how he pulled a 'sting' on a local numbers man about a week after the shooting. On the basis of that we got a search warrant and went through the fucker's apartment."

"What did you come up with?"

"We got the dead man's policy play stuffed in the bottom of a garbage bag that the super had been too lazy or stupid to throw away, and we came up with almost thirty-five hundred bucks in small crumpled bills, and best of all, we found a box of .38-caliber bullets, which is the kind that was dug out of the dead man's gut."

"Did you find a gun?"

"No. But once we had a line on the super and pulled him in, it wasn't too long before we got the actual killer. A young girl who lives in the building, a real looker, admitted to the detective that she was in the super's apartment the night before the killing, visiting the super's wife or something. Anyway, she admits that she saw the super holding a little powwow with this guy who turns out to be the killer and that the guy had a .38-caliber revolver. She heard them talking about the guy who was killed, and she knew the name of the killer, which led to his arrest and the lineup."

"Any confessions or statements?" Murcer asked.

The bureau chief laughed. "Are you joking? Both of these bastards have criminal records that go back to when you were sucking on your mother's tit. They told the detectives to go fuck themselves."

"Well, with bad records, I suppose that the defendants probably won't take the stand."

"Probably not," the chief agreed. "If they do though, that's the best thing that could ever happen. You could spend half a fucking day questioning each one about his priors, and by the time you were done, the jury would figure that they had to be guilty, if not of this murder then of some other one. That would flush them right down the tubes."

Murcer felt that he had to make an offer.

"Does your man want to cop a plea to manslaughter one with a zip to twenty sentence?" he asked the lawyer representing the trigger man.

"I wish I could get him to take a plea," came the answer. "But I'll tell you something funny—he swears that he's innocent, really swears it, so that I almost believe him. Usually these bastards swear up and down that they didn't do it, and then when you start talking about plea bargaining opportunities, they get real thoughtful. Later on when I work out a plea I tell them that they're going to have to admit guilt in order to take a plea and that they can't do that unless they're really guilty. That's when they usually own up to me. But this guy's different. He won't even talk plea with me, and I don't think he ever will. And that's downright unnatural. This guy is forty-eight years old and he's spent half his adult life in and out of jail. He knows the score better than you or me. So I almost believe he's innocent."

"So?"

"So, I'm suggesting, why don't you give him a lie detector test?"

"And if he passes?"

"Then dismiss the indictment."

"And if he fails?"

"Then you'll know you're convicting a guilty man."

"Will he agree to plead guilty to murder and take his life sentence if he fails?"

"No. He won't plead."

Murcer shrugged. "No test," he said.

"Tell your client," Murcer told the super's lawyer, "that I know that he didn't pull the trigger. And because of that I'm willing to give him a break. I'll take a plea to manslaughter two and recommend only a zip to five sentence, which is a pretty good deal."

"It's a great deal," the lawyer answered. "What's the catch?"

"Very simple," Murcer answered. "All he's got to do is to agree to testify against the trigger man."

"No deal," came the reply. "I broached that possibility a long time ago with my man and it's out of the question. There's no way my client's going to do a zip to five-year jolt labeled as a stool pigeon. He's not going to do a zip to five months that way. It wouldn't be good for his health.

"Anyway he gets really uptight every time I suggest his cooperating. Maybe he's scared of the trigger man. Maybe it's something else. But I can tell you that he won't cooperate."

It appeared that the case would have to be tried, and Murcer set about methodically preparing. He went with the detective up to Harlem and walked all over the roof of the apartment building, and then down the stairs to the sixth-floor landing, getting in the process a feel for the layout of the crime scene. He had a forensics man take a slew of photographs.

Then he sat down with his witnesses. The police officers who had executed the search warrant on the super's apartment, the deputy medical examiner who had done the autopsy on the numbers man, and above all, Esther MacKenzie, his almost-eye-witness, and Olivia Brown, the young woman who had seen the defendants plotting together the night before. He spent hours, days, with them, getting each ready to withstand cross-examination.

Olivia Brown was a looker. The bureau chief had been right. She had long straight jet-black hair worn loose, high cheekbones, and sloe eyes. She wore Chinese-style dresses with slits up the sides reaching close to her hips.

"You're going to have to wear something different when you come in to testify," he told her one evening as they were about to quit for the day.

"Too sexy, huh?"

"Yeah. The next time I see you, I want to see you wearing some kind of nice baggy, dull old skirt that reaches down to about your ankles. And maybe a white blouse and woolen sweater. It wouldn't hurt if you wore a brassiere either. And don't wear any makeup."

"Really?" she asked him. "Don't you like the way I look?"

"Sure. It's just that I'd like it a lot better if you dress the way I ask. We don't want the jury thinking you're a whore, do we?"

She smiled.

He smiled back.

Murcer got more nervous the nearer he came to the trial. It was always like that. He got gun-shy before it began, worried about a hundred things, tried to cover every angle, to answer every question.

He was convinced that the defendants were guilty. They had to be. One had been identified by a virtual eyewitness. The other had been caught with the fruits of the robbery, had been heard plotting the killing. They had to be guilty. Murcer had convinced himself, which he knew was the first step toward convincing the jury. He had to believe in his case, because if he didn't, if he had the slightest doubt, the jury would see it instantly. And if they saw that he had doubt, then they would have doubt. And if they had doubt, a reasonable doubt, then they would acquit. And that would be no good.

It was Friday night. The trial was scheduled to begin Monday morning. He was sitting in his office with the detective who originally had investigated the case, the same one who had executed the search warrant, who had arrested both defendants. They had worked closely together getting the case ready for trial. They had become friends.

"Is there anything we haven't done yet, Greg?" Murcer asked. "I don't know why, but I just have a feeling that there's something we're overlooking, something basic."

"I know what you mean," the detective answered. "It's bugging me too. Like there's something wrong. To be honest it's been bugging me from the start."

"Anything particular that you can think of?"

"The only thing I can think of is the super. His family really. He's got a kid about fourteen, fifteen years old, a boy, and I hear that he was around the time that the killing happened, that he knows the way it came down. The one time I saw him he was real tense and withdrawn, tightly wound, and I had the impression that if I pushed he would explode and tell me all kinds of things that I might want to hear."

"But you didn't push?"

"No. I felt kind of sorry for the kid and I didn't want to fuck him up any more. I didn't need to pump him in order to make my case. Besides the home situation was so messed up that I just laid off. You see, the kid's mother, the super's wife, who is still a pretty attractive woman, was shacking up with some new guy and the kid really resented that. There were some bad problems between the kid and the mother's boyfriend, and I can guess that it was particularly bad because the kid was visiting his father in prison after the old man was arrested, and probably had to lie to his old man about how things stood at home. I talked to the super's wife, and it was pretty clear to me that she didn't give a shit if her husband stayed in jail forever. It was a bad situation so I laid off."

"And now you're thinking that maybe you shouldn't have?"

"Yes."

"So am I."

"Tomorrow morning?"

"Yes."

"Your father is going on trial for murder Monday," Murcer began bluntly. He and the detective were seated in the dinette of a tiny apartment with the super's son. The wife and her boy-friend, a big hulking man, had absented themselves from the apartment when Murcer arrived. They were alone.

No answer, just hatred. The boy stared back at him with hard eyes.

"Did you hear what Mr. Murcer said?" the detective asked, menace in his voice. He knew his business.

"Yeah, I heard. And yeah, I knew."

"I thought you might know something that might help your father, or maybe the guy who's going to be on trial with him? That's what I thought," Murcer said.

"You thought wrong." The boy answered too fast. His eyes said what his mouth wouldn't. The hardness cracked and the hurt showed, the impossible, unjust pressures. He was only fifteen years old. "I don't know a thing."

"That's too bad," Murcer replied. "It would be nice if you could help your father."

Murcer hated the cruelty of it, the taunting irony, the unfairness of leaning on a defenseless lonely troubled boy. But he wanted the truth, wanted to be sure of what he was prosecuting. In three years as a prosecutor he had learned to be hard, learned to ignore his more tender sensibilities.

"You know," he told the boy, "somehow I just think you know something important, something that I need to know, something that will maybe help me, or maybe that will help one of the guys I'm trying to send to jail. Maybe I'm wrong. But maybe you want to lead the rest of your life knowing that you didn't speak up when you should have. It's your choice."

No answer. The eyes were hard again. Murcer had lost him, had said something wrong. They all knew it.

"Okay," Murcer left it. "Think it over. Here's my phone number and here's where my office is. If you change your mind just call or stop by."

The trial went well. Murcer and the defense lawyers spent two days picking a jury and when they were done Murcer liked their looks. They were male and white and middle-aged. They were lower middle class and law-abiding and uptight. A prosecution jury. A jury that would have no trouble convicting.

His witnesses stood up well. The "eyewitness" was terrific, frightened and convincing. "That's the man!" she said, pointing to the trigger man. "I swear to God almighty, that's the man I seen coming off that roof with a gun in his hand. I'll never forget it! Never!" The jury believed her.

Olivia Brown was excellent too. She came into court dressed like an old-fashioned schoolteacher, gave her testimony humbly, answered the cross-examination questions patiently, like a lady. The defense lawyers never touched her.

The cops, the medical examiner, the dead man's widow, the forensics man, all testified. And the defense lawyers barely laid a glove on any of them. Murcer was about ready to rest his case. Then the defense would be put to its proof. The defense lawyers would have the unhappy choice of either putting their clients on the stand, subjecting them to withering cross-examination in which Murcer would parade all of their past criminal misdeeds before the jury, or else they could refrain, letting the jury imagine all the reasons why they might be afraid to testify. It was a no-win situation. A guilty verdict seemed assured.

The boy was waiting in Murcer's office the evening Murcer was to sit down and prepare his summation. In the excitement of the trial he had forgotten about the super's son.

"It's you," Murcer said, surprised.

"Yeah."

He was silent, waiting for the boy to speak.

"You're sending the wrong man to jail," the boy said. "I was in the apartment the time that numbers man got killed, in the same room as my dad, and I saw the man who did the killing come running into the apartment and it wasn't the guy you got on trial. It was another friend of my father's, a guy named Ernie Jackson, who looks just like the guy you got on trial. Those two dudes could be twins. The lady on the sixth floor picked out the wrong man."

"Why didn't you tell us this a year ago?"

The boy looked at him as if he were demented. "My father is the other man on trial," he said simply.

"And he was in cahoots with this Ernie Jackson."

No answer.

"And by telling me about Ernie Jackson you're giving up your father, right? Because now I'll have to put you on the stand and ask you about your dad and even if you lie, the truth will come out."

Still no answer.

"Are you willing to take a lie detector test?"

"Very well," the judge stated the next morning. "Are the lawyers ready to begin their summations?"

"No, your honor," Murcer replied. "A most extraordinary thing happened last night and I am now going to make a strange application. I must ask for a mistrial."

"What?"

"Your honor, last night a new witness came forward who told me for the first time that there might be a case of mistaken identity here. This witness, who also saw the actual killer fleeing from the building, identified him as one Ernie Jackson, not as the man now on trial.

"Late last night I went to the Bureau of Criminal Identification and pulled Ernie Jackson's photos. Here they are, and here are those of the man now on trial. The resemblance is uncanny.

"Early this morning I confronted my eyewitness, the lady who lived on the sixth floor, with the photos of the defendant and the photos of Ernie Jackson. She could not differentiate between them, could not say which was the one she saw."

"Well what do you propose?" the judge asked.

"I spoke with counsel this morning and he will agree to a mistrial. I propose to give his client a lie detector test and if he passes it, I will move to dismiss the indictment. If he fails, then we must simply retry the case."

"And what about the co-defendant?" the judge asked. "Do you want a mistrial as to him?"

"No. As to him, I would ask that my case be reopened to call just that one newly discovered witness."

At that moment, by pre-arrangement, the detective entered the courtroom accompanying the super's son. And the super blanched, began to shake.

"This is the co-defendant's son and I have him here under subpoena and he will be obliged to give testimony against his father."

"Very well," the judge said. "Let's call for the jury."

"No!" the super yelled, staring at his son. The boy was crying. The man who was on trial as the trigger man was crying.

"No!" the super cried. "Don't put him on the stand. Leave him alone. I done it, and Ernie Jackson was in on it with me. Jus' leave my boy alone."

And the super began to cry too. They brought the boy up and let him embrace his father and they all looked away embarrassed.

When it all sorted out the supposed trigger man passed his lie detector test and was released. The super pleaded guilty to attempted manslaughter in the second degree, and took a five-year sentence. Ernie Jackson was arrested six months later. The case was assigned to someone else.

Murcer was the big winner. He was shaken by the prospect of nearly having convicted an innocent man. But not shaken enough to prevent him from making sure that the newspapers all got the story about how he had had the courage to do the right thing and push an investigation to free an innocent man and cost himself a sure conviction. It made good copy, good publicity. Five months later, the story helped him win first the Republican nomination and then the general election to the state senate. Ted Murcer was on his way.

26

Sabotnik found a job working for the house counsel of a large insurance company that wrote automobile liability policies. It was a job. It earned him a living. He hated it.

For six months he sat in an office, a tiny cubicle really, writing pleadings. He drafted answers to automobile accident personal injury cases that had been served upon the company's policy holders. Then he graduated to doing motions, motions to compel the plaintiffs to appear at pre-trial depositions, motions to dismiss complaints due to the failure of the plaintiffs to do something or other. It was all unspeakably dull, repetitious, boilerplate-type work. There was no opportunity to excel, no opportunity to learn much. There was nothing.

Then he was finally assigned to work in court and things began to improve. Slightly.

It was the civil court in Brooklyn, the lowest and least glamorous rung on the ladder. The cases he was asked to defend were never greater than five thousand dollars in value. They were the hit-in-the-rears, the fender benders, the pedestrian knockdowns, the minor accidents where even the plaintiffs wouldn't have the gall to claim that the injuries were serious. They were the cases of the fake whiplash, the slight sprain, the recurrent headaches for which the physicians could find no reason. The minor complaint.

Sabotnik was given a crushing caseload, almost two hundred fifty files to deal with. Far too many for him to possibly learn, even casually, the facts of each case. Instead he would run around the courthouse from courtroom to courtroom, conferencing these cases in front of the various judges, glancing at each file for a moment or two before going up to either settle the case or set it down for trial. He learned to make snap judgments on scanty information, learned to talk to judges, to plaintiffs' lawyers, to negotiate, to give a little, take a little, to try to get a result. He learned to talk to the claims men back at the insurance company, to get authority to settle a case, to talk them out of a settlement he considered too high. He learned skills of a sort.

He also learned how to try cases. They were small cases. Unimportant cases. The stakes were negligible and there was no chance to be a hero or a goat. The judges were, as a rule, the least experienced and least learned judges imaginable, and the evidentiary rulings he received were often bizarre. He frequently had to deal with blatant favoritism, and sometimes he thought that he was in a fish market rather than a courtroom. He developed polish and poise, learned to prevail in spite of everything.

Still he hated it. He never got over the feeling of sleaziness, the sense that he was not really practicing law properly. He just knew that if he were given a chance, the opportunity to prepare cases properly, to try them before some of the better judges in the state supreme court, or even the federal court, he would make out well.

Then things began to get ugly. He had been working for the insurance carrier for a year and a half, almost two years, and had pretty much gotten himself accepted as one of the boys. He was approached by Jim Kawolski, one of the senior claims men in charge of the civil court cases to which Sabotnik was assigned.

"Phil," Kawolski began, calling him aside at the end of a working day, "how much is the company paying you in salary these days, sixty-five hundred a year or so, right?"

"Yes," Sabotnik answered.

"Would you like to earn more?"

"Sure. Who wouldn't."

"Well, I know an easy way that someone like you could maybe double his salary."

Sabotnik didn't answer and the claims man went on cautiously.

"This is all hypothetical of course, but you know that there are certain plaintiffs' lawyers out there who bring lots of bullshit cases, cases that you wouldn't think of paying out any real money on. Well, hypothetically speaking, some lawyers here might just think about maybe letting some of those cases get settled for a little bit more than they might be worth, say maybe three thousand dollars or sometimes forty-five hundred dollars. And again, hypothetically speaking, maybe some claims men here would like to approve such settlements."

"And then?" Sabotnik asked. The claims man smiled.

"Why then the plaintiff's lawyer earns his one-third fee of a thousand or fifteen hundred dollars. And it wouldn't be out of line for that grateful lawyer to make a gift of oh, say ten percent of that fee, a hundred or a hundred fifty dollars in cash, to be divided between the claims man and the defense lawyer, kind of a tax-free gratuity."

"And forty or fifty little settlements like this a year, and our hypothetical lawyer has put an additional three or four thousand in cash into his pocket?" Sabotnik asked.

"That's the idea. And no one's the wiser."

"And what if our hypothetical lawyer refused?"

"Well that might prove embarrassing to him. Especially if he wanted a future with the company. It would disappoint a lot of people and make a lot of enemies; bad enemies if you catch my drift."

Sabotnik stayed with the insurance company only three more months. There was nothing else to be done. He would take no bribes and was too smart to try to turn in the claims man who had approached him. There was no proof he could offer except his own word. He had to get out. It was a bad time.

Sam Horowitz was a young lawyer with one of the better, more successful plaintiffs' firms. He had graduated from NYU Law School the same year Sabotnik had graduated. He was a dynamic restless kid, unpolished but bright. Like Sabotnik he had been assigned to try small cases in Brooklyn civil court, assigned to get seasoning. And like Sabotnik he had shown promise. The two men had met, had opposed each other, had negotiated settlements, and had become friends. They had talked together about going out on their own. Now Sabotnik pushed the discussions in earnest.

"Sam, I think that we should go into practice for ourselves now," he told Horowitz, saying nothing of the special reasons he had for leaving the insurance company. "We're young, we're single, neither of us have any real responsibilities to hold us back. There will never be a better time."

Horowitz needed no persuading.

"If we do this, Phil, I want to do it right. I don't want to have a hand-to-mouth practice where we have to run our asses off just to make ends meet. I want us to become specialists, doing what we do best, which is personal injury work. I don't think that we should try to get involved doing divorces, or real estate closings, or criminal defense work. We'll stretch ourselves too thin if we try to do everything and then we'll end up being nickel and dime."

"Sounds right to me," Sabotnik agreed. "I suppose that we should specialize in representing the folks who get hurt. At least that's what I'd prefer. I wouldn't really want to work with insurance companies as my clients, selling them my time by the hour."

"Exactly," Horowitz cut in, their thoughts dovetailing. "There's a lot more money in plaintiffs' work. We'll represent our clients on a one-third contingent fee, so if we settle a case for say thirty thousand then our fee would be ten thousand. Do you know how many hours it would take us to generate ten thousand dollars in fees? We can do that in one case, and not an especially big case at that."

They talked every night for several weeks. Each man raised five thousand dollars from their families to start up with. They looked around for office space and finally rented a small three-room suite on Chambers Street in downtown Manhattan. They hired a secretary, printed up stationery, purchased used office furniture, put in a telephone, bought insurance, and gave notice to their employers.

They flipped a coin on the day they decided to go into partnership. Sabotnik called heads and won the toss. That made the firm Sabotnik and Horowitz. So it would remain.

They began their practice with only four tiny cases they had managed to scrounge up, and with a small annual retainer to do some legal work for Sabotnik's uncle. There were days and even weeks in the beginning when they sat around waiting for the telephone to ring, trying to figure out ways to attract business.

27

Mary Ann Salisbury met her second husband at a cocktail party. Max Braverman was a professor of psychology at New York University. He was forty-seven years old, drank too much, had written three well-regarded books, and spent most of his time doing research into the dynamics of social coercion and brain washing. He had interviewed and written about a number of American servicemen who had been prisoners of war during the Korean conflict, and was working on a study of concentration camp survivors designed to demonstrate why some of the inmates had come to identify with and even imitate the SS in their conduct. He was fascinated by issues of power and power-lessness, authority and social structure.

"Tell me about your work," he asked her, leading her to a corner, out of the crush of the party.

"I'm with the Civil Division of the Legal Aid Society."

"Doing what?"

"Mostly landlord-tenant work. I've been representing tenants in disputes with some of the municipal housing authorities. Disputes of heating, and repairs, fighting eviction notices."

"So you fight city hall."

"There's a lot to fight. For instance, I've got a number of women clients who live alone with their kids in the projects. They're divorced, or never got married, or maybe they were deserted by their husbands. Anyway in one regard or another these ladies manage to violate some regulation of the housing authority. One of them earns a little too much money and falls out-

side the guidelines on income. Another wants to keep a dog in
the apartment because she's afraid of burglaries. A third has a
twelve-year-old son who's a discipline problem and has been
spraying obscene graffiti on the walls of the lobby and keeps getting caught."

"Yes."

"So it turns out that a pair of housing policemen worked up
dossiers on these women and then confronted each of them,
threatening to get them evicted unless they had sex with them."

"Blackmail."

"That's right, and soon these cops, and half the bloody pre-
cinct, were fucking those poor women. One of them even somehow was made to prostitute herself for a little while. It was all so
pathetic."

"And it happens all the time," he said, while getting himself
another drink. "Authority figures, no matter how petty, can be
pretty well relied upon to abuse their positions in one way or
another. Bosses screw their secretaries, both literally and figura-
tively, and so on right down the line. But the thing that has always intrigued me is why the victims submit. I know that your
clients were afraid that they would lose their apartments, but
they must have known that those cops were bluffing. Or that it
was really unlikely that they ever would be evicted what with
obnoxious legal aid lawyers like you to defend them. And even if
they might be evicted, there are other places to live in the city.
And is it really worth it to give in to that kind of bullshit and
give some cop a blow job just to keep a lousy apartment?
There's something else at work there. A kind of submission to
authority that's really dangerous."

Mary Ann could not tell whether he was sober or drunk as he
talked to her. Or whether he was serious or joking. He finished
his scotch and immediately got yet another and they kept talking. There was something cynical and mocking in his nature.
And also something attentive and sympathetic. He was not too
drunk to listen to what Mary Ann had to say, to ask intelligent
questions and make interesting observations. He was aggressive.
And challenged what she said, made fun of her political enthusi-

asms, put her on the defensive. But there was something wounded about him. Vulnerable.

"You'll come home with me tonight," he said eventually. It was a statement more than a question.

"Yes."

And they made love. Briefly. And he fell asleep. Mary Ann lay beside him into the night wondering who he was.

In the morning he awoke and dressed before Mary Ann had opened her eyes. And provided her with a cup of fresh-brewed coffee when she did. Then he proposed that they go to a Chinese restaurant that he knew.

"For breakfast?"

"Certainly. Chinamen have to eat in the morning too, don't they? This place makes unbelievable breakfast dumplings, which go wonderfully with tea, and are a hell of a lot better than bacon and eggs."

And he was right too.

Sitting over breakfast she began to tell him about the case she was working on that troubled her most.

"It's a divorce case with a custody fight. My client works as a night porter at a midtown hotel. His wife has a very bad psychological problem. She drinks and neglects their kids. They've got three boys.

"Anyway, there are times he told me when he calls home and the oldest boy, who's only seven, answers and says that his mother has gone out and no one knows where she is. The kids have been left alone and when he comes home at eight in the morning, he's found the little one, who's one and a half, lying in his crib crying, covered with shit.

"He wants a divorce and he wants to send the kids back to Puerto Rico to live with his aunt, his mother's sister, who raised him and who's willing to raise them."

"So what's the problem?" he asked.

"The mother won't agree. When my client suggests sending the kids away she tells him to go fuck himself. She's not Puerto Rican and she doesn't want the children that far away. But then she keeps on drinking and neglecting them. He stopped giving her money because he thought she was spending the grocery money on liquor. And now he suspects that she has sold her body to get drinking money."

"Well can't he win the custody fight?"

"I doubt it," Mary Ann said. "Judges don't take small children away from their mothers no matter what the facts are. And besides if we end up with a trial and he tells all of his stories about his wife, she'll probably just bring in some girl friends who will lie and accuse him of being twice as bad. He'll lose."

And the professor smiled his sardonic smile as she told him about the case. "Another case of the legal system and the courts being out of touch with reality," he said softly. "Shakespeare, or whomever, was right when he said that if you want justice you should start by shooting all the lawyers and judges."

"Well what would you do then?"

"I'd tell him to fuck the courts, and not go anywhere near a judge or lawyer. And I'm surprised that any sensible Puerto Rican hotel employee was stupid enough to go see a lawyer. What he should do obviously is grab his kids and put them on a plane to Puerto Rico. Maybe he should quit his job and go down there himself and get a job. I mean if he loves his children, and if the situation is the way you describe it, he's crazy to trust in lawyers. He should just do what's right himself. That's what I'd tell him to do."

He was right. Mary Ann knew that as he spoke. And it disturbed her to think that she had so quickly become programmed to "think like a lawyer" that she could not see beyond the technical problems of the court system to the practical realities underneath. She was so mired in the workings of the law that she had become blind to its limitations.

She found herself drawn to the professor. He was attractive in a tousled, unkempt sort of way. His eyes were bright, and his mind was like a steel trap. She knew she would spend more time with him.

And she did. Not moving in with him but spending two or three nights a week, most weekends at his apartment. They drank and they made love and they talked. Sometimes it was no good in bed. Especially if they drank too much. Sometimes it was better. Sometimes she lay in bed beside him and felt lonely. Other times she felt warm and protective. Sometimes she did not know what she felt.

And then she became pregnant. It wasn't planned. She had had too much to drink and got careless about her diaphragm one night. And she knew almost right away.

"Let's have the baby," he said when she told him, and then she said she was thinking about an abortion, that he shouldn't worry, that she would take care of it. "Let's get married and have a little boy and raise him to be as screwed up as we are," he said, smiling.

She could see that he was truly happy, that he wanted a child. That made her feel happy too. And besides she had always wanted to have a baby.

So they were married at City Hall two weeks later. Married and moved in together. Mary Ann kept her maiden name professionally though.

28

Cleveland Daniels graduated from high school, the first member of his family to have ever done so. His mother and Ralph, her boyfriend, attended the graduation. They took photographs of Cleveland in his cap and gown.

"You're going to have to get yourself a job now," Ralph told Cleveland as they sat down to a restaurant dinner after the graduation. "If you like, I think I can probably get you a good job with the Transit Authority. There are spots available and you could get training as either a motorman or a conductor. The pay is pretty good, and the benefits are excellent. There's health insurance and a pension and lots of paid vacation and personal time off. And the union, the TWU, is real tough, and looks after its own. It's a pretty good job. It's been good to me. And I'd be glad to get you a start with it."

Cleveland didn't like Ralph. He never had. Ralph had always treated him well, had never given him cause for the dislike. More important, he had always treated Cleveland's mother well. He was a decent man. Still Cleveland disliked him.

"No, Ralph," he answered a little too quickly, "I don't think I'm cut out to work my whole life under the ground. I mean I don't even much like riding in the subway as a passenger, if you know what I mean. But thanks anyway, man. I appreciate it."

It was a lie of course, and they both knew it. Cleveland had nothing against the subways. It was a terrific opportunity, a better one than anything Cleveland was apt to turn up on his own. He was turning it down because he didn't want to owe Ralph. He was going to make his own way.

After two months of looking he found a job as a night watchman and porter at the Sages of Israel, a Jewish nursing home in Yonkers. The pay was awful, but it beat nothing. From midnight to eight in the morning, six days a week, he was supposed to wander around the dismal six-story building doing whatever pushing or shoving or carrying the graveyard shift of nurses or orderlies required.

A lot of the old folks at the nursing home didn't sleep too well. "You don't sleep too much when you get old," one of the residents told him. "I'm eighty-seven years old and my body just doesn't need to sleep much anymore. Sixty years I ran my dry cleaning business and I used to get up five-thirty in the morning and work till nine, ten o'clock at night. So I never really got much sleep. It's a matter of habit."

The old man was named Morris Itzkowitz, and he and Cleveland became friends. The old man had a kind of palsy that made his hands shake, which made it difficult or even impossible for him to light the Camel cigarettes that he chain-smoked. Cleveland used to sit up with him in the small hours, lighting his smokes for him. They sat in one of the common rooms and watched old B-grade movies on the television together. They spent a lot of time talking. Itzkowitz was the one who first clued Cleveland in on the way things were at the nursing home.

"Things aren't too bad now in September, when the weather's pretty nice. But wait until January or February when it gets real cold. Comes around five or six o'clock, when the owners go home, the heat drops down to fifty-five maybe sixty degrees at the most so that they can save money on fuel.

"And I can tell you right now, at this moment, that there are a good half-dozen nurses and orderlies that are too busy fucking one another in some of the empty rooms to pay attention to their patients. Some of the people here need special medication and they're too senile or forgetful to take it themselves. A lot of them never get what they're supposed to get, 'cause no one on the staff cares about getting it for them.

"You're all right, kid," Itzkowitz ended up, "but you're an exception. I'll bet that half the people who work here drink or take drugs while they're on duty. The rest aren't much better."

It was pretty much as the old man described it. Perhaps it was worse. Cleveland learned that the nursing home was owned by a man who styled himself as a rabbi, who, along with his family, owned a string of five or six similar homes. Their object, and their sole object, was to extract a maximum profit with a minimum of expense or effort. Accordingly, the homes' so-called kosher kitchens were presided over by Filipino chefs with poor command of the English language. The food purchased for preparation was of the worst quality, often rotten when purchased and always disgusting when prepared. Cleveland watched the staff, also the dregs, ignore the patients, saw old men lying in their own excrement because no nurse or orderly had come to help them with bed pans.

He watched patients die, some peacefully, others struggling, resisting to the bitter end. He watched some of them languish, abandoned by children too busy or too distant to see to the dignity of their parents' last years. He grew hardened to it. It was a necessity.

Then he found a girl at the home, a nurse trainee from Bedford Stuyvesant in Brooklyn who worked the same night shifts he did. They set up a little nest for themselves in the custodian's room, with a folding cot and some linen that they borrowed from the home's supplies. He bought a fancy radio and kept it at work so that they would have music, and soon he too was taking three- or four-hour breaks from work so that he and his lady friend might play.

He was down on the ground floor making it the night that Itzkowitz died. He had been sitting with the old man earlier that night, lighting his cigarettes and shooting the breeze. Around two-thirty he had lit the old man one last cigarette and had gone downstairs to party. When he returned upstairs at four-thirty he learned about the fire.

"That old Itzkowitz guy," one of the orderlies told him, "must have fallen asleep with his cigarette going. Anyway his clothes and the fuckin' couch an' everything caught fire an' we're god-damned lucky that I noticed it before this whole fuckin' place went up in flames."

"What about the old man?"

"He's burned real bad on his face, and his hands, and all over. They took him to the hospital, but he ain't gonna make it. He's probably dead already."

Cleveland got up and walked out of the nursing home and never returned. He didn't even put in for payment of the wages for the three days that week that he had worked.

29

Petrakis had gone to Regis, McCormick, and Letterman when he left the Supreme Court. His justice had been friendly with Ed Regis and it was easily arranged for Petrakis to become a privileged associate assigned as an aide to Regis himself. It was a relationship that prospered.

Regis saw in Petrakis a kindred spirit. Hard-working, ambitious, hungry, both men were realists. Both were devoid of ideology, had little patience for posturing and rhetoric. Regis was a doer, and a fixer, interested in results, priding himself on a ruthless ability to accomplish what others could not. He had made a great deal of money and was independently wealthy, but that was largely beside the point. It was the exercise of power that he loved. Petrakis watched Regis carefully, admired him, and modeled himself after him. Professionally he enjoyed himself, expected to make a career at the law firm. It was Regis who decreed otherwise.

"George," he told him one day, "I don't think that it makes sense for you to stay here at the firm."

It was a blunt statement and it shocked Petrakis. He had been doing well. He knew he was doing well. And he expected to make partner. Maybe not for four or five years, but he knew he would make it. Now, suddenly, for no apparent reason he was being told he would not make it. It was inexplicable and his face showed it.

Regis laughed. "Don't look like that, George. You can stay if you like. And you'll become a partner too. I can assure you of that. It's just that I don't think that that would be what you would want. What I have in mind makes a lot more sense."

"What's that?"

"Before I tell you, let me tell you why you don't want to stay here. First, it would be five years before I could make you a partner, because if I do it sooner it would bend the other associates out of shape and there's no point in making the troops angry. So you would have to wait. And even after you made partner, there would be the junior partners to think about, and the not so junior partners. You'll be mired in the pecking order, and frustrated. I don't see it for you.

"You're the type who's cut out to be on top of any organization. And you can't do that here."

"Because you're the boss here?" Petrakis asked.

Regis laughed. "Exactly."

"So what do I do?"

"I've given it a lot of thought, and I believe that the best move for you now is to move over as the executive assistant to Paul

Reynolds. The general counsel at Transcontinental Communications."

"Why Transcontinental? They're pretty small, aren't they?"

"Yes, but they're cash rich, and they're about to start on a program of growth that would make your head spin. Acquisitions and mergers, that's what it's going to be all about in the next ten years and that's what Transcontinental is in a great position to do. For instance, they're just about to acquire Lefcourte Labs, you know, the pharmaceutical house, and are negotiating a merger with one of the big California agribusiness outfits that grows and markets avocados and lettuce. Transcontinental has a strong central core in computers and transistorized technology. In ten years it's going to be one of the largest conglomerates in the world."

"And what about the management? Why do they need me?"

"In a sense they don't. The management at Transcontinental is sharp and they're doing just fine. But they're old. Paul Reynolds, the general counsel, is sixty-eight, Ben Peterson, the chief executive officer, is sixty-four, and Lee Richardson, the executive vice-president in charge of finances, is sixty-two. They're all relatively old."

"And they don't have good talent in house to replace them?"

"Exactly."

"And how do you come to know this all so intimately?"

Regis smiled again wolfishly. "Because I'm on the board of directors of Transcontinental."

"And you're going to look after your company by sending me over there."

"Exactly."

"And you'll look after me that way too."

Another smile. "I don't think you're going to need much looking after."

Petrakis worked long hours. That would always be his way. But through it all, he always made time for his daughter. She came first. Or if not first, at least equal to his work.

He made it a point to be home in the evenings before she went to bed. She waited for him to walk in the door, dropped everything to run to him. They had secrets. He told her stories, wonderful invented stories about princes and princesses and dragons and magicians. He would take off his jacket, unbutton the vest of his suit, loosen his tie, and sit by her bed with the lights off, the night light on, and tell her stories.

Saturdays he usually worked, but Sundays were his daughter's time too. He took her on adventures, to the circus, Christmastime to the *Nutcracker* ballet. He took her to the movies, to see all the Disney animated features. They saw *Pinocchio, Snow White, Lady and the Tramp*, all of them. He took her to see *Peter Pan* and watched her eyes open wide as the children flew through the air. They went to the top of the Empire State Building and took a boat ride around Manhattan Island. Diana at the age of four was a beautiful and precocious child. She was his escape and diversion.

"She's not your daughter, she's your mistress," his wife told him half jokingly. Petrakis didn't answer. It was too nearly true.

He wanted another child. A son perhaps, to carry on his name. Or another daughter. It didn't matter. He tried to talk his wife into another child.

"I don't want another child," she told him. "I don't want to be awakened in the middle of the night by a crying baby and I don't want any more dirty diapers and I don't want to spend any more time wiping someone else's behind. I've had enough thank you."

He offered to hire help, a full-time baby nurse or a housekeeper. "You won't have to do those things," he promised. "You'll be able to write your books and do your free-lance work. I'm earning enough money now."

"No," she answered. "That won't work. I don't want to have a baby so that some West Indian woman or something can bring it up. It's all right for you to come home at seven o'clock each night like some kind of hero, to be a good guy to Diana, to take her out for treats, but that's not the way I do it. I'm the one who has to discipline her, to force her to get dressed, to fight with her. I'm the one who takes her to the pediatrician and who sits up with her when she's sick. And I'll be the one who will have to sit up with a new baby if we have one. I know you, George.

When the baby cries in the middle of the night, you're going to roll over and grunt and say that you have to work in the morning. And I'm going to have to get up and I'll resent it terribly. And I'll resent you. And I'd rather not. Because I love you."

She would be crying by then, and he would hug her. But three or four days later they would begin the same debate again.

In the end, when Diana was five years old, Petrakis won. Emma became pregnant.

30

The little firm of Sabotnik and Horowitz did not take a long time to prosper. It was only two years before they made their big breakthrough.

It started innocently enough. Sam Horowitz's mother had a Greek cleaning lady who worked for her one day a week. That lady had a grown son who worked as a steel and structural painter and sandblaster. "He's a good boy," she told Horowitz. "He just got married to a nice girl and they got a baby on the way."

"So what happened?" the lawyer asked.

"He was working on a scaffold painting a part of some bridge that the buses go over when they leave the bus terminal."

"Yes."

"Anyway, he fell off the scaffold. They were trying to move the scaffold while he was on it and it jumped or something and he fell about twenty-five feet and broke both his legs and his hips. He hurt his insides bad too. They had to operate on him twice already and I don't think that he's ever going to walk again without crutches or a cane. Tony's only twenty-four years old and he never even graduated from high school. How is he going to support his wife and the baby when it's born, if he's a cripple?"

Horowitz and Sabotnik both went to the hospital and met the

painter. He retained them on a one-third contingent basis, and they set to work together on the case.

They investigated the accident, spoke to the painter's co-workers, took a look at the type of rigging and scaffolding that had been used. They discovered that the scaffolding had been grossly inadequate, and had violated an entire host of provisions of the New York State Labor Law, a statute enacted to protect laborers such as painters, sandblasters, and construction workers. They started a suit against the Port Authority of New York and New Jersey, the owner of the terminal, claiming that its violation of the Labor Law and especially its failure to provide the painters with safety belts, caused the accident to occur.

Preparing the case for trial, Sabotnik and his partner met with the painter's doctors, and learned that their client would be permanently disabled; they met with officials from the local of the painter's labor union, got his work records as well as copies of the union's collective bargaining agreements over the past ten years, demonstrating how wages and benefits had increased. They prepared their case meticulously for trial, made ready to show that over the rest of his lifetime their client had been deprived of an enormous amount of lost income, that instead he would be forced to endure a life of pain, disability, and frustration.

And when they tried the case, it all paid off. Sabotnik took the lead role at the trial. He was low key, earnest, almost boyishly appealing, and the Manhattan jury loved him. The trial went beautifully, and the jury deliberated and after three hours returned with a verdict of $375,000, an absolutely phenomenal result in 1965.

"And it was a clean trial too!" Horowitz shouted as he hugged Sabotnik. "It will stand up on appeal. Goddamned, we just made ourselves $125,000, Phil! And that's not chopped liver!"

It was the following day that Horowitz displayed himself as a shrewd businessman. He bought five bottles of fine scotch and went down to the local and gave the union officials the bottles as a gesture of thanks for the help he had received in prosecuting the case. He made sure that the union men knew of the fantastic success they had accomplished for their member, made the point that they would like to represent any other members who got hurt.

And the message got through. In the next few years they got a steady diet of scaffold cases. They did well with them too, made out like bandits. Soon both men were earning more than they had ever dreamed of. They were on their way.

Sabotnik had not wanted to go to the party. It was a Friday night. It had been a long week and he and Horowitz were closing up the office for the weekend. Horowitz had been invited to the party by a girl he knew, who had told him to bring his friend. It was to be an open house. Sabotnik tried to beg off. He was tired. Horowitz insisted.

It was a crowded smoky party in a small East Side apartment. The men were on the make, looking for something fast. The women were more cautious, looking for something serious. Sabotnik decided to leave soon, have a drink maybe and go home.

Then Marilyn walked in. Her hair was cut short, looked stylish. She walked in and she saw him. They froze. He walked up to her.

"Marilyn."

"Phil."

They talked. The party buzzed on around them and they ignored it. Horowitz left with a woman he had picked up, and Sabotnik barely acknowledged him. Sabotnik and Marilyn talked and it seemed as if they had never been apart. They left the party and they continued to talk.

"Where do you live now?" he asked her.

"Not far from here. I share an apartment with two of the girls I teach with. It's a two-bedroom place over on Second Avenue and we take turns. Each semester one of us gets a bedroom to herself. How about you, Phil? Where do you live?"

"On the West Side. I've got a floor of a brownstone near the Museum of Natural History. It's quite nice really. It's got fifteen-foot-high ceilings, exposed brick walls, and a fireplace in both the living room and the bedroom. It would be really great if I ever got around to furnishing it nicely."

"I'd love to see it."

"Now?"

"Sure," she said, and she smiled.

They made love all through the night. And it was as if they had always been together. They knew each other instinctively, could laugh at one another, could talk about things that mattered. By morning they knew they would marry. They knew more than that. They knew that the marriage would be good, that it would endure. They would have children. None of it was stated, not in so many words. It didn't have to be. It was implicit.

"I had an affair two years ago," she told him. "It was with one of the guys I worked with, a social studies teacher. He was divorced and he lived with his parents. They ran a delicatessen and they used to work until one o'clock at night. So we would go back to his folks' house and stick around until eleven or twelve." She smiled. "I always had to be gone before they came home. Silly, wasn't it? At least I started to think it was silly. Or maybe that I was silly. Or that he was silly. So I broke it up."

She told him the rest of her stories. And he told her his. A week later she moved in. A month later he bought her a ring.

31

Sabotnik was pleased and surprised when his secretary told him that George Petrakis was on the phone. It was years since he had spoken to Petrakis, not since graduation. But he knew that his classmate had clerked at the Supreme Court, that he had gone on to the Regis firm and then to some fancy corporation. He assumed that Petrakis was calling to refer a case and that pleased him.

"George, how are you?" he said.

"Okay."

"What can I do for you?"

"I hear that you've been specializing in medical malpractice cases lately."

"Yes."

"And you've been doing pretty well at it."

"I've had good results."

"I know. And I'm afraid I have a case for you."

"A client?"

"No. Me."

"You."

"No, my wife, Emma. She died in childbirth last month. Her doctor killed her."

"Oh, my God, I'm sorry, George." What more was there to say.

Petrakis came to Sabotnik's office to discuss the case. He looked older to Sabotnik, still lean, well tailored, but his face was lined, his eyes more guarded. He was also beginning to go gray. It looked good on him.

"Emma's pregnancy, it was her second, was basically uneventful," Petrakis told him. "The first pregnancy had been fine and our daughter, Diana, had been born after only a six-hour labor."

"How long ago was that?"

"Six years, almost six and a half now. Anyway, Emma went into labor early in the evening and we called the obstetrician, Dr. Edelman, the same one who delivered Diana, and he told us to get into the hospital. So we called a neighbor to watch Diana, and we took a cab to the hospital, and she checked in."

"What happened then?"

"Well this time the labor was much longer and Emma seemed to be having a lot more pain. She really didn't seem to be able to get on top of the contractions this time the way she did with the first pregnancy."

"You were there?"

"Both times. We were doing the Lamaze natural childbirth routine."

"Yes."

"So the labor went on for about fourteen and a half hours and during that time that goddamned Edelman, the son of a bitch, only came in to examine her three times. There was a young resident there, an oriental doctor named Kim, who kept popping in and out, but I could never get a straight story out of him. He kept clucking his tongue and muttering about how it was an interesting case, but he wouldn't answer any questions and told us to talk to Dr. Edelman.

"Anyway, later on they decided to give her something called an epidural, which is a kind of local anesthesia injected into the spine, that leaves you awake, but eases the pain. An anesthesiologist came in but it turned out that Emma's vertebrae were so close together that they couldn't get the needle in, and that only hurt her more."

"And then?"

"Another hour or two went by and Edelman showed up and conferred with Kim and told us that they would have to do a Caesarean, that the labor was taking too long, and he was afraid that the baby might be getting into trouble. So they took her away."

"Yes?"

"And then three hours later they came back and told me that both Emma and the baby were dead. Kim came back to tell me. Edelman didn't even have the decency to talk to me that morning. It was right around the time the sun was coming up."

"What happened? Do you know?"

"Of course I know. I spoke to the nurses who worked the operating room that night, and I also had some of the doctors who work for one of my subsidiaries look at the record. Emma had an unusual condition it turned out, in which the placenta, instead of sloughing off the uterine wall and coming away easily after the delivery, had actually grown into the uterus so that it wouldn't come free.

"Anyway, the bastards waited so long before doing their surgery that the baby was stillborn, and then with this placenta condition, instead of doing a hysterectomy, which is what should have been done I'm told, right away, they tried to detach the placenta, which caused a lot of hemorrhaging. She was bleeding heavily for almost forty-five minutes before Edelman woke up and started to do the hysterectomy that he should have done in the first place. She went into shock from blood loss, and they couldn't save her after that. I've got the hospital record with me, and I insisted upon an autopsy. I have that report too. I think that you'll find it an open and shut case."

He handed a large manila envelope to Sabotnik. All through his recitation, Petrakis had been in perfect control of himself, presenting the facts in a fairly straightforward manner. Now that he was done though, Sabotnik could see the strain on his former classmate's face, signs of the struggle to keep control.

Sabotnik offered to handle the case, and told Petrakis that he would take it at a 5 or 10 percent fee, something nominal, just to cover expenses and the time that would have to be put into the case. "I'd feel funny," he told him, "making any kind of profit from your tragedy. You're an old friend."

"No," Petrakis answered. "I want you to charge me your normal fee. I don't really need the money from the lawsuit, and frankly whatever we recover I'm going to put into trust for my daughter. And even she really doesn't need the money, since to be honest, my wife had inherited some money before she died, and that now passes in trust to Diana. I really want to bring this suit to punish the bastards who killed my wife, and that's what I want you to do. Make their lives miserable."

And that's what Sabotnik did. As Petrakis had said, it was an open and shut case. Sabotnik hauled Dr. Edelman into court and cross-examined him for two grueling days as part of his pre-trial discovery, leading the doctor step by step through the long night of Emma Petrakis' death, challenging him minute by minute to justify where he was and what he was doing, asking him again and again whether his failure to operate earlier, or his failure to run certain diagnostic tests earlier, was negligent. The doctor, with the help of his defense lawyer, tried to defend himself, justified his conduct, refused to acknowledge his negligence, insisted that he had exercised his best judgment under difficult circumstances. But Sabotnik kept hammering away, implacably, hour after hour, pinning the doctor down, catching him in contradictions, making him look bad.

With discovery completed, Sabotnik put the case on the trial calendar to await its day in court. They waited fourteen months until it worked its way to the top of the list. Then the defendants tried to settle the case.

"I'll give you $250,000 to settle," the defense lawyer told Sabotnik. "That's a generous offer and you know it is. If you want anything more you're going to have to get it from a jury, because we're not going to pay it voluntarily."

The judge, who was sitting in on the settlement conference, recommended that Sabotnik accept the offer and Sabotnik agreed that it was fair. He said that he would call his client to seek authority to settle.

"No way, Phil," Petrakis replied. "I don't care if their offer is reasonable, or even if it's generous. I want my day in court, and I want to watch that son of a bitch sweat. I'm quite prepared to live with the jury's verdict. No settlement."

So there was a trial. Sabotnik punished Edelman on the stand for two more days, this time before the judge and jury. Then he called a professor of obstetrics from the University of Pennsylvania Medical School to explain why the doctor had committed malpractice. Petrakis gave testimony about his wife in a subdued, understated effective way. Diana, now aged eight, was brought into the courtroom and introduced briefly to the jury. She was dressed in a jumper with her hair tied back in a ponytail.

The defense case was brief and not terribly effective. And then they summed up to the jury, the defense lawyer first. Then Sabotnik.

He started slowly, almost dispassionately, lecturing them on medicine, reminding them of all the particular acts of carelessness and delay that had come out during the trial. "This woman died in childbirth," he kept repeating. "She was a young and healthy woman. She had had an earlier uneventful pregnancy. And now she's dead. In this day and age, that's not supposed to happen. And I think that you on the jury know that it happened only because of the shocking neglect and carelessness of Dr. Edelman. I think that you know that if he had been careful, if he had been on top of the case, Emma Petrakis and her baby would be alive today."

He started to pick up steam, sensing a receptive jury, and turned to the question of damages.

"Some of you," he said, looking at two women on the jury, "have had children yourselves. You don't need to be told that even under the best of circumstances childbirth is no picnic. It is painful. Imagine then, how many times more painful and hellish Emma Petrakis' experience must have been as hour after hour she was negligently permitted to suffer! Think on it, and then remember that we are entitled to recover for the pain and anguish that she suffered before her death caused by this negligence. You must put a substantial dollar value on that.

"But that's the least of it. Think now about the talented artist that this woman was, about the books she authored. She earned good money before she died. You've seen her tax returns and her royalty statements. She was making more and more each year, earned $13,000 in her last full year of life. My God, she was only thirty-two years old and she should have lived over forty more years. You've heard what the life-expectancy tables for her were. Suppose she had continued to write for another thirty years, until she was only sixty-two, and suppose that she never did better than $13,000 a year. Why then her death has cost her family thirty times $13,000 or $390,000.

"And that doesn't even begin to take into account this woman's value as a wife and mother. You saw little Diana. What is the value you put on the loss of care and guidance that she must suffer all the remaining days of her life. And George Petrakis? That good man must lead his life deprived of the society, the companionship, the love, and the affection of the woman he married. You must place a value on that loss, upon all of these losses. And then you must come back into this courtroom and face George Petrakis and face Diana Petrakis. You're going to have to face them and tell them in dollars what Emma Petrakis was worth to them. I wish it wasn't in dollars that you had to give your verdict. But then I wish that Emma Petrakis wasn't dead.

"But she is dead. And you do have to give your verdict in dollars. That's the way it is, and I know that you are going to give a verdict to the Petrakis family. And I know that you're going to give them a lot of money, an awful lot of money. And I know that whatever it is that you give, it won't be enough.

"Thank you."

Sabotnik sat down exhausted. The courtroom was silent.

The jury came back after less than one hour with a verdict of $920,000, by far the largest verdict Sabotnik had ever obtained up until that time.

Later, while the appeal was pending, they settled the case for $750,000, rather than face the risk of a reversal. Sabotnik's fee worked out to almost $250,000.

Petrakis came up to Sabotnik's office one last time, on the day that the papers were executed setting up the trust fund for Diana.

"Phil," he said as he was about to leave. "You know that I want to thank you for seeing this thing through for me. I know that no one could have done better. Anyway, I've been thinking about how to thank you and I think I know how. What you should do, Phil, is take the fee that you just earned and invest it in a little over the counter stock called Ehrenkrantz Computers. It's selling somewhere between one and two dollars a share right now. Within a year or two it will be on the big board trading for ten to twenty times that."

Sabotnik took the tip, and invested $50,000 of the firm's money and $10,000 of his own in the stock. And Petrakis' prediction proved conservative. Within two years the stock was trading at $45 a share, the price at which the company was acquired by Transcontinental Communications.

32

It was not an easy pregnancy for Mary Ann. She had morning sickness in the early weeks. Her breasts swelled and became painful. And she put on lots of weight. Later in the pregnancy she developed varicose veins in her legs and hemorrhoids. One way or another she was uncomfortable nearly the whole time.

She tried to persuade her husband early in the pregnancy to join her in taking a natural childbirth course and met a blanket refusal. He refused to even discuss it and eventually she gave up trying. As it turned out the debate was academic because she delivered by Caesarean. She had been in labor eighteen hours without really dilating sufficiently and the obstetrician told her that he was concerned for the child. So they took it by section. Mary Ann was given a general anesthesia through the IV. "Count backwards from a hundred, dear," the nurse told her. "One hundred, ninety-nine, ninety-eight . . ." Mary Ann was determined not to fall asleep.

She woke up suddenly. Feeling nauseous.

"You have a beautiful healthy daughter, dear," the nurse told her. "A real pretty one."

Where was she though? And where was Max? And where was her mother, Mary Ann thought, still groggy, not oriented. "Can I see her now? Please let me see her," she asked the nurse.

"She's in the nursery, darlin'," the nurse told her. "So you just rest and take it easy now. You'll be seeing plenty of her. Rely on it."

Mary Ann began to cry then.

Mary Ann tried to nurse her daughter. The baby would cry and she would get up to nurse her. She would put on her bathrobe quietly, careful not to wake her husband. He was a heavy sleeper however, and there was no need to be quiet. He never seemed to hear the baby cry. Still she was quiet.

She had set a rocking chair in the baby's room, next to the crib. She would lift the baby up, put it to her breast, and rock while the baby nursed. But five or ten minutes into the nursing, about long enough for the milk to reach and affect the baby's stomach, it would all break down. The baby would cry, fidget, reject her nipple.

She was allergic to milk, it turned out. A simple thing, an allergy. But it took Mary Ann four months to figure it out. For four months the baby cried, burped, had gas. For four months Mary Ann went without a night's sleep, catching an hour here, two hours there, dragging herself from bed, doggedly offering the baby her breast. And each time the baby would take the nipple, and suck for a while. It pacified her to suck. And then five or ten minutes would go by and she would start to cry. It cut Mary Ann to the heart. This little creature, out of her own body, crying, taking no comfort, judging her, she thought, finding her lacking. It made her crazy, depressed, and lonely.

Then she switched the baby onto a bottle, to a soy milk formula, and the baby slept. Mary Ann slept. And she decided to go back to work. She hired a housekeeper, a middle-aged Haitian woman who seemed to be experienced and responsible. The baby seemed to like her.

Mary Ann felt guilty about returning to work. Guilty about how much she enjoyed returning to the Legal Aid Society. And guilty about being away from her baby. Anxious that something might happen, that a stuffed nose or a sore throat might turn into something worse, that she would not be there to do the right thing.

She tried talking it out with her husband, tried to express her ambivalence.

"You cannot win, Mary Ann," he said simply. "You want a career. And you want to be your own person. And you should want that, even if it's a little selfish or self-centered. You're intrinsically every bit as important as little Christine. But you also feel obligated to her, to mother her and somehow surrender up your own personality and freedom to nurture her. There's that instinct in you apparently."

"But don't you feel it, Max?"

"No. I don't have any maternal feelings. I thought I might. But honestly I don't. When I'm teaching my courses or working on my articles I don't usually think about the baby. Or about you either, for that matter."

He was drinking when he said this. And it made him honest. "It's not that I don't love you both. I like playing with Christie.

And I like playing with you. But it doesn't conflict with my being who I am. It doesn't conflict with anything. That's your problem."

And it was her problem. And Christine's problem. She stopped talking to him about it.

Mary Ann's involvement with the day care movement came by accident, although later it seemed to have been inevitable. She was coming out of Family Court, having just argued a custody case to an acting supreme court judge, when she ran into Karen Dubinsky, an older woman whom she had first met down south doing civil rights work. They went for coffee. Karen raised the subject.

"There's a black community group up in the Fort Washington section of Manhattan that would like to establish a day care center," she told Mary Ann. "They are mostly working mothers, many of whom are divorced or widowed or deserted by their husbands, and they need a place where they can leave their children confidently while they go to work. The idea is to provide the kids with all of the things at the day care centers that they don't get at home or on the streets. There can be enriched or remedial education opportunities starting at the pre-kindergarten level, so that these kids can make out okay when they get into public schools. Another feature of the program that could be terrific would be to provide the kids with nourishing hot meals at lunchtime. That would help with a lot of dietary and nutrition problems that these kids have. There should also be a nurse, a trained licensed nurse at the center to monitor the children's health. That way any problems that show up can be referred right away to the outpatient clinic at Harlem Hospital and nothing will be neglected.

"And the best thing of all," Dubinsky went on, glowing with enthusiasm, "is that the center can be run by the community itself. There's been some legislation sponsored by Rockefeller up in Albany that makes state and local money available to open up and run these centers. A board of directors of community people can be set up to run the center, to hire and fire and to spend the money, only subject to state review. Think of it. The centers can become perfect vehicles to politically mobilize parents in these minority neighborhoods. They can teach them all kinds of management and political skills. They can also provide jobs, ease unemployment, and deal with a pressing social problem."

Karen Dubinsky's enthusiasm infected Mary Ann instantly. Day care was an issue that was immediate and concrete, something Mary Ann could grapple with in New York. It was something constructive, something that would help—not the kind of crisis management, the divorces or rental disputes or eviction problems, that she was used to. She seized the opportunity to serve as unpaid counsel to the Fort Washington community group, and in the weeks that followed she threw herself into the task.

Mary Ann read the statutes and met repeatedly with the state and city officials who administered the program. She drew up incorporation papers and got the group organized as the board of directors of a not-for-profit corporation. She negotiated with the owner of an old shut-down movie theater to lease the building on a long-term basis for conversion to the center. She and board members met with a prestigious architectural firm and were able to persuade them to donate time on a *pro bono publico* basis to draw up plans to convert the building. In the process, she learned all about the health and educational codes that governed the way the child and infant care facilities had to be constructed. She met with more officials with her architectural plans, taking it step by step until she had the approval that permitted the group to sign the long-term lease with state money, and to begin to hire contractors to effect the conversion. Then she and the board members interviewed the contractors and negotiated terms to do the work. Mary Ann was there on the day that the workmen began to gut the inside of the theater.

She spent much of the next month helping the board members interview prospective employees for the center. They interviewed for a custodian or janitorial position, they interviewed for a dietician-cook, and for a nurse. They looked for teachers, and teacher's aides, and mother's helpers. And after the interviews they would sit up until late at night debating each decision.

It was the best time of her life. That first center was her love
child as surely or more surely than Christine. It was Mary Ann's
way of combining law and her maternal instinct. Towards other
people's children.

And for a time she got Max and the housekeeper to shoulder
the major burden of watching the baby. And Max was good
about it too. His academic schedule was very light that year.
And he could work at home. And their daughter was at a quiet
stage—no real problem.

33

It cost a lot more money to run for Congress than it had to run
for state senate. There was a bigger district to cover, more
voters, higher stakes. Ted Murcer took the plunge. He printed
up the flyers, the handbills, the brochures, and the bumper
stickers. He paid high school kids to work putting up posters. He
rented an office in two key neighborhoods and put in phone
banks. He had volunteers working from voter registration lists
calling to identify potential support, building to the big push on
Election Day to get that vote out. He planned for three mass
mailings, the last one occurring four days before the election. He
bought and handed out thousands of campaign buttons and he
even hired a political pollster to do a modest survey of the district. He tried to learn something of the public's mood, something about his basic name recognition. It cost a lot of money.

Murcer had raised money for his earlier campaigns largely by
throwing cocktail parties or teas at which friends and supporters
paid twenty-five or fifty dollars to attend. That, plus a little
money out of his own pocket, plus a little money from the Republican party campaign fund, had done the trick in the first
campaign. His reelection had been easier. He had been an incumbent and more people had been willing to contribute. In addition
his opposition had been weaker. He had worked his senatorial

district hard those first two years, made friends. But running for Congress was different. That called for big dollars.

Murcer found himself taking more and more time off from sidewalk campaigning to raise money. Through the governor he had access to the old-line Republican Wall Street contributors. They were receptive to Murcer. He was their type—safe, Ivy League, with a progressive veneer. But still they had to be wooed. There were luncheons to attend at private clubs, understandings to be tacitly reached.

"What do you think about this business in Vietnam?" he was asked at one of these meetings at the Union League Club. "President Johnson has been sending quite a substantial number of troops there, hasn't he?"

Murcer took the Rockefeller line. Vietnam was not a hot issue that year. His poll told him that and he hadn't given the war much thought.

"I support the President and I support his efforts to preserve South Vietnam from communist aggression." He looked at his audience, seeking clues, finding approval. "I don't believe," he went on, "and I am not naïve enough to pretend that Thieu is a great democrat or a great civil libertarian, and I don't think that South Vietnam is a wonderful democracy. But they are our allies. We have an obligation to the people of that country to help defend them from communist aggression. And I think that we must honor that obligation. I believe that in this world both our friends and our enemies must know that our word is good, that we will not shrink from the sacrifices that we must make to defend our way of life. I do not like the war, but for now I support it."

And he won polite applause. More importantly he got his contributions.

Murcer met George Petrakis at one of his fund raisers. It had been five years or more since they had last seen each other.

"I heard that you left Regis, McCormick, and Letterman," Murcer said as they had a moment alone. "And now, that you're with the house counsel to Transcontinental Communications."

"Not exactly," Petrakis replied. "I was with Transcontinental, but I've moved over to Lefcourte Labs, the drug company, which is one of Transcontinental's wholly owned subsidiaries. We bought out Lefcourte's stockholders about a year ago, and I was sent over as general counsel and as a troubleshooter to help shape things up."

"That's terrific, but aren't Lefcourte's executive offices in Denver or someplace? Did you have to leave New York?"

Petrakis smiled. "They used to be in Cleveland, not Denver. But now we run the company out of New York. I've got two floors of a building on John Street, and the way things work out I don't have to spend more than four or five days a month in Cleveland."

"So you stay pretty close to the main action at Transcontinental in New York," Murcer observed mildly.

Petrakis didn't answer the unstated question, just smiled thinly. Murcer was shrewd, he thought. He had instantly realized that Petrakis had his eye on moving to the top of the conglomerate, realized that in the fierce world of corporate internal politics it was essential that Petrakis not isolate himself in Cleveland running a subsidiary. Murcer realized immediately what half of Petrakis' rivals at Transcontinental had failed to grasp. And Petrakis realized just as instantly that Murcer was a man to watch, a politician who would go far. There was a sense of recognition that passed between them, the recognition of ambitious young men who could easily become bitter and formidable rivals to one another. But there was also the recognition that their respective ambitions lay in different directions, that there was no reason for rivalry. They might be able to help one another.

"You need a lot of money to pull this election out," Petrakis said bluntly.

It was Murcer's turn to smile, and not to answer.

"I can tap the political action committees at Transcontinental for you," Petrakis continued. "I could get say a hundred of our middle-level executives to contribute say a hundred dollars apiece to your campaign. That would be ten thousand dollars, and I would then have Transcontinental reimburse the executives by giving them bonuses. That way the corporation gets a tax-deductible business expense out of the contribution, and your opponent doesn't get to embarrass either you or the corporation by falsely claiming that you're being bought by Transcontinental."

They were both smiling now. "What do you say?" Petrakis asked.

"I say," Murcer replied, "that twenty thousand would be even nicer than ten thousand. Do you think you might be able to find two hundred executives instead of one hundred?"

"Sure, I can," Petrakis answered.

And he did.

Murcer was elected by a comfortable margin. He outspent and outcampaigned his opponent, a social worker who had mobilized the reform wing of the Democratic party and successfully challenged the organization-backed incumbent in the primary on an antiwar platform. In the general election, Murcer was able to paint his opponent as a radical of the left and reaped a rich harvest of conservative Democratic ethnic votes. He also received covert support from the old-line Democratic organization, the old bosses and district leaders being far more willing to see a Republican elected than to see a hated reformer attain public office.

There were many reasons why he won. But in the end, he won for the simple reason that he was the better candidate.

34

Cleveland Daniels took to stealing cars. It was easy. He would wait until three or four in the morning when the streets were deserted. He worked the back streets, the ones that were poorly lit, used a thin wire to pick through the window and open the lock. Then, using a slammer, he would punch out the ignition switch and hot-wire the car to get it going. He would drive to Spanish Harlem where he knew a mechanic who cannibalized stolen autos to sell their parts in the back of his garage. He paid Cleveland between a hundred and two hundred dollars, depending on the make and model of the stolen car.

There were weeks when Cleveland cleared close to a thousand dollars. And the risk was small. It took him less than two minutes to steal a car from the moment he opened the lock until he drove away. The chances of his being caught were slight. Small risk and no violence. Besides no one was hurt. Insurance would pay back the owners of the cars he stole, so they would only be inconvenienced. No one got hurt. And finally, once the car got to the garage and was broken down into parts the evidence was gone.

Then he got caught. He was driving a Buick station wagon down the Grand Concourse and a cop pulled him over. It was plain dumb luck. It was a slow night, the cop was bored, Cleveland drove by, and the cop waved him over. One look into the car and Cleveland was finished. The cop's eyes went immediately to the ignition, focused on the dangling wires.

"I think you'd better get out of that car, boy. I really do think you'd better do that. And I think you'd better have a license and a registration for this car. I really think that."

He was arrested, fingerprinted, strip-searched, photographed, and then booked. Grand larceny auto was the charge. Possession of stolen property. A felony. Possibly four years in state prison.

"What's gonna happen, man?" Cleveland asked his legal aid lawyer, a fat, balding little man, who seemed to have trouble paying attention to Cleveland.

"Probably nothing much today. First we've got to wait around and see if the guy whose car you stole bothers to show up to press his complaint. The odds are that he won't. Most of them don't."

"And if he doesn't show?"

"Then the DA will ask me to agree to stipulate to the owner's testimony that he didn't give you permission to drive his car. And I'll agree."

"Why?"

"Because in return he'll agree to reduce the charge against you to a misdemeanor."

"And then?"

"Then we'll start to talk plea."

"Suppose I want a trial?"

"Then you'll get convicted and the judge will send you to jail for six or maybe nine months if he's in a bad mood."

"But I don't even have a criminal record, man. I never been arrested before this, an' he's gonna send me to jail for nine months?"

"If you go to trial, he will. Because they punish you if you go to trial. It wastes the court's time."

"And if I plead guilty?"

"Then I'll see what kind of deal I can make."

"No jail?"

"If you're lucky. It depends a lot on the judge and the DA, on what they had for breakfast, or whether they got laid last night, if you know what I mean."

"I don't wanna go to jail."

"I'll see what I can do, okay?"

"No jail," the legal aid lawyer said when he came back down to the holding pens. "They've got something different in mind for you."

"What's that?"

"They want you to join the Army."

"What?"

"The deal is that you plead guilty, and you get a conditional discharge. The condition is that you have to enlist in the United States Army. There's a recruiting sergeant upstairs, and he's looked over the complaint against you and your arrest record, and he's willing to sign you up."

"And I go in as a regular soldier?"

"Yup. Infantry. And you'll end up in Vietnam."

"Mr. Cleveland Daniels?" the judge asked.

"Yes."

"I have been advised by your lawyer that you wish to withdraw your plea of not guilty and plead guilty to the charge of petty larceny, a class A misdemeanor."

"Yes."

"Have you discussed this with your lawyer and are you pleading guilty of your own free will?"

"Yeah."

"Do you understand that by pleading guilty you are waiving your right to trial by judge and jury, and your right to confront the witnesses against you?"

"Yeah."

"Have any threats or promises been made to you by me or anyone else to induce you to plead guilty, other than the understanding that if you plead guilty, it is my intention to sentence you to a conditional discharge, conditioned on your enlisting in the United States Army?"

"Yes. I mean no. I mean no threats or nothing like that."

"Okay. Are you pleading guilty because you are in fact guilty?"

"Yes."

"And did you in fact steal the automobile that you are charged with stealing?"

"Yes."

"Very well then. I will accept the plea."

Nine months later Cleveland Daniels was in Vietnam.

35

After his wife died, Petrakis hired a housekeeper and a governess to help him look after his daughter. With the life he was leading, the long hours, and the unpredictable crises, with the frequent business trips he was forced to take, he had no real alternative.

He had known from the outset that he would not remarry. By

degrees, even before his wife's death, he had allowed the pursuit of corporate power to become his dominant passion. And whatever need he had for human warmth and affection, whatever need for love, he more than received from his daughter.

Nurses, nannies, governesses, tutors, and boarding schools notwithstanding, Petrakis always found time to spend with his daughter, always made certain that he was the most important person in her life.

He bought property in the Berkshires, a seventy-four-acre working farm, which he paid a neighboring farmer a healthy fee to maintain and run. The farm was a good investment and an even better tax shelter. He got a low-interest loan from the Department of Agriculture, and was able to buy the farm on favorable terms. But its real purpose, and its real value to him, was that the farm provided an ideal retreat, a place for Petrakis and his daughter to vacation each summer. For three weeks and on long weekends each summer they would be up at the farmhouse together. They would help to work the farm, milk cows, feed the chickens, collect the eggs, tend to the vegetables, spray the apple trees in the little orchard. It wasn't especially hard work, the neighboring farmer still did most of what had to be done. But the work that they did do, the satisfaction and the good times that they had doing it, forged tight bonds beween father and daughter. The farm fronted on a small lake, and on hot days they would swim or sail in a tiny Sunfish that Petrakis bought. He bought a pony one summer, and taught Diana how to ride.

For Petrakis, the farm became his one escape, the place to recharge his energies.

There was a war being fought in Southeast Asia, a dirty little expensive war. It was a war motivated in part by noble sentiments, by patriotism and anticommunism, by treaty obligation, by the need to fight aggression. It was a war that just happened, step by step, inch by inch, without any real plan or design, almost by accident. It had a life of its own, a logic of its own that transcended individual or collective understanding. And like all dirty expensive little wars, it superheated the economy, made for full employment, for government spending. And there was money to be made too, lots of money. George Petrakis understood this. He thought long and hard about how he might use the war to make money for Lefcourte Labs.

Petrakis arranged to be invited to a Washington cocktail party where he might meet the deputy surgeon general. He had done his homework well. The deputy surgeon general was sixty-two years old, poor, a career serviceman, with five children, two of whom were in college, the other three in expensive private schools. He was a brigadier general, who had been twice passed over for his second star, a man who had reached his highest rank, a man a little bit bitter and a little bit resigned. He was a prime candidate for recruitment into the private sector.

"General," Petrakis asked solicitously, "have you ever given any thought to what you're going to do after you retire from the military? I know that you're a licensed doctor, but it's probably been a good ten or fifteen years since you actually practiced, hasn't it?"

"God, it's been longer than that," the general answered. "I think that it's been almost twenty years since I have personally examined or treated a patient. I've really been a medical administrator all these years, mostly involved with the oversight of the delivery of health care to servicemen and their dependents."

"That's what I thought," Petrakis went on. "And I also thought that there must be a place in private industry, like at Lefcourte Labs, for a man like you with a lifetime of administrative experience in the health care field. You've had years of background in procurement of health supplies, in cost overrun, and quality control, and research and development of new products. You've been in on the negotiation of many drug procurement contracts, and you know what it's all about. Which means to me that you would be able to function damned effectively as a businessman. Have you ever thought about that?"

"Yes." The general was noncommittal, cautious.

"The remuneration at the top of the corporate ladder can be very sweet," Petrakis went on. "There's a six-figure salary, plus an almost unlimited expense account. We've got an extremely generous executive retirement fund where we contribute a sum equal to twenty percent of your salary into the fund each year. Then there are stock options, bonuses, and incentives. There's also health insurance, life insurance, disability insurance, and just about every other kind of fringe benefit you can imagine. And we do it all pursuant to an executive employment contract. So there's perfect job security. You can enforce the contract in court."

"It sounds sweet," the general said.

"It is sweet," Petrakis answered. "So sweet that we try to be very careful about who we hire as our senior executives. We try to make certain that the people we bring on board are capable. We want men who have something to contribute."

"Like good contacts with the federal government?"

"Yes."

"Or maybe with the Defense Department in particular."

"Or the Food and Drug Administration," Petrakis added. "We can always use friends there."

"I understand," the general said. "I have many friends at Food and Drug."

It went no further that night. The two men drifted apart, chatted to others at the party. The seeds had been sown though. For Petrakis, it was a good night's work.

It took another eleven months for Petrakis to put the deal together. Even before he first approached the general, Petrakis had known that Lefcourte Labs held the patent on Trioxsone. He had read preliminary reports by his research people, based on laboratory and animal studies, that Trioxsone might prove to be the next multi-purpose wonder drug. He also knew that it would take three or four years and hundreds of thousands and possibly millions of dollars to test and win approval of the drug before it might be marketed and make a profit. He was also aware of confidential Defense Department reports out of Vietnam, that a shockingly high percentage of combat troops were being rendered ineffective by a veritable medley of jungle maladies. In addition, he had information, based upon a rush study he had secretly commissioned, that Trioxsone looked like it might prevent most of those diseases. The preliminary report was terrific.

For eleven months Petrakis made phone calls, set up meetings with the government officials he called, pulled strings. He made promises and kept promises. Trioxsone became a pet project.

The general was the key to his strategy. The general came off as disinterested at all the meetings. He wore his uniform and his ribbons and he argued persuasively that the Army needed to cut bureaucratic red tape to get the right medicines to his troops in Southeast Asia.

"I've got boys dying in Vietnam because we don't have drugs for them that prevent jungle fever. I've got units understrength that are getting cut to pieces in those rice paddies because they don't have enough effectives to do the job right. And I cannot wait two or three years for the FDA to drag its way through its testing program to okay a drug that we all know will do the job now. We're at war now. A real shooting war and my boys are dying. I want a way to get Trioxsone to my troops."

He was persuasive. He had a point and he made it well, made it well because he had rehearsed it over and over secretly with Petrakis. He made his pitch well because he believed in it, believed that it was the right thing to do. It was easy to believe, easy to believe that he was acting in the public interest. After all, the evidence did seem to show that the drug would work, that it would save lives.

"Why can't the lawyers work out a way to get around the FDA regulations? Couldn't we declare some kind of national defense medical emergency to expedite things? I'm sure something can be worked out."

The general was sure, because he knew that Petrakis had already worked out the details of how to circumvent the regulations. He knew of Petrakis' scheme to create an agreement by which the FDA would abdicate its regulatory authority to the Department of Defense when "military health emergencies" were declared. He knew that the documents to implement the scheme had already been planted with a sympathetic lawyer at the proper government agency. And while he didn't know it, he suspected that that lawyer stood to profit personally if the scheme was implemented. Indeed, he wasn't at all surprised a year later when he learned that the lawyer had left government service to accept a lucrative junior partnership at Regis, Mc-Cormick, and Letterman.

The pieces all came together for Petrakis. The red tape was eliminated and the Defense Department declared its health emergency.

Then the procurement officers had to come to Lefcourte Labs to buy the drug, and to buy it in bulk. After all, the government wanted to feed the drug to almost a half million men every day.

"I'm not geared up to produce that much Trioxsone," Petrakis complained to the procurement officer. "None of us at Lefcourte ever dreamed that there would be such a phenomenal and instant demand for it," he lied. Then he paused for effect.

"Of course, if you tell me that Trioxsone is essential for national defense, then we'll make it somehow. We at Lefcourte would like to think of ourselves as patriotic.

"It will be expensive though. It's going to cost us a lot of money to make Trioxsone. And that means that it will cost you a lot of money to buy it from us," he told the procurement officers.

That turned out to be an understatement.

36

Sabotnik and Horowitz continued to grow. The cases came in and they continued to get good results. There was more work than they could handle and they began to turn cases away. They became selective, specializing more and more in the large medical malpractice cases. They learned to refer to other lawyers more and more of their smaller business, and in making those referrals they made friends. And in time, those friends began to refer cases back, large, complicated, lucrative cases. Even by specializing, and limiting themselves to the very best of cases, they still found that there was more than they could handle. They had to grow.

They hired a young lawyer as an associate, then another, and another. They had to hire more secretaries, and they had to lease new office space. They had to hire a messenger boy to deliver papers to court and to help serve subpoenas. They had to hire a receptionist and a switchboard operator, and they had to buy or lease office equipment, furniture, and typewriters, photocopiers, and eventually word processors. They hired more lawyers and made two of their best associates into junior partners. And they could not continue to do their own books. That too became time-consuming. They had to hire a bookkeeper and then an office manager to ride herd over the growing numbers of secretaries, paralegals, and messengers.

Still they grew. Eventually they had to leave the downtown Wall Street area, and they signed a long-term lease, taking a whole floor in a modern midtown Madison Avenue office building. At first they sublet part of the floor to another law firm in order to ease the burden of the big lease. But eventually they ended up using the whole floor themselves. They even, in time, took a lease on a second floor, sublet most of it, and slowly took it over for their own use. They hired a firm of real estate lawyers to represent them in these leasing and subleasing agreements.

From the start they had used an accountant to go over their books and prepare their tax returns. But eventually that wasn't enough. They were earning too much money and they were paying too much of that money in taxes. So they retained tax attorneys to advise them. They became involved in a series of shelters, investing money in cattle-feeding or pig-farming or oil-drilling schemes that were not designed to earn money, but were highly leveraged to permit enormous depreciation deductions with tax savings many times more valuable than the original investment itself. Eventually they were persuaded to change the firm from a partnership into a professional corporation. That allowed them to set up a deferred compensation retirement plan that in turn let them put aside a full twenty percent of their income, tax free. The money that built up in their retirement fund quickly became substantial, added to their security.

Not slowly, and not by degrees, but almost overnight, Phil Sabotnik found himself not only a trial lawyer but also a businessman and a boss, an employer. It could not be avoided.

37

Max Braverman's academic career was going nowhere. He had tenure and job security. He was well regarded by his colleagues and could go through the motions of teaching courses, conducting seminars, writing monographs, effortlessly. But the flame was gone. Ten years earlier he had been doing important original research. Earlier still he had written two provocative books that had been more than promising. In his late twenties the academic world had been at his feet and it was predicted that he would have an important career. He was seen as certain to become the chairman of the department. Maybe dean of the faculty, maybe more.

But he had burned out early. Lost his insight, the spark of creativity or the self-assurance that made his first work distinguished. He lived on his reputation instead, putting out pieces that were pedantic rather than original. And in time everyone knew it. He remained with his academic appointment but without further advancement. He began to drink heavily.

Mary Ann had not understood about Max and his work when they met. He had dazzled her with brilliant insights that were ten years old. And she had no way of knowing his inner panic over the fact that he had been saying the same thing repetitiously for a decade. She had accepted the alcohol as part of his style, as something that maybe released his creative energies. It took her a long time to appreciate that there were no creative energies left there to be released.

He wasn't an attentive father, Mary Ann felt. He was self-centered and could shut Christine out completely while he worked, or drank, or read. The irony was that child simply adored him. More often than not it was he that she called for at night when she was frightened. It was Max who she insisted give her her baths and shampoos. "Mommy, you don't do it good," she would say. "You always get the soap in my eyes. And it hurts. Daddy never hurts me."

And when he paid attention he was a very good father. He could play silly games with Christine that made her laugh. He could play piggyback or tell stories and she would listen with wide eyes and dream of princesses and handsome princes who came to rescue them. Needless to state the princes almost always looked something like Max. And they were always nearly perfect.

It was Mary Ann who had to discipline the child. She was the one who dealt with the temper tantrums and the bad behavior when Christine was feeling bored or neglected. She had to scrub clean the living room walls after Christine had spent an afternoon crayoning all over them.

Then she discovered that he had been unfaithful. In the nastiest possible way. Symptomatically. Her gynecologist was blunt.

"You contracted gonorrhea," he said simply. "It's not serious medically. We should be able to clear it up in a week or so with antibiotics. But, of course, you will have to curtail your sexual activities for a couple of weeks. And I think you'll have to tell your husband or whomever you've been with to see a doctor. You've got to do that."

She took it calmly. It wasn't until Mary Ann left the doctor's office that the shock and the anger set in. She found herself walking down Riverside Drive literally shaking with anger, with a sense of violation.

She returned to their apartment to find her husband happily giving their daughter a bath, rubbing soap on her back and bottom. There was a flush to his face. He had been drinking.

Mary Ann was shaking violently.

"Get out," she almost whispered. She was unable to make her voice louder. "Get out."

He didn't turn around. Seemed to be unaware of her presence.

"Get out," still hardly more than a whisper.

And Christine turned in the tub and saw Mary Ann. She was laughing and happy.

"See, Mommy," she said, "Daddy's real good at giving me a bath."

Mary Ann took to sleeping on a convertible couch in her living room. She left Max the double bed and the bedroom, moving her clothing out into a hallway closet. She never let him touch her after that.

Max started to drink even more heavily, to deteriorate visibly. He was on sabbatical then, supposed to be doing research, which was fortunate, since it was unclear whether he would have been able to maintain even his light teaching schedule.

They barely spoke. But for days on end he never left the apartment. Then he'd be gone two or three days, abruptly and without explanation. Only to return for many more days of apparent immobility. He was without appetite and Mary Ann actually found herself cooking meals for him, dishes she knew he liked, setting them before him without comment. Later she would pick up the plates untouched or barely picked at. Also without comment.

Christine never asked what was wrong, and neither of them could bring themselves to try to explain what they themselves didn't completely understand. Instead she began to have frequent hysterical nightmares, to wake up shrieking. "There are monsters in my room, Mommy," she would sob when she calmed down enough to get anything out at all. "There were dead monsters that started out being beautiful butterflies. Then they got dead and became monsters."

Mary Ann held her in her arms and rocked her. Over and over. "Don't worry, baby. Don't worry. It's only a dream. It's not real and Mommy's here. Butterflies are beautiful." She rocked Christine until the child fell asleep, or until she thought the child was asleep. Mary Ann would set Christine quietly in her little bed, sit by her side for a time, alone in the small of the night, crying without sound. But sometimes before the crying stopped, before she had taken herself back to the living room couch, the nightmares would start again. Christine's body would go rigid, and she would shriek hysterically.

Mary Ann would stop crying then. She would hold the child and rock her.

Mary Ann realized that she was becoming guilt-ridden over Christine. And over Max too. That she imagined they were blaming her for their pain. That she was the strong one who was supposed to make everything all right. And she had failed them.

Finally Mary Ann decided to seek help. She thought about a psychiatrist and settled upon a lawyer. There just wasn't enough money for the former. She knew that she had to end the marriage, and had to do it before they were all destroyed.

Typically, Max refused at first to see a lawyer, refused to even discuss it. Finally she put it bluntly. "If you get a lawyer, we'll negotiate some kind of decent separation agreement. You'll get generous visitation rights with Christine. I won't ask for any alimony, and I won't seek unreasonable child support. We can try to work out something fair about the apartment. I'd like to keep it and stay here with Christine. But we can work it out if you feel differently.

"But, Max I swear to God, if you don't get yourself a lawyer, then I'm going to get an uncontested divorce and I swear I'll have you declared unfit so that you'll never have a right to get near Christine. And I'll soak you for all the alimony I can get. I'll take the apartment and everything else. And then I swear I'll sell the co-op and take Christine back to Indiana, or out West. And you'll never see her again."

In the end she did get him to see a lawyer. And then the two lawyers met and arranged a separation agreement. Max then found another apartment and moved out.

Work was Mary Ann's salvation during the months of the divorce. She would escape to work in the morning and lose herself in whatever task presented itself. And at night she took paper-work home with her as a distraction to keep her mind working.

A year went by. And then another. The little day care center she had helped to establish was a success. It had attracted publicity and Mary Ann attracted publicity. She was one of the few law-yers who knew how to set up a day care center, one of the few who had actually done it. She knew the bureaucrats, and the community leaders, the landlords and the contractors. She was very much in demand.

Mary Ann found herself devoting a great deal of time to rais-ing money to help organize new day care centers, or fund new programs in existing centers. She was a natural. Not only with the government officials, but also with the private foundations. She made the rounds, smiled, made pleasant small talk, and then presented her proposals with an earnestness and attention to de-tail that won over most of her listeners. She had the knack of being assertive without being threatening.

Mary Ann's dream at that point was to establish a center to coordinate and give advice to low-income day care centers throughout the metropolitan area. She wanted an organization of her own, a place to hang her hat, a central place to assemble the expertise that she had developed. She decided that she needed a grant of roughly $150,000 a year for three years. She needed money to lease office space, to hire a secretary or two, to pay herself a salary, to hire a junior lawyer as an assistant, to retain an occasional consultant—$150,000 a year would do it. So she wrote up her proposal with care, put on her best suit, and set out to see if she could win the grant. It was a lot of money. She knew that. Still it would be worth the try.

George Petrakis had moved back from Lefcourte Labs to Trans-continental Communications. He was general counsel now, and an executive vice-president of the conglomerate. He had general troubleshooting responsibilities. He also, as part of his patronage power, had been made a member of the board and chairman of the new grants committee of the Transcontinental Foundation.

He had a decisive influence in disbursing over $12.5 million a year.

Petrakis read Mary Ann's proposal, one of literally hundreds in a large manila folder. He caught Mary Ann's name, pulled the proposal, reread it carefully. He had his secretary call Mary Ann and make an appointment for her to come up to his office the following week.

She was ushered into his office, took in the walnut-paneled walls, the oriental carpet, and the French Regency furniture. There were large picture windows looking out from the fifty-fourth floor of the Wall Street building, south across New York Harbor. She looked across the room at Petrakis.

His face was the same. Intelligent, but expressionless eyes, unblinking and searching. He was still slim, still intense, but somehow changed. He was beautifully tailored now, in an expensive charcoal gray three-piece suit and a custom-made silk shirt. He carried it well. She had noticed random strands of gray in his thick black hair. And that looked good too. There was something about him that had become attractive, an aura of self-confidence and power.

And she knew that she looked good to Petrakis too. It was something she could feel, a kind of tension. He stood up from his desk and walked across his office to her. Smiling. He offered his hand. Simply. She had wondered if he was going to kiss her in greeting but was glad he didn't. They walked to another corner of the large office, sat down in easy chairs, and began to talk. He asked her about her proposal.

"George," she answered, "the day care center concept, for low-income and minority women, is potentially one of the most important and constructive programs that your foundation could get involved with. If it works, it could potentially free hundreds of thousands of capable women, who are now on welfare because they must watch their children, and allow them the dignity of work. In addition, it could give the children the advantage of an educational head start. If we get them early, we can teach them foundation learning skills. We can socialize them to like school rather than to reject it. Besides, we can help see to it that

the kids in the center can get a balanced diet. And we can monitor their health care, have nurses around to check them out. We
can get them to doctors, or to a clinic. Maybe we could even get
a dentist, or a dental hygienist, to examine their teeth once a
year. There is virtually no end to the kind of things that can be
done."

"But why a centralized organization?" he asked. "Wouldn't
you do just as well to fund some of the programs you want,
rather than to set up some kind of new centralized bureau-
cracy?"

"No. The problem is that right now there is no clearinghouse
or place where day care people can get together to share their
experiences. To find out what's working and what isn't working.
It makes no sense, say, if we're trying out a program in one center, for instance, of giving a nighttime course in diet and hygiene
and neo-natal care for expectant mothers, to have some other
center inadvertently run the same experimental program before
the first one has been evaluated. It would be better for the second center to set up a different experimental program, maybe
one to teach the children black or Hispanic history to foster a
sense of pride and positive self-image. That way we would have
two experiments going instead of one, and double the chances of
hitting upon good programs. I see my proposal as one that would
permit a coordinated and logical development of the day care
movement."

"So you would hold periodic meetings at which the heads of
the boards of the various day care centers around the city would
meet to discuss their problems?"

"Yes. And also so that we could present programs and seminars to them to teach techniques in bookkeeping and administration and everything else."

"The day care people who you're talking about are all community leaders who are pretty well respected in the minority
areas they come from?"

"Yes."

"So you would have a fair amount of political clout with your
organization?"

"Some. Our day care people do tend to vote and control votes in their neighborhood."

"Do you intend to do any political lobbying as part of what your organization does?"

"Yes and no," Mary Ann answered. "We certainly will act as intermediaries between the centers and government bodies to assist the centers in getting set up and in getting funds. I also think that we will lobby the various legislatures on behalf of legislation that will help the day care movement. What we will not do is to campaign as an organization, or formally support any particular party or candidate in any particular election."

"And you'll be the head of the organization?"

"Yes."

"And you'll control its operation?"

"Yes."

Petrakis stared at her directly. "Do you have any plans to run yourself for public office?"

Mary Ann laughed. "Good God, no. You couldn't get me to run for all the tea in China."

Petrakis nodded. He looked thoughtful.

A week later Petrakis called. Mary Ann had been on edge expecting it, expecting to be asked out, wanting to be asked out. Worried. Knowing that if he asked her out she would never be able to get around the fact that he held the purse strings that could get her project going. She didn't want to face that issue, didn't want to face the proposition she thought he might make, at a time when saying yes or no could profoundly effect her career. It was all terribly muddled in her mind. It was many months since she had seen a man that way, and Petrakis was not unattractive. Under other circumstances she would have welcomed an advance. Now she wasn't sure.

He called, and asked her out.

"Yes," she answered. As she knew she would. Yes, she decided. And she would go to bed with him if it came to that. Because she wanted to. And because she wanted the grant. It wasn't all thought out. But there it was.

When they met the following evening—he seemed to know her mind.

"Look," he said right at the beginning, "before we do any-thing or say anything, let me tell you that the foundation has approved your grant. The approval was ratified and here's the formal notification. It's a done thing. And it was done on the merits with no strings attached and no obligations, except to do a damned good job."

Then he looked at her seriously and lowered his voice. "Maybe someday, you and I might begin to see each other. I think that you know what I mean. But not now. This isn't the right time to start. It would feel too much like a business deal. And it would be a mistake. So let's be friends. Good friends."

And they were. They ate dinner together, enjoyed each other's company, felt free of tension. And in the times that fol-lowed, Mary Ann never failed to get support and advice from Petrakis. He taught her administrative and business skills that helped her run her centers more efficiently, and he saw that adequate funding was always available. They remained friends, neither of them wishing to jeopardize something good with the uncertainties of an affair.

38

Cleveland Daniels found himself part of a unit that was dug in to make a perimeter around an airbase near Saigon. Six, seven, eight hours a day he found himself on guard duty, marching around, looking for Vietcong. The rest of the time he was more or less free to sleep or relax, or play, as the mood seized him. It was quiet in his sector. No battles, no firefights, hardly any incidents.

About forty percent of the men in his company were black. There were bars and restaurants and clubs in Saigon where black GI's congregated. Where there was soul music and an attempt at home cooking. There were girls who for a few dollars and a few minutes would try to make you forget that you were far from home. Cleveland didn't like making it with the whores. He didn't

like making it with someone he couldn't really talk to afterwards, with someone he couldn't really tell what made him feel
good. He didn't like making it with someone who he couldn't
make feel good. And how in hell was he going to make some
eighteen-year-old Saigon whore who'd been tricking since she
was thirteen feel good? Chances were he couldn't make her feel
at all. Good, bad, or indifferent. Still, it was a way to kill time.

It was a time of new strategy. There was always a new strategy.
This one was something about strategic hamlets. Some idea of
taking key villages and making them secure against Vietcong
infiltration.

"You know how to make a fucking slanty village secure?" one
of the men told Cleveland over some beer. "It's the way the
Republic of Korea troops we've got over here do it. Those
fuckers are tough, an' you know what they do?"

"What?"

"They move into an area and they set up a little base next to a
village, right. They dig their trenches an' set up their machine
guns an' mortars. Then they go into the village an' call for the
head man and they tell him the first time any VC shoot at them
he dies. Well, after a while, sooner or later they get shot at, and
they go looking for the head man, only, of course he's gone. So
they pick out someone else and shoot him about fifteen or
twenty times until he's dead an' tell everybody that they shot
him because the head man ran away. Then they pick out another
guy and tell him that he's the new head man and that if the VC
shoot at them he's going to get killed. Usually pretty soon after
that there's a real peaceful village there. Real peaceful."

Finally, after months of tedium, the company was relieved, was
sent up north in turn to relieve some other company that had
sustained too many casualties. Cleveland almost welcomed the
change. He was still young enough to have no real fear of death.

Then he found himself out on a patrol. Platoon strength.
There was a lieutenant in command. ROTC. From Iowa. And a
sergeant. A tall skinny guy from Alabama with a down-home
drawl and an unhurried manner. Fifteen maybe twenty men

loaded down with food, supplies, ammunition. If Cleveland was ever told, he soon forgot and never could remember the purpose of the mission. They just marched through the jungle, through the fields of shoulder-high buffalo grass, through swamps and semiflooded rice paddies which smelled of decaying night soil. Day after day toward some distant objective. Night after night, trying to sleep in 100 degree temperature. High humidity. Cleveland got some kind of crud or mold or rash between his toes that itched like hell at first and later hurt, and even bled a little. He had some ointment that they gave him to put on the crud, which helped a bit, but didn't make it go away. Then he ran out of ointment and it came back worse than before.

They were careful at first. Very careful. Looking, listening for an ambush. Jumpy. Fingers near triggers. Nerves stretched taut. A sudden noise in the bushes drew a burst of automatic fire. No more noise. The sergeant went to look. "We killed a goat, boys," he shouted back. "Looks like we done some farmer out of a goat."

Still they were careful. They had been warned about traps. Sometimes the VC stuck sharp-pointed sticks covered with shit into the ground. Then covered the sticks with leaves. The sticks, pungee sticks, would go right throught the sole of a combat boot and leave a truly nasty wound. There were guys who lost a leg to gangrene after stepping on one of those sticks. They were careful about where they stepped.

No enemy. Nothing. Day after day. There were supposed to be enemy units in the sector. Intelligence had told them that. Still nothing. Just the heat and the humidity and the jungle rot.

They got hit late one afternoon. They had been resting in a clearing, sitting up against some trees, guards down just a touch, when a sudden burst of fire and a grenade wiped out half the platoon. One second Cleveland was sitting under a tree thinking about taking his boots off and picking at his toes. The next second he was running, diving headlong into the brush, rolling, scrambling, anything to get cover.

It was too fast for him to be frightened, too fast for him to think. He shouldered his rifle and fired a blast, realizing that he had no idea of what he was firing at, stopped.

Others were firing too. The same panic. Stopping. He heard cries.

Cleveland Daniels then saw the sniper. A small figure, less than a hundred yards away, crouched in the low branches of a tree. He saw the sniper and knew that he himself had not been seen. In slow motion, without thought, he raised his gun, sighted, aimed, and fired his first true shots in anger against another human being. The sniper fell from the tree.

Again without thought Cleveland Daniels ran up to the sniper. He was a small brown man, twenty, twenty-five, thirty, forty years of age. He couldn't tell. Dressed in black cloth peasant clothes. His left leg was broken at the knee from his fall, twisted at a grotesque angle, and a shattered piece of leg bone protruded from his upper shin. His belly was ripped open by one bullet and another had entered his side, midway up the rib cage. There was a bloody foam at his mouth as he drew breath and his eyes were open, surprised, dilated, unseeing. He didn't cry and gave no evidence of pain. Cleveland would never know if the sniper was single or married, if he had parents or children, if he was loved. He would never know the sniper's name. He just stood there staring, rooted to the ground, giving no help to the sniper, nor worrying that the sniper, or another, might shoot him in his exposed position. He stood there, and was standing there still when the sergeant walked up to the now quiet scene, walked up to the sniper, ignoring Cleveland, placed a gun to his sightless head, and blew his brains out. Cleveland Daniels sank down on his knees and began to vomit. He retched until there was nothing more in his stomach and he began to spit up bile.

They gave him a medal for killing the sniper. Not a big medal, but a decoration just the same, for valor and bravery. There was a ceremony in Saigon where they gave the decorations out, and Cleveland attended in dress uniform. And at the ceremony were a group of congressmen who had come to Vietnam on a fact-finding junket. One of them was Ted Murcer.

39

Ted Murcer found himself getting restless. He had no power as a junior congressman, had uninteresting committee assignments and virtually no voice in the shaping of events or even legislation. He was in the wrong party, and as likely as not, even if he stuck around for twenty years and gained seniority he would still be in the minority. The chances were that somebody else, on the other side of the aisle, would have the committee chairmanships and the power and the perquisites that went with them. He had won an election or two by now and had pretty well secured his seat. He was the incumbent, with name recognition and the ability to raise money at will to finance his local campaigns. And he had set up a good district office to service the needs of his constituents. So he was safe. Safe and restless. Going through the motions. Casting votes that by and large didn't matter.

He looked around. But there was no place to go. Both Senate seats were filled, and a gubernatorial race was unthinkable. He wasn't crazy enough to wish to be mayor of the City of New York. And anything else would be a step down. He certainly wasn't likely to get himself a high appointive position. He was in the wrong party.

At first Murcer's preoccupations were largely domestic. Tax reform. Mass transit subsidies. Urban renewal. Rewriting and modernizing the federal criminal law. There was plenty to focus upon closer to home and it was easier to leave the war to the Administration, politically prudent to keep a low profile, to let others be up front and draw the fire.

Still it was there. Not going away. On the nightly news, in questions at political gatherings. "Congressman Murcer, what do you think should be done about draft dodgers who run away to

Canada or Sweden?" "Congressman, how come rich kids get
draft deferrals so that they can go to college while my boys have
got to go?" "Congressman, how come forty to fifty percent of
our army in Vietnam is black or Spanish while only sixteen or
seventeen percent of the country is that way? Why aren't there
any minority officers in the Army or Navy?" "Congressman
Murcer, why are we fighting over there anyway? What did they
ever do to us anyway?" "Congressman, aren't there some big
companies that are making a lot of money in defense contracts on
this war? With the taxes we're paying, how come we can't do
any better over there?" "Why don't we bomb the hell out of
those commies, Mr. Congressman? That's what we did to the Japs,
and that's what I say we should do to them Vietcongs. Congressman, why are you guys in Washington tying up the hands of our
soldiers who are trying to do a job?"

Many questions. No answers.

He went to a Veterans Administration hospital to meet with
some wounded Vietnam veterans from his district. It was supposed to be a publicity stunt, a photo opportunity for his next
newsletter report back to his constituents. They brought him
into a darkened room to meet a nineteen-year-old former Marine
named William Boyd, who had been blinded by a fragmentation
grenade. Murcer took one look at the boy, a handsome kid, lean
and muscular with blond curly hair and dark glasses. He took
one look at the blind man's cane and he sent the photographer
away. Murcer went in alone to talk to the boy.

"Will, I'm Congressman Ted Murcer," he said, taking the veteran's hand, "and I wonder if I could talk with you."

"Sure." There was an ill-disguised bitterness and indifference
in his voice.

"How are they treating you here at the hospital?"

"Okay. They don't hassle me much."

"Are you getting any rehabilitation?"

"Yeah, I'm learning to eat with a knife and fork instead of
with my fingers. It's easy. All you've got to do, Congressman, is
close your eyes and think of your plate as a clock. Then try to
remember that the meat is at three o'clock and the vegetables are

at six o'clock and the potatoes are at nine o'clock. It's a lot of fun. Want to try it?"

"No."

"Me neither. But I have no choice."

"You were in the Marines?"

"Yes. I volunteered when I graduated from high school. I thought it would be good for me. Help me grow up. And then when I got out, I figured that I would go to college."

"I see."

"I thought that I might get a degree in education, specialize in physical education and become like a high school gym teacher. Possibly I could have coached high school basketball. I lettered in basketball myself, you know. Even got an honorable mention for all-city. That was my junior year."

"How was it in the Marines, Will? Do you mind if I ask?"

"Over there?"

"Yes."

"I mind."

"You don't want to talk about it."

"No."

"Let me ask you something then. Knowing what you know, do you think that I should support the war?"

No answer. How do you ask a nineteen-year-old boy to evaluate the cause that cost him his eyesight?

Eventually Murcer went on a junket to Vietnam. To see for himself. He attended briefings conducted by articulate colonels and distinguished-looking generals, briefings complete with slick graphics and colored charts. He learned about kill ratios and pacification programs, saw demonstrations of sophisticated new weapons systems, heat-seeking missiles and infrared night scopes, all sorts of impressive hardware. And in the evenings there were the diplomatic receptions thrown for their benefit by the South Vietnamese. Fine old-style French affairs, complete with haute cuisine and cultured conversation, complete with the opportunity, once the evening began to wind down, to visit, free of charge, the most exclusive brothel in Saigon. An old restored colonial mansion filled with absolutely breathtaking Eurasian women. Professionals. They at least seemed to be good at what they did.

Ted Murcer came out againt the war. Cautiously. Privately excusing himself to the governor and other party elders. "It's partly a matter of conscience," he explained apologetically. "But it's also a matter of my constituency. It's turning pretty violently against the war. And I'll lose my seat if I continue to favor the war. I'm going to come out against the war. I have to. But don't worry. I will not embarrass you."

He had done it the right way. And when he denounced the war, he did not alienate the powers in the party. He got major coverage for the speech he delivered at a meeting of the American Jewish Congress stating his opposition. It was a well-reasoned, restrained presentation, a responsible presentation, and it went down well with the newspapers, the *Times* and the *Daily News*, the *Post* and the *Wall Street Journal;* and even with the news magazines, all of whom seemed to see his speech as an act of courage. His timing was exquisite. He anticipated by a number of months, what would soon be a flood tide of revulsion and opposition. In the process he won an enduring reputation as a progressive on the basis of his antiwar stance. It turned out to be great politics.

40

Mary Ann had never given any serious thought to becoming a judge of any sort. It wasn't one of her fantasies. It was not anything that she had ever consciously prepared herself for. Not a possibility to be reckoned with.

The idea took root slowly. Being in the right place at the right time. A woman. And there were so few women of a plausible age. An Ivy League law degree with honors. Law review, even if she had resigned in her third year. Mary Ann had credentials.

"The President is looking for qualified women to put on the federal bench," they told her. "He made promises during the primaries to the women's organizations, and now he has to deliver on them. There are openings on the United States District Court in Manhattan, and the Administration, and both senators, are anxious to name a woman. That could be you."

She had resisted the idea. "I'm not really qualified," she said. "I've never had anything to do with criminal law. I'll make an ass of myself. I'm not sure that I even want to."

But she wasn't sure that she didn't want to either. There was job security, lifetime tenure. And prestige. The robe and the dignity. And the power. Federal judges ran school systems sometimes. Or prisons. Sometimes they broke up large corporations or forced state legislatures to draw up voting districts that permitted minority representation. That kind of potential power was frightening. It was also difficult to resist. Especially after decades of fighting for one cause or another. Fighting and losing sometimes. Winning sometimes. But always on the outside. Begging from the system. Threatening or bullying or cajoling or begging things. Reasoning with those who had the power to give what she wanted for society. For others. For an abstraction. But to have that power herself. To be begged or cajoled or bullied. To be reasoned with. Or persuaded. That was difficult to resist. Even at the cost of possibly making an ass of herself. A challenge.

So she gave in. Told them she would be available, that she would accept the appointment. They asked her whom she knew outside the women's movement who might back her candidacy, give her more of an appearance of having a broader base of support. "George Petrakis," she told them. "At Transcontinental Communications. And years ago I was close to Ted Murcer."

They were each contacted, and they gave their support. Mary Ann was interviewed by blue ribbon panels from the major bar associations, investigators from the Justice Department, and from the Senators' Screening Committee.

Then there was the nomination. Some newspaper coverage. An almost perfunctory hearing before the Senate Judiciary Committee. And one day the United States Senate voted its consent. It was a done thing.

Then came the day of the swearing in. The crowd of friends. Twelve-year-old Christine all dressed up in a navy blue jumper. Mary Ann's mother, come all the way from Indiana, smiling nervously. Day care people. Feminists. Standing around. Buzzing. The clerk of the court entered.

"Oyez! Oyez! Oyez! All rise! The United States District Court for the Southern District of New York is now in session! Let all those who have business before the court draw near and let them be heard! God save the United States and this honorable court."

And in walked the judges of the court. Over twenty of them. White-haired and stately. In black robes. Some of them legends, great scholars. Others lesser men, still impressive in appearance. Secular priests on high state occasion.

The clerk again.

"I bear greetings from the President of the United States." He read Mary Ann's commission.

The chief judge rose. And Mary Ann stepped forward, beautiful still in her black robe. A Bible was held out for her, and she placed her left hand on it, raised her right.

"I, Mary Ann Salisbury . . ." the chief justice began.

"I, Mary Ann Salisbury . . ." she spoke clearly.

"do solemnly swear . . ."

"do solemnly swear . . ."

"that I will administer justice without respect to persons . . ."

"that I will administer justice without respect to persons . . ."

"and do equal right to the poor and to the rich . . ."

"and do equal right to the poor and to the rich . . ."

"and that I will faithfully and impartially discharge and perform all the duties incumbent upon me as a United States district judge according to the best of my abilities and understanding . . ."

"and that I will faithfully and impartially discharge and perform all the duties incumbent upon me as a United States district judge according to the best of my abilities and understanding . . ."

"agreeably to the Constitution and laws of the United States . . ."

"agreeably to the Constitution and laws of the United States . . ."

"so help me God."

"so help me God."

SECTION
FOUR

41

"I don't really see how we can go on like this," Nancy Revering told Murcer.

"Why?"

"I thought I could handle it when we began. I figured that I could keep things separated and I figured what the hell. We could have whatever we could have. And the office would be the office. Work would be work. Your life would be your life. My life would be mine. And we would touch where we could or when we could. I thought I could be cool about it."

"And?"

"I can't, Ted. I can't talk to anyone about us. Not to my girl friends. And not to my parents. And certainly not to anyone at work. And I can't talk to you about us. Not in any way that will give me perspective. It's getting so that I can't look at myself in the mirror. Or maybe I've started to look at myself and I don't like what I see.

"I have a cousin who is my age and she grew up near me and we were very close, Ted. And I also had a best girl friend who married her high school sweetheart. Anyway, a few years later my cousin started sleeping with my girl friend's husband. And eventually we all knew about it except for my girl friend. And no one in my family ever said anything to my girl friend even though we all loved her and we all hated what my cousin was doing. I remember once trying to talk my cousin into stopping it and she told me that she loved my girl friend's husband and that I didn't understand and that I couldn't understand. And I said that it didn't matter what I understood. That you just don't take your pleasures off the backs of other people. That it was dirty and wrong. And you don't do it."

"And what did she say?"

"Nothing. And I knew she wouldn't listen. So I told her if she didn't quit I wouldn't talk to her again."

"And she didn't."

"No."

"And you stopped talking to her?"

"Yes. And then my girl friend found out. And later she got divorced. And her husband married my cousin. And now nobody in the family talks to her."

"And now you're having trouble talking to yourself?"

"Yes. Because what we're doing is wrong. And what I'm doing is wrong. Because I've become a hypocrite and a liar and I don't like that."

"Who do you have to lie to?"

"No one. Not in so many words. And not like you probably have to lie to your wife. But it's a lie when I have to pretend that you aren't in my life. Or that I don't care about you when we're with other people. And it's a lie when I fight my feelings and make myself not love you although I have to do that to keep myself sane. But I have to do it. Because we're going nowhere you and me. And I know that. And I want more for myself than what you have to offer."

"Even if I tried to offer . . ."

"Don't say that," Nancy cut in. "Don't say it because you don't mean it and I don't want you to lie to me. And if you did mean it, I wouldn't want it. It wouldn't work. You would be torn up by guilt and what we have would not survive that. So just don't say it."

"That means we're done?" he asked.

"I think so," she said. And he could see her eyes go wide and watch her fight back the tears. He had never seen her cry. He waited until she had control.

"I don't believe we're through," he said quietly. "I don't feel that and I don't think you feel that." He searched for the right words and she stared at him. He felt her eyes boring into him. Felt them and knew he was right, that she would not leave him.

"I know that we are hypocrites. And I know that we are deceitful. I lie and I know that there are nasty words for what I am and what you are and what we do." He was almost whispering.

"And I feel more guilty than I think you do. I am more guilty than you are. And I'm terribly afraid that what we're doing will hurt innocent people I also love and who don't deserve to be hurt. So I can't argue with you. And if you want us to be through I won't fight you and I'll try my damnedest to make that work. But I don't believe in it. I love you, Nance, and I want you. And there is still magic between us. And I can touch you and feel that you want me. And know that when we go to bed together it works for us. And there's a truth to that too. And a truth to the kind of talk what we're having now. And to our rapport. And it would be a lie to stop it. As much of a lie as if we keep going on.

"And I don't know what to do. I don't know if I promise to stop that I will keep that promise. And I don't know if you promise or make me promise that we wouldn't end up in worse trouble in the long run if we repress what we have and then it gets the better of us. I don't know."

They stared at each other across her darkened apartment. He held out his hand to her and waited. She got up slowly and went to him.

Later, holding her. Again almost in a whisper, "Tell me you love me."

"I love you," she said.

They slept.

In the morning they were shy with each other. Nothing was solved. Murcer began to talk about himself. Not about his work, which she knew. Or about his family, which she imagined. About himself.

"I'm selfish, I suppose," he said. "Ambitious and self-centered, which you probably have to be to get where I am. For instance I look at my wife and the boys and I think that I should sacrifice my career for them, or perhaps sacrifice my life to them, that if I spent more time with them they would be better or happier for it. But actually I haven't neglected them, not in any extreme sense. And if I have, to some degree, does it follow that the extra time I spent, which I would resent, and which would make me surly and unpleasant, would be any good for them? It would certainly be bad for me. I count just as much as they do. I'm no less a person and my life should be as full as I can make it. Shouldn't it?"

She did not answer.

"I'm under consideration for a position on the Supreme Court of the United States," he said, switching the subject. "That's in confidence of course, but Justice Smith is going to either resign or die soon, and there will be other openings in the next two or three years, and I've got strong support with the Administration and in the Senate that can put it together."

"Do you want it?" she asked.

"What lawyer doesn't?"

"It's very passive work though. Reading briefs, writing opinions, fighting with the eight other justices, making a few speeches. And that's about it. It's cerebral work mostly. Do you think it suits you?"

"It's a chance to make history. How can you say no to it?"

"But it hasn't been offered to you to say no to. You're reaching for it, campaigning, I suppose. And I wonder if you got it whether it would be good for you. I don't really see you in that role. I think you could be stifled or bored there. Maybe I'm wrong."

She looked at him and understood that it didn't matter one iota whether he would be suited to the job or not. He wanted the advancement, the honor, and the prestige and the power. And he would struggle and ultimately excel at it if he could, because he would keep looking to advance, to feed his ambition and his ego. He would never be satisfied. He was a prisoner to his ambitions. And for the first time she found herself feeling sorry for him.

"I think you are wrong," he said.

Later that day, she came into his office to talk about the Trioxsone case.

"I think I've pieced it together," she said simply.

"Yes."

"I think that Lefcourte Laboratories bribed Defense Department personnel to get the drug used in Vietnam. I think that they were bribed with lucrative job offers for the future. And I can show that the officials who were responsible for approving the use and purchase of the drug are now either highly paid executives at Lefcourte or else are partners at Regis, McCormick, and Letterman, the firm that represents Lefcourte."

"And who engineered this conspiracy?" he asked uncomfortably.

"I believe that it was George Petrakis, who was then general counsel to Lefcourte. He's now . . ."

"I know who George is," Murcer cut in. "Do you have anything hard against him? Or is it just suspicions?"

It was her time to be uncomfortable now. "Not hard evidence," she admitted. "But not just suspicions either. I've found some memoranda written by General MacCauley, who was then with the surgeon general and who's now at Lefcourte. He states that he met with Petrakis and discussed Trioxsone. The memoranda are vague about what was discussed exactly. But they imply that Petrakis was extremely interested in pushing the drug for use on the troops, and he states his skepticism about using an untested drug like that. Anyway three months later, the general is Trioxsone's biggest booster, without the files showing one drop of evidence that he was persuaded to change his mind on the merits. Less than a year later, six months after the deal goes through, he's at Lefcourte earning in six figures. And, of course Lefcourte made millions."

"And now you want power to empanel a grand jury?"

"Yes."

"And see if you can indict George Petrakis and the others?"

"Yes."

"And you know that Petrakis is one of the most powerful and influential business leaders in the world."

"Yes."

"That he was responsible for raising almost a million dollars in contributions for the last presidential election for my party."

"Yes."

"And that he's made important contributions to more than half the United States Senate?"

"Yes."

"Did you know that he contributed generously to my campaigns? And beyond that, that he was my law school classmate and friend?"

"No."

"Well, he was and I've known him a good many years. And I can tell you that he's a thoroughly engaging person. But I also think that he's ruthless. And if you try to make a criminal case out of something that happened fifteen years ago, a case that would destroy his career and wreck his life, watch out, because he will destroy you. And if you think that you're going to build a criminal prosecution out of some equivocal memoranda, forget it. You're not going to be able to bully these people into making confessions. And after all these years, when they answer your questions with 'I don't remember' or 'I don't know' or 'I'm not sure,' that will be believable so you'll get nowhere trying to stick them with perjury charges."

"So I can't have my grand jury?"

"I'd rather not."

"Because it would hurt your chances of going to the Supreme Court if you authorized an investigation into the background of one of the President's biggest supporters?"

He looked at her.

And suddenly they were at a crossroads again. She was wrong, he thought. Or at least not entirely right. He was afraid of losing his chance for the appointment. But not that afraid. It was more the first thing. That he knew in his heart that the investigation would go nowhere, that it was a pointless exercise that would only end up hurting her and probably him as well.

But he also knew deep down that she was probably right in her suspicions. And he could see that he would lose her if he said no. That maybe he had lost her already.

"You can have your grand jury," he said softly. "Come back to me in one week with a thorough and persuasive explanation of why there should be a grand jury and what you hope to accomplish and I'll give you your grand jury and the resources from the Criminal Division to try and build a case."

She left his office then.

At home that night. And the night after that. And the night after that. Alone. The doubts came back to Nancy Revering. She was out of her depth with Ted Murcer. It wasn't making her happy. When they were together it was one thing. Then he could almost make her believe that it was all right. But then she would be alone and it weighed on her. It was too heavy and too complicated. And she wanted her life to be simple. To meet some guy whom she could see whenever she wanted. Someone she could take home at Christmastime. Or walk with on the streets and hold hands without worrying about who might see. She decided again to put an end to it. Rehearsed a speech to give to Murcer. To tell him that it had to be over. That just like they learned to love each other and handle the strains of not telling anyone or not showing anyone, now they would have to learn how to stop.

Still, she wanted to love him. To be his friend, and confidante. But not his mistress. She decided that she had to tell him that.

Murcer at home thought about telling Karen about Nancy. He didn't like being deceitful, didn't like lying even if only about little things. He didn't like not desiring his wife because he had someone else he loved better that way. He didn't like it at all.

Karen was his wife. She was his age. They had raised children together. She understood him better than anyone else would ever be likely to. They were part of one another. Had lived together so long that he could not contemplate living apart.

And the boys. He loved the boys. He thought about walking away from the house for the last time and being shut away from the boys forever. Having them turn against him. Having them raised maybe by some other man.

He thought about leaving Karen for Nancy. He wouldn't mind the scandal, he thought. No one took these things that seriously anymore. It was old news. But marrying Nancy wouldn't work. She was too much younger than he. He wouldn't be able to deal easily with her friends. They would think him old and stiff and formidable. And she wouldn't be able to interact easily with his social network. It wouldn't work. She would want children. And he couldn't go through that again.

Still he could see himself escaping somewhere with her. For a week or a month or a year he could see them impossibly happy.

Making love, talking, walking along moonlit beaches, or maybe visiting galleries on the Left Bank of the Seine in Paris.

It was all dreams, of course. But dreams that could easily be true if he had the will to act on them. She would come with him, he thought. And it would be as he imagined. Still dreams though.

She was right, he thought. They should end it. But he still wanted her badly. Perhaps in the end it was nothing more than the sexual attraction, the madness, and the need, the entering and the sharing and the tenderness, the feel of her hands caressing his back while he was in her. The sense of emptying himself into her, of falling asleep beside her, of sometimes being awake and watching her peaceful and asleep beside him. Of watching her shower and dress in the morning. He wasn't about to surrender that easily.

Ted Murcer was in trouble. And he knew that. He could feel his control of the situation weakening.

Tell Karen, he thought, Let her decide what should be done.

Or break up with Nancy and try to go back to the way it was.

Impossible.

Through it all he quite totally forgot about George Petrakis and the Trioxsone case.

42

Ed Regis was in his mid-seventies and looked nearly ten years younger. He still held himself erect and his stride was purposeful as he walked into Petrakis' office. The two men shook hands. His grip was still firm. Petrakis came directly to the point.

"How bad is the trouble with the Trioxsone case? Is the criminal investigation a serious thing? Or is it a ploy to annoy me, or to produce some political squeeze?"

"Any criminal investigation is serious," the lawyer answered. "There's never any telling what some damned half-baked, wet-behind-the-ears assistant prosecutor with a compliant grand jury might do. You can always get yourself indicted without any real difficulty. That's easy. And once you're indicted then there's a bushelful of very bad publicity. And a bad loss of face. To say nothing of a host of stockholder derivative and class action lawsuits claiming that management defrauded the company by their misconduct. There is always a lot of potential aggravation in these things."

"Yes, but is there any chance that the Justice Department might be able to build a serious prosecution that actually could send anyone from Transcontinental, or from your firm for that matter, to jail?"

"Like yourself?" Regis asked.

"Like myself."

"Let me ask you a question. Do you think there is any document in existence, a memorandum or something, that records your role in the Trioxsone business? Did you leave any tracks?"

"I don't think so."

"But you're not sure?"

"No. It was a long time ago and I've wracked my brain. I can't remember anything like that. But then I don't really remember thinking that there was anything too wrong about the whole deal then. Remember the way it was then. We were building Transcontinental and I was supposed to be turning Lefcourte Labs around fast so that I could get back to the home office. Things were slow, but we had this new drug that was supposed to be the next penicillin. I was pretty well persuaded at the time by our research people that we would be doing mankind a great service if we got the drug out. It was possible that we might save lives."

"So maybe you didn't cover your tracks," the lawyer said.

"Maybe."

"And it's possible, I suppose, if the pressure gets serious enough, even your friend the former general could turn on you."

"Possible, but unlikely," Petrakis answered, thinking that it wasn't that farfetched, that the general was pretty weak, that he could fold under pressure.

"So what do you suggest?" Petrakis continued.

"First off, I would try to get rid of the civil action as quickly as I could. I would offer that fellow Sabotnik more money than he or his client could turn down. Sabotnik is dangerous. He has the resources to make a lot of trouble. And he's a seasoned lawyer. I wouldn't want to see him making common cause with the young woman from the Justice Department."

"That's Nancy Revering?"

"Yes."

"What is she like?"

"Bright. Ambitious. Cold. And dangerous."

"Naïve and idealistic?"

"To a point."

"Can she be reached?"

"Probably not."

"And her superiors?"

"Ted Murcer, you mean?"

"Yes."

"I don't know."

"He wants a Supreme Court seat, doesn't he?"

"Yes."

And Petrakis began to think.

Petrakis found it difficult trying to decide what, if anything, to do about the Trioxsone situation. He had been through ticklish situations before. He had trimmed his sails or cut corners before, taken risks, and always he had come out all right. He would emerge in one piece from this one too, he felt. He was just too well protected and insulated, too bloody wealthy to be personally vulnerable. Still there was a threat in the air.

It was something else that bothered him though. Not a guilty conscience. Nothing that overt. He had long ago rationalized the Trioxsone deal—decided that his motives, if mixed, were certainly not evil. He had thought the drug would help save lives. Perhaps it had. It had been, as those things went, a clean deal. A lot cleaner than many things he had seen over the years. A profit had been made, of course. A couple of million dollars. Not too much in the grand scheme of things. Not enough to produce a guilty conscience.

It was more subtle. Hard to articulate. A kind of nagging doubt that he normally could repress with little effort. He was past fifty years old. In his prime and at the top of his world. For more than twenty years he had been climbing a steep corporate ladder, intent upon the ascent, reasonably oblivious to the consequences. He had lost a wife and raised a daughter alone and none of it had hampered his rise.

And it had happened largely without introspection, without questioning whether the prize was worth the game. How much wealth was enough? How much power? To what use could they be put? To what use should they be put? They had been there to be taken. So he had reached for wealth and power. Made them into habits.

He would be losing Diana soon. She would meet someone, would love him and marry. She would have a career. And she would have children. They would mean more to her than he would. Which was as it should be, he thought. He wanted that for her, was unselfish in his love for her. Still he felt that he only had two or three years with her, five at the outside. He found himself wondering what she would think of Trioxsone if she knew the whole story. She could be made to understand, he thought. She would understand and accept his role, he thought. But it would cost her her innocence.

The case was full of old faces. Phil Sabotnik, Mary Ann Salisbury, Ted Murcer. Good people, he thought. Possibly not as bright as he. He had done better in law school and had gone farther in the world than they. But they were very solid people, each of them. They had accomplished plenty. And now, without any of them really knowing it, they were arrayed against him. Or they might be.

They had been as near to friends as he had made over the years. And none of them was truly a friend. Not in the sense that he could call them up and unburden himself.

He was without friends, he realized. Instead he was surrounded by colleagues, acquaintances, adversaries, protégés, and assistants, all of whom he manipulated. And who in turn manipulated him.

There was Ed Regis, of course, whose protégé Petrakis himself was. But in twenty years the two men had done little except plot business deals and manage crises. Petrakis could not honestly say that he knew what Regis did for recreation, or even if he had recreation, whether he loved his wife or what he especially enjoyed eating for dinner. What he did know, even after twenty years, was that Regis' loyalty was ultimately to himself and to no one else. And if he ever made the judgment that Petrakis had to go down the tubes, that he was a dangerous liability to Regis or his law firm, then the old lawyer would not shed a tear. He would cut Petrakis loose in an instant.

Petrakis sat up late in his apartment puzzling it all out. He thought of retiring, of disengaging himself, trying to spend more time with Diana, perhaps to find a wife. It wouldn't work. He had no talent for leisure. He would age, or die, without work and power. He was riding on the tiger's back, and he knew that if he got off it would devour him. Because then he would be indicted. A nice powerless symbol of corporate evil. A politically safe and attractive target, a former executive. While his successors, whomever they might be, would conduct his business as usual.

So it was settled before it began. In the morning Petrakis called Regis and gave him authority to attempt to settle the civil action with Sabotnik, to spend as much as a million dollars, if necessary. He also agreed to let him use whatever influence as might be brought to bear to either squelch or limit any criminal investigation.

Then, by an act of will, he pushed Trioxsone from his mind, and by habit, went on with the business of running his conglomerate.

43

Sabotnik drove up to the Bronx to visit Cleveland Daniels. Other than an occasional trip to the courthouse and an even more occasional visit with his son to Yankee Stadium he had not been to the Bronx in ten years. It was a place he passed through on the railroad up to the suburbs. The streets were the same as when he was growing up though. They were poorer, more run down, the people's skins were darker. But he did not get lost.

"How's it going, man?" Cleveland asked him as he ushered the lawyer into his mother's apartment. "Can I offer you some tea or coffee or something? Maybe a piece of fruit?"

Cleveland was wearing a pair of cotton chino pants that looked two sizes too big on him. He had a belt clinched tight to keep them up, which accentuated their bagginess. He was wearing a white T-shirt, a blue terry cloth bathrobe and slippers. His hairline had receded since Sabotnik had last seen him and he had a stiff old man's walk.

"No thanks, Cleveland. I ate before I got in the car to drive up here."

"Well what's doing then? How's my case going?"

"Truthfully?"

"Yeah, truthfully."

"Not so well. I've been buried in paper by the lawyers for the drug company, and the government lawyers have been almost as bad. They've moved to dismiss your case and filed briefs in support of their motions that are each over a hundred pages long. I've had to fight like a tiger to squeeze every piece of paper out of the government, and I'm still sure that they're holding out their best stuff on me. And as for the drug company, I still haven't got my first useful or relevant piece of paper from them. They make motions about attorney client privilege, complain that their records are too voluminous and that they cannot or should not be forced to search through them. Then they say that they've lost or cannot find the relevant records. Then they ask me to formulate more precise requests, and I do it, and we start all over again."

"It sounds terrific."

"Yeah, it's great. But that's not the half of it. They've served interrogatories on me, for you and me to answer, in which we have to set out our theory of the case. I've got them here in my briefcase. They run seventy-five pages in length and I think there are three hundred twenty questions in total. But each question is broken down into half a dozen to maybe a dozen subparts, which really makes for over a thousand questions. And that's before we even get to start taking depositions of the various witnesses."

"So we're whipped then. And that's what you came up here to tell me?"

"No. That's the thing of it. We're not whipped at all, even though by rights we're in way over our heads. The truth of it is, and the reason that I came up here, is that yesterday Ed Regis, the lawyer for the drug company, actually offered me money to settle the case, and I've got to tell you about it."

"He offered you money?"

"Not me, Cleveland. He offered you money and asked me if you would settle. Let me tell you what he said. He told me that this lawsuit was a pain in the ass to Lefcourte Labs. He said that the publicity was bad for business, and that the cost to the company of being forced to pay lawyers to defend the case was very high. He offered you a hundred twenty-five thousand dollars to settle the case and leave him alone. That is a nuisance value to them. But it is a lot of money to you and your mother so I thought that I had better come up here and talk to you about it."

"How much would I clear, man? That hundred twenty-five includes your fee, don't it?"

"Yes. You would clear a little more than eighty thousand."

"And that's what my life is worth, eighty thousand dollars?"

"That's for you to decide, Cleveland. It's your choice whether you settle, not mine. All I can do is advise you."

"Okay, so what do you advise? Should I settle?"

"Personally I wouldn't, Cleveland. But I'm prejudiced and I should say that to you. I think that from what I know, what happened to you really stinks. And I suspect that there are hundreds more like you and that they're hoping to keep it all quiet by paying you off and shutting me up. Oh, I forgot to tell you. One of the terms of the settlement is that the court files have to be sealed, and I as your lawyer have to promise to take no more Trioxsone cases and not to publicize my involvement in the case."

"Can they do that?"

"They can do whatever they like in making a settlement. That's a contract freely entered into between you and them."

"But what about you? Can they shut you up?"

"I'm your lawyer. I've got an obligation to do what's best for you even if I don't like it."

"And if settlement is the best?"

"Then we settle."

"Even if it means that you don't get to find out about the other veterans who might be growing cancer because of the damn drug."

"Even if it means that."

"And you don't want me to settle."

"No."

"And if I don't, what then?"

"Well they might offer you more money. And they might withdraw their offer altogether. And then we'll go forward with the case and maybe we'll win. More probably we'll lose."

"And you don't want me to settle."

"No."

"You know what eighty thousand dollars would mean to my mama?"

"Yes. I think I do."

"And you want me to say no."

"Yes."

"The money isn't for me, man. I'm not going to live long enough to enjoy it. You know that."

"Yes."

"And I'm supposed to say no to it because of that. I'm supposed to be a hero an' let my name stay on the case so that you can be a bigger hero an' help all us servicemen an' get yourself headlines, right? Tell me, if we settle you get forty-five thousand and that's the end of it, right?"

"Yes."

"But if we go on you might end up with hundreds of cases and might finish making millions."

"Yes. But I could also spend a hundred thousand dollars and come up empty too. You've got to remember that."

"And you want me to say no?" Cleveland looked searchingly at his lawyer. "You want me to turn down the settlement offer."

"Yes."

A pause.

"Okay. No. Tell them that they can go fuck themselves."

They sat down together and went over the interrogatories then, spent almost two hours on it. After Sabotnik left, Cleveland Daniels fell asleep exhausted.

44

Behind the scenes, discreetly, Homer Anderson, the ninety-two-year-old circuit judge, was using his enormous prestige to see if Mary Ann might be named to the seat soon to be opened on the Supreme Court.

He had been a federal judge for almost fifty years, had authored literally thousands of opinions, had seen dozens of his ringing dissents become the basis, sometimes decades later, become the basis for major new Supreme Court decisions. It was a mark of the high respect that he enjoyed that he was one of the very few lower court judges whose decisions were identified by their author's name in opinions written by the Supreme Court justices. In effect, his very name on an opinion carried with it a prestige and the presumptive conclusion that the decision reached was not only correct but flawlessly reasoned. Over the years he had sat on the circuit court with the likes of Learned Hand and he had held his own with all of them. And on the fiftieth anniversary of his graduation, Yale had dedicated a copy of its law journal to him, had a series of eminent scholars write learned articles analyzing his career, trying to measure his many contributions to American jurisprudence. He was a marvel. So old that he was no longer controversial. Just great.

He should have been a Supreme Court justice himself was the universal view. And he would have been too, it was said. Franklin Roosevelt had promised it to him in 1945 the story went, and would have named him to the next opening. But the

President had died in April. The promise was forgotten, and Harry Truman had had his own far less qualified candidates. It was a pity. Everyone knew that. But the old judge never spoke of it.

He did speak out on Mary Ann's behalf though. Eloquently. And with a sincerity and conviction that could not be questioned. He was a tall man, now stooped with age. Bright blue eyes peering out from behind wire-rimmed spectacles. Deep-set eyes in an old wrinkled face. A fringe of white hair and bushy eyebrows. Nondescript business suit and old-fashioned bow ties. He walked slowly with his cane from one office to another, traveling down to Washington to make his case in person, forcing by his presence those with power and influence to sit still and listen respectfully to what he had to say.

Even the President of the United States gave him time, let the old man be ushered into the Oval Office. His pitch was naïve. But not ineffective.

"I'll be blunt, sir," the old judge began. "I'm an old man, and I think you know that I'm beyond partisan politics. I have been a judge for almost five decades and a lawyer for almost seventy years. I have devoted my entire adult life to the law and to the service of my country. And I think that I have done so with love. And not without distinction.

"I'm here, as you well know, to urge you to appoint Mary Ann Salisbury to the Supreme Court of the United States. We both know that my old friend Justice Smith will be required to resign soon, and I know that your Justice Department people are preparing a list of possible successors.

"You'll find no one better than Judge Salisbury, sir. She's not a Republican. I know that. And she's not thought of as a political conservative, whatever that means. But these things mean nothing in a judicial context. You must know that. Long after the politics of the moment were forgotten. You'll forgive me if I say that long after the Presidents who appointed them were dead, those justices were performing valuable services.

"And that's why you should appoint Mary Ann Salisbury. I know this woman, sir. And I can tell you not only that she's a fine legal scholar. There are many fine legal scholars around. But she's also a fine human being. She cares. She has compassion. And she has common sense. She does what has to be done. And she's a realist.

"Most importantly, sir, she's a great judge. I've seen many, many, judges over the years, and I can't think of more than a handful who deserve to be considered in her league. A lot of the so-called great judges are intellectually arrogant bastards who are so swept up in their own brilliance that they lose sight of the human realities that they're dealing with. Others are good men and women who try to do their best, but who lack the intellect to fully appreciate the consequences of the precedents they are setting. There are damn few who put both qualities together. Intellect and compassion. Mary Ann has both.

"I remember when Franklin Roosevelt appointed Felix Frankfurter everyone foretold that he would be one of the great liberal justices, left-wing reform type and all that. And in the end he became one of the great conservative proponents of judicial restraint, and a darling of the right wing. And then there was Eisenhower appointing Earl Warren, thinking that he was getting a nice safe conservative to middle-of-the-road Republican politician.

"I once heard Ike say that appointing Warren was 'the worst damn fool thing' he ever did. Well let me tell you, it was the best thing he ever did for this republic. That and appointing Brennan. The same was true when Hoover appointed Benjamin Cardozo, who was a Tammany Hall Democrat and a Jew, to the Court. Or when Calvin Coolidge appointed Harlan Fiske Stone. They weren't playing politics with their appointments. They were just putting the most qualified, best-suited individuals they could find on the Court. And the nation benefited from those appointments."

The President listened quietly, noncommittally, and made no attempt to interrupt, which was a bad sign the judge thought. Still the man seemed to be attentive, possibly thoughtful.

"Well, your honor," the President said, standing up and thus indicating that the interview was over, "what you say is interesting and I just might do what you suggest. But, of course, Justice Smith hasn't resigned yet. Still it's very interesting.

"But now you will have to excuse me. I have a meeting of the National Security Council to attend."

The judge's final appointment in Washington was with Justice Smith himself. They had known each other fifty years—back to a time when the justice was a trial lawyer with the government and had appeared to prosecute one of his first criminal cases before Judge Anderson, then a newly appointed district judge. They had been friends ever since.

"You know I'm dying," the justice said grimly.

"Yes," Anderson answered. "And so does everyone else in Washington."

"I imagined as much. Although almost no one in this miserable city has the courage to look me in the face and talk about it."

"Do you want to talk about it?"

"Not really."

"Are you going to resign?"

"Not yet. Would you?"

"Can you still function?"

"Yes."

"Then I wouldn't resign."

"Cancer grows slowly at our age," the justice went on. "And I can't see just sitting around and waiting to die. So I plan to keep working as long as I am able. Since Louise died, this work is really all I have anyway."

"It's much the same for me," Anderson replied.

"Ah, but you're still up and about and busy meddling in politics, aren't you? After all you're down here promoting some candidate for my seat, aren't you? Just the way, twenty-two years ago, you were busy promoting my candidacy. Do you remember?"

"I do."

"Well who is it now, Homer?"

"Mary Ann Salisbury."

"The young girl on the Southern District?"

"Yes."

"Pretty?"

"Yes. But she has a good head and a good heart. The Court needs her."

"And I suppose that it's time to put a woman on the Court."

"It's inevitable."

"She'll never make it, Homer. Not with this Administration. They'll name a woman, I suppose. But not anyone controversial in even the slightest degree—it will have to be someone from the Midwest or the Far West, certainly a conservative Republican and preferably someone whose public record is pretty heavily silent on any sensitive issue.

"I know that in your own uniquely shrewd and naïve way, you will promote this woman and try to make everyone feel guilty about even contemplating someone less well qualified. But once you leave, they'll just go back to thinking about politics, and they will pretty much forget what you had to say."

"Will you support my candidate?" Judge Anderson said simply, ignoring his friend's tirade.

"Yes."

"You'll speak to the President?"

"At the right time."

"And the Attorney General?"

"Yes."

The two men looked at each other.

"Does it hurt much?"

"No."

"Are you frightened?"

"A little. But less than I would have thought. I'm tired. And the work on the Court has lost all of its excitement for me. Things that I remember I used to care about don't seem to matter so much anymore. I used to worry about my place in history, about how I would remembered. Would I be a great justice, or someone obscure whose name no one would remember five years after I'm gone. Now I'm pretty sure that I don't care. When I look back at it all I know is that there were many things that I did that were pretty good. And many more things that were damned mediocre. Early and late, I did more than my share of compromising and trimming. You have to do that when year in and year out you're trying accomplish something in tandem with eight others. It's not the greatest job in the world you know."

"I know," Judge Anderson said softly. "I know."

45

"How has your criminal investigation into Trioxsone been going?" Murcer asked Nancy Revering. He wasn't sure that he cared how it was going. But he did care about being near her, listening to her talk, looking at her.

"It's going nowhere," she answered. "Trying to subpoena records from Transcontinental is frustrating as hell. They make motions and drown me in mountains of paper. They ask me first to be more precise about what I'm looking for, accusing me of being vague. Then I redraft the subpoena in the most precise way I can, and I'm met with a motion attacking it as unduly long and burdensome to comply with. So I go back and try again and finally get the judge to order compliance. Only they don't comply. Instead they move for reargument, which takes another two weeks before it's denied. Then when they finally produce documents, it is worthless junk that doesn't really comply with what I'm looking for. So I have to go to the judge once again for a new order. And they just find a way to evade it again."

"That's Ed Regis' firm?" Murcer asked.

"Yes."

"It's pretty much what I told you would happen."

"Yes."

"Have you made any progress trying to get any witness who will break down and turn state's evidence?"

"No. Regis has covered all the bases. Everyone who might know anything is represented by counsel, and nobody is talking without promises of immunity."

"And they won't even tell you what they might have to say if you did give them an immunity bath."

"Correct."

"So you can't give anyone immunity because you're operating blind and might inadvertently immunize a prime suspect."

"Yes."

"And you're up against a stone wall?"

"Yes."

"Are there any Defense Department documents or FDA documents that help?"

"No. Or they're missing. I spent a couple of days in a warehouse trying to make heads or tails of the old records. It is impossible, almost as if they had been deliberately messed up."

"But you can't prove that?"

"No."

"Did you try to talk to George Petrakis himself?"

"Yes."

"And?"

"When I asked to talk to his client, Regis politely told me to go fuck myself."

"And now?"

"There's the civil case."

"Before Mary Ann Salisbury?"

"Yes."

"That's a dangerous case before her," Murcer remarked, looking away out his office window. She sensed the change in his mood. It was the first time he had looked away from her.

"She's a very good judge," Nancy said.

"That's what I hear."

"And the plaintiff's lawyer is very good too."

"She could rule that the government might be liable for this Trioxsone business, is what you're saying."

"She could."

"And then she would be reversed on appeal."

"Probably."

"Definitely."

"Why?"

"Because there is no way that the circuit court or the Supreme Court in today's conservative environment is about to judicially sanction untold thousands of lawsuits seeking tens of millions of federal dollars. Particularly not in a military context where concerns about discipline and national defense might be involved."

"I'm not so sure," she answered.

"Do you really think Mary Ann will rule in the veteran's favor?"

"Yes."

"If she does it will destroy whatever chance she has of being appointed to the Supreme Court. It would confirm the lurking suspicion that she might be a dangerous radical. Which of course, she is."

"You know Judge Salisbury? And she's under consideration for a Supreme Court spot?" Nancy asked.

"Yes and yes," he answered. "I knew her a long, long time ago.

"Can I come to your apartment tonight?" he asked after a moment, changing the subject.

"No."

"Tomorrow?"

"No, I don't think so. Not ever."

"Never?"

"That's right."

"Why?"

"Because it's over."

"Why?"

"Because I need to be free of this. It is too heavy for me, and I don't feel good about it."

"Don't you love me?" Softly.

"I don't want to love you," more softly, "and I wish you didn't love me."

"But I do love you."

"I'm sorry."

"And you love me."

"I'm trying not to."

She could see the hurt in his eyes.

"I'm trying not to, and if you'll let me, I think I can. I've been through it before. At first its hurts from the moment you wake up. And when you open your eyes, the first thing you think about is the pain. Then one morning maybe you don't think about it until you're taking a shower or eating breakfast. Maybe a few weeks later you can get all the way to work without thinking about it. And then one day you don't think about it at all. It's there. And if you look for it you can find the place where it hurts. But you can go on living."

"Without me?"

"Yes."

"And without the things we can do together?"

"Without that too. I won't hitch myself to your star, Ted. I know what you are, and how you can light up a whole lot of the sky with what you're probably going to be. But I have to be my own star. And I have to light up my own little corner of the sky. Even if it's a real little corner and a real faint light. I've got to do it myself."

"And that's what you aim to do?"

"Yes."

"What's the matter, Ted? For the last several days you've been like a turtle pulled into a shell. Is there something I can help with?"

He looked at Karen. And saw that she had no idea of the reason for his hurt, that she did want to help, that she cared deeply. She was his wife, and he took her for granted, knowing that she was there for him. And now if he told her why he hurt, it would only be to hurt her too. And in hurting her he would only hurt himself further. But he hated to lie to her. And even if his affair was itself a kind of lie, she had never asked questions or sought explanations that made him lie. But now, when it was over, and when a lie would suffice, he found he couldn't. And he looked at her sadly. "Karen, I think I'd better tell you something," he began.

And there was something in the tone of his voice that said it all. Murcer watched his wife pull herself together, brace herself, as if waiting for a blow. She knows, he thought to himself. Or if she doesn't know, it's just come to her. I don't have to speak. If I don't say anything, we can live with it. He thought to lie, or to talk of something trivial. She looked at him.

"I'm in love with another woman."

No answer.

"I have had an affair with her for about a year now, and it's over, and I don't know why I'm telling you this, because I don't want to hurt you. I don't want a divorce. And I don't want you to divorce me. I love you and I love the boys, and I want to live with you and I wish I didn't have to say this . . ."

He looked at her. She was still pretty. Almost fifty years old and she still had her figure. He should never have loved anyone else, never needed to love a girl half their age. He waited for her to speak.

She didn't. Instead she struggled for control, and lost. Her shoulders began to shake and he sat and watched her, unable to go and comfort her. He watched as she let out an almost animal moan, as she got up and ran out of the room.

He found her on the floor of their bedroom, crumpled on the floor, sobbing. And then he took her in his arms and cradled her. And she let him. In a sense it was simple as that. They would be up all night talking. She would be angry, and frightened, and jealous. She would tell him that she loved him. She would offer to divorce him on amicable terms. She would ask him to try to explain why it had happened, whether she was at fault.

"Who was it?" she asked in a soft voice.

He shook his head no.

"In your office?"

He didn't answer.

"It was in your office," she repeated, as fact, not as a question.

"I'd rather not say."

"And it's over?"

"I think so."

"But you're not sure?"

"The truth?"

"Yes."

"I'm not sure."

"And what am I supposed to do?"

"I don't know."

"Just love you and be understanding," her tone somewhere between sarcasm and concern.

"I don't know."

Round and round. Every night for a week they talked. They made love with passion neither had felt in years, and they fought with an honesty that also had been long lacking between them. In some ways things were actually better than they had ever been. But a faith and a trust had been destroyed, and could not be easily mended. They would be wary with one another, cautious. Still they would go on.

46

The briefs had been written at great length. Additional briefs and memoranda had been filed in opposition to the original applications. Then reply briefs were drafted and filed to rebut the arguments in the opposition briefs. Affidavits were prepared and signed and submitted to make a factual record in support of the position taken by each party. The pleadings, briefs, affidavits, motions, complaints, and answers were all neatly typed on eight and a half by fourteen-inch paper, page after page, stacked up inch after inch of paper, a pile seven inches high, over a thousand pages. Mary Ann's clerk read her way through every page, then sat down and drafted a twenty-five page memorandum summarizing it all. Then Mary Ann sat down and read the memorandum, and began to work her way through the pleadings. Finally, she decided to set aside an entire morning to hear oral argument in *Cleveland Daniels* v. *United States and Lefcourte Laboratories*. She sent letters to counsel scheduling the argument three weeks into the future.

It was a bright spring morning. Mary Ann awoke early, ate her breakfast in her sunlit dining room, drinking coffee, munching on toast, daydreaming about being named to the Supreme

Court. Going to Washington. Limelights. Starting a new life. Independence. A place in history.

Christine walked in wearing a short nightgown, frowning, tentative.

"Have you finished your college applications yet?" Mary Ann asked.

"No."

"Aren't they due in this week?"

"Maybe."

"You mean you don't know the deadlines?"

"I'm not sure. I mean I'm not even sure that I even want to go to college next fall. I'm not sure that I'm ready for four more years of school. I probably wouldn't do too well at it. I need to grow up."

"So you want to enlist in the Marines?" Mary Ann asked. And they both laughed.

"No, but I'd like to try to see if I could get a job with a television news station on a film production company or something. Maybe I could get some experience in something interesting. Maybe with a radio station."

Mary Ann looked at her daughter. Then she looked at the clock on the kitchen wall. Something important was happening. Christine was opening up to her. It was in her eyes. A wariness. Not trust. Not yet. But an openness. A willingness to talk.

It was time for her to be leaving for court. There was the oral argument. Government counsel would be flying in from Washington. She had never once voluntarily been late to open court. She looked again at the clock and then at her daughter.

"You've got to go to work," Christine said flatly, following her stare.

"No, I'll be late today. Let's talk."

Phil Sabotnik rode the train down from Westchester County that morning. He made notes on three by five cards as he waded through his highlighted copies of the briefs. He was nervous. He was still always nervous anyway before an important day in court. But this was different. He would be arguing before Mary Ann Salisbury, whom he hadn't seen in over twenty years. He could remember last seeing her, remember very well. He was determined to do well.

Nancy Revering awoke early and alone that morning, dressed, and caught a cab to the airport.

She thought about Ted Murcer, about quitting. The Trioxsone case was going nowhere. Maybe her career was going nowhere. She was in love with a married man and she could tell no one about it. She felt as if she couldn't easily love some nice single guy. She wanted a career. She didn't want to get married. She wasn't sure that she wanted children. It was all a muddle. She hated the idea of quitting, of failure. But she also hated facing Murcer every day. She hated making herself hard to him, hated being unresponsive when he looked at her. And she would never find a job that she loved as much as this one. She felt trapped.

Ed Regis was met at his doorway by his firm's limousine, rode in the back seat as the car purred its way downtown to the federal court. He was at ease. He knew where the bodies were buried, and he knew how it was bound to turn out. He looked forward to the court appearance.

Cleveland Daniels was not aware that that morning had been set down for the argument of his case. But he woke up early just the same, staggered into his mother's bathroom, leaned over the toilet, and began to vomit. When he was finished he returned to bed and went to sleep.

47

Sabotnik arrived at the courtroom a little early. It was an old-fashioned wood-paneled courtroom, not one of the new marble and concrete ones, and it was empty. Near the front door a calendar was posted. It had one entry: 10 A.M. *Daniels* v. *United States*—Motions to Dismiss—Oral Argument—Status Conference. Sabotnik was reading the calendar as Nancy Revering walked in.

"Are you here for the Daniels case?" she asked.

"Yes."

"Are you Phil Sabotnik?"

"Yes."

She introduced herself and they shook hands. It was often like that. One lawyer filed an action, served a summons and complaint. Another lawyer was assigned to defend the action. Answers were filed. Then motions were made, briefs were written, telephone calls were made back and forth. Weeks, even months, might go by and the lawyers would begin to know each other in a way, to learn each other's writing style, their intellectual honesty, or lack of it, their sense of humor even. All this without meeting. That happened later, early one morning, in empty courtrooms, before oral arguments.

She was very pretty, Sabotnik thought. But she was a good lawyer, he knew. Her briefs had been excellent. Terse, well phrased, to the point. He wondered how much the Justice Department was paying her, whether she might ever be lured to New York to work at Sabotnik and Horowitz. They needed good young associates, especially with solid experience. Finding them was always a problem. She was well dressed. Primly almost. In a gray skirt, a matching jacket, and a high-collared white silk blouse. Her honey blond hair was pulled back into a bun. No wedding ring.

"Have you ever been before Judge Salisbury?" she asked innocently.

"No," he answered truthfully. "Never since she's been on the bench. But we were law school classmates many years ago." He left it at that.

"I've never appeared before her either. But I understand that she's just terrific. She's supposed to be very smart and from what I hear she treats the lawyers before her very decently. I've been looking forward to today."

Before they could go on, Ed Regis walked in followed by a young associate carrying a large briefcase. He too introduced himself and the three of them stood around waiting for the judge. The stenographer and the court clerk arrived next and took their names, made sure that everyone was present who needed to be there. Everyone except the judge. She as it turned out was forty-five minutes late.

"All rise!" the clerk called out.

And they all stood up as Mary Ann entered from her robing room, black robes trailing behind her, and took the bench.

Her blond hair had touches of white, just a bit, Sabotnik noticed. It made Sabotnik think of his own years, of the gray in his own hair. She still looked good though. It was the same Mary Ann. He felt a strange surge of emotion as he remembered their past. Suddenly it did not seem so long ago.

"You may sit down," Mary Ann told them as she sat down herself. "Let me apologize for the delay in my arrival. A personal matter arose suddenly which could not be avoided."

The clerk stepped forward. "Your honor, the case on the calendar this morning is Cleveland Daniels against the United States and Lefcourte Laboratories, Civil Action Number 8723."

Mary Ann looked down at them, turned toward Sabotnik and smiled, turned back to look at all of them.

"Folks," she began, "before we begin, I would like the record to reflect that Mr. Sabotnik and I were classmates in law school. We were friends at that time. That has nothing to do with this case, nor will it have anything to do with how I preside over this case. But I thought I would state the fact so that if any of you have any objection, and that means you too, Phil, to having this case assigned to me, you will be able to make it. There's no reason that I know of why I should disqualify myself. But I will entertain any applications to have me disqualify myself."

She looked down at them.

"Your honor," Ed Regis began, always composed, "Lefcourte Labs is delighted to have you preside over the case. We have no objection."

"The government has no objection either," Nancy Revering said.

Silence.

"And you, Phil?" Mary Ann asked.

"None, your honor. No objection."

"Okay, then," Mary Ann said. "Let's get to work. I've read your briefs carefully, and I would like to approach the issues one at a time. Let's start with the government's motion to dismiss this lawsuit on the grounds that it is barred by the doctrine of sovereign immunity. I will hear from Ms. Revering on that first."

"Well, your honor," she began tentatively, "from the very beginning of our republic, and really going back long before that to the very origins of the English common law, it has been axiomatic that the crown, or the government, cannot be sued in their own courts unless they have specifically given consent to be sued. That's the doctrine of sovereign immunity.

"And to be quite blunt, your honor, Congress has never given consent to be sued by servicemen for injuries that they have sustained while on active duty, let alone in time of war. And for that reason, I must take the position that with all due respect, even if Mr. Daniels' claim is perfectly justified, even if he has been wronged, and please understand that we do not for a minute concede that there is any merit to this claim, even if he is right, he still cannot seek relief in this court."

"Are you saying, Ms. Revering, that I am without power to even consider this case against the United States?"

"Yes, precisely. I think that you lack jurisdiction."

"Because Congress has not passed any law enabling me to consider it."

"That's correct, your honor. But I would like to add, if I may, that Congress has not been indifferent to the fate of our servicemen, and has not left Cleveland Daniels without a remedy. As you know, with the passage of the Veteran's Benefit Act, many years ago, a comprehensive system of benefits and pensions and payments has been established to provide no-fault relief to servicemen who sustain a service-related injury or illness. And of course, the Veterans Administration hospitals stand ready to give Cleveland Daniels free medical care for his illness regardless of whether it is service-connected or not. So Cleveland Daniels is not without remedies. It is simply that he cannot seek a remedy here."

"But tell me," Mary Ann interjected, "you are not arguing that veteran's benefits, which are limited, are as good a remedy, or as adequate, as the type of verdict that Mr. Daniels might get from this court or a jury if his claims are true. If he's right, and he was wrongfully given cancer, he would certainly get a lot more here. And if he were a civilian he would be allowed to sue the government here, wouldn't he?"

"Yes, it is true that Congress, when it passed the Federal Tort Claims Act, consented to waive sovereign immunity for lawsuits by injured civilians. But the Supreme Court said in the case of Feres versus the United States that the Tort Claims Act does not apply to the potential suits by servicemen. The Court said, and this makes sense, your honor, that it could destroy military discipline to allow soldiers and sailors to start questioning the orders of their superiors, and to allow them to come into a federal court and start a lawsuit every time they get injured, or think they have been injured. You just can't run an Army and defend this country if every decision made can be second-guessed in a federal court."

"So I can do nothing, no matter how outrageous or disgusting the government's conduct toward its soldiers was, correct?"

"I'm afraid so," Nancy Revering said, holding her ground.

"Even if a military officer were to decide in cold blood to murder a soldier, to order him to march off a cliff to his death, even if that officer ordered that soldier motivated by something as perverted as racial or religious prejudice, you are still saying that the soldier and his family cannot sue the government in this court?"

"Your honor, no one has alleged in this case that anyone intended to give Cleveland Daniels cancer. And certainly no one has alleged that there was any race or religious prejudice involved. Soldiers of all races, religions, creeds, and social classes took Trioxsone."

"I know that, Ms. Revering," Mary Ann shot back, "but I would still like you to answer my question. Are you really saying that I have no power to give tort relief, even to a soldier who is maimed or killed for racial reasons? I would like to know that."

"The answer is yes."

"Okay, I thought it was. I think I would like to hear from Mr. Sabotnik on this." Turning to her old friend, Mary Ann went on, "Tell me, why do you think that I have authority to decide Cleveland Daniels' case, in the face of the two-hundred-year-old sovereign immunity doctrine, and the two or three dozen Supreme Court decisions that the government cites in its briefs which support that doctrine. How can I, as a lower court judge, avoid the holdings of those decisions? I am legally bound by those decisions to dismiss this case, no matter what I might think, isn't that true?"

"No, your honor," Sabotnik answered. "You are not bound, your hands are not tied, because this case is fundamentally different from the Supreme Court cases that the government relies on. You see, in those cases, they were talking about simple negligence lawsuits, automobile accidents, medical malpractice, things like that. But here we are talking about something totally different. Cleveland Daniels alleges that he was the victim of unlawful medical experimentation. He was made into a drug guinea pig without his knowledge and certainly without his consent. What was done to him was no simple act of negligence. It was not an accident. It was deliberate and it was vicious. And it fundamentally violated his constitutional rights.

"Your honor," he went on, picking up a head of steam, "I would like to talk about the doctrine of sovereign immunity, and to show why Ms. Revering is dead wrong when she says that it applies here. You see, sovereign immunity does go back to old English common law, and it is usually associated with the maxim that 'the king can do no wrong.' Well that's the point. We have no king here. A revolution was fought in 1776 to ensure that no man, or indeed, no government or Parliament or Congress, can act free of the law. And when our Constitution was drafted in 1787, and the Bill of Rights enacted shortly afterwards, the whole point was to establish certain fundamental freedoms and rights as paramount and inviolable. And I challenge your honor to search the entire Constitution from top to bottom to find a single reference to sovereign immunity. I would ask Ms. Revering to tell me where in the Constitution it says that the federal government cannot be sued without its consent. I would ask her to tell us where it says that the government may violate fundamental constitutional rights with impunity, and with no fear that the injured party may come into this court and seek redress. Your honor, under the Civil Rights Act of 1871, a citizen may come into this court for a remedy when a state or a local government violates his constitutional rights. It is time, and long past the time, that it should be made clear that the federal government no less than the governments of the fifty states is legally responsible. Under Article III of the Constitution, and under acts of congress, this court has jurisdiction over cases arising under the Constitution and laws of the United States. You will never have a case before you that more squarely arises under the Constitution than this one."

Mary Ann sat listening to Phil Sabotnik and found herself remembering a tall, skinny, curly-haired boy at a moot court argument, so many years earlier. He had been nervous beforehand. But he had been good. There was something intense and naïve and honest about him still. So she let him go on.

"I would like to focus on the human experimentation aspect of this case, to show you how disgraceful the government's position in claiming immunity is. In 1945 and 1946, at the express order of President Truman, a United States military tribunal at Nuremberg, Germany, sentenced Karl Brandt and a host of Nazi doctors to death for medical experiments they conducted at concentration camps on innocent peoples of many nations. Those Nazi doctors were acting at the behest of their own sovereign government in time of war. Their victims were by and large, and I believe entirely, not United States citizens. And yet an entirely American court—not an international tribunal—in the medical experimentation case, had no trouble imposing the death penalty on those doctors.

"Now, I am not questioning what happened at Nuremberg. Far from it. Nor am I saying, or would I ever wish to say, that what happened in Vietnam with Trioxsone sank to the total moral depths of Auschwitz. But what I am saying is that if you read the Nuremberg decision, and look at the principles and laws that were used by the court to send those Nazis to their death, you will see that those very same principles were violated by our Army in Vietnam when it fed dangerous untested drugs to our soldiers without giving them warning or obtaining their consent. I feel that it would be the height of hypocrisy if we were unwilling to at least give to our own citizens and soldiers a civil remedy against our own government when we are perfectly willing to sentence the officials of other governments to death."

"Let me ask you," Mary Ann finally interjected. "You aren't just asking for money for Mr. Daniels in this lawsuit, are you? You also started a class action in which you asked me to order the government to warn the veterans who took Trioxsone that their health may have been endangered?"

"Yes, and to offer them diagnostic and therapeutic medical care free, so that any cancers that do develop will be treated as quickly as possible."

"Yes, and what I would like to know is whether you draw any distinction between the class action part of your lawsuit and your suit just on behalf of Cleveland Daniels?"

Sabotnik paused a moment before answering. He had expected this question, and he had prepared his answer, but he was trying to gauge Mary Ann's reason for asking. He was afraid that she, or any judge, might be tempted to be Solomonic and give him the class action relief of notification and medical care, while denying the right to money damages. And that would do Cleveland Daniels no good at all. He looked at Mary Ann. There was nothing that he could read in her face.

"There are distinctions, your honor, but both actions are based on the Constitution, and both are equally valid."

"But isn't the class action seeking an injunction in which I order the government to affirmatively take certain actions?"

"Yes."

"So it is an equity action."

"Yes."

"And aren't there certain Supreme Court decisions that seem to give me the power to compel the government to take actions to remedy constitutional violations in an equitable context?"

"I cite them in my briefs."

"Yes, and there are also certain laws that Congress passed, particularly the Administrative Procedure Act, that you argued were waivers of sovereign immunity which allow me to issue injunctions against the United States."

"Yes."

"But there are no statutes, and there are no cases, which allow a lawsuit for damages against the United States by a soldier?"

"None, your honor. Just the Constitution."

"But the Constitution doesn't say anywhere that a soldier can sue the government, does it?"

"No."

"Well let me ask you this, don't you agree with Ms. Revering that permitting lawsuits like this will disrupt military discipline and undermine the defense of our nation, and of the Free World? Isn't there something to that?"

"Yes there is, your honor," Sabotnik conceded. "And that is why I would agree that where you are talking about an automobile accident or some simple act of negligence, committed on an isolated basis, perhaps the requirements of discipline should take precedence over giving the injured soldier his day in court.

"But here we're talking about something different. We're talking about human experimentation, perpetrated as a matter of policy, at the very highest levels of government. And somewhere, your honor, military discipline, however valid and worthwhile it is as an abstraction, must give way to something more fundamental, namely the protection of basic human rights. The United States is not, and God willing, never will be a military dictatorship, and quite simply this case is far beyond the line where courts can step aside and blindly accept a military discipline argument."

Mary Ann turned then to the third lawyer. "Mr. Regis, you've been mighty silent through all of this. I'd be quite interested to hear what you have to say about the viability of this lawsuit."

The old lawyer got up slowly, walked even more slowly to the podium, paused, looked around, paused some more. He knew how to dominate a scene without saying a word.

"Your honor, there are many things I might say. But I suppose that I should begin by observing that it is nearly obscene to compare in the same breath the unspeakable atrocities of Auschwitz and what was essentially a humanitarian effort to save American servicemen from the ravages of tropical diseases. I would make the observation that before this drug was used in Vietnam we were losing dozens of soldiers and marines each month to these illnesses. Once the drug was employed though, the incidence of the diseases fell off to practically zero. I wonder how many men are alive today because of Trioxsone? I think that we should put this into perspective when we talk about the case. There is nothing to it."

Mary Ann did not go for the bait. "Mr. Regis, I am not interested in hearing from you how weak Mr. Daniels' case may be. That would be for a jury to decide after complete pre-trial discovery and a full trial. What I care about now is more fundamental. I want to know if Mr. Daniels has the right to sue your client at all. Would you like to comment on that?"

"Certainly. We do not think that Lefcourte Labs can be sued because of the circumstances under which the sale of Trioxsone was made. As you know, the Defense Department directed Lefcourte to provide it with the drug. It told what quantities it wanted, what dosages it wanted, the exact chemical compositions it wanted, the manufacturing processes and degrees of purity it wanted. And we had no choice in the matter. Lefcourte Labs could no more refuse to sell to the Army than any defense contractor. Not in wartime. And there was a war going.

"Your honor, Lefcourte Labs had no say over how Trioxsone would be used. We did not hide from the government the state of the research that had gone into the development of Trioxsone. The government knew that it was largely untested. That was well documented. We certainly cannot be faulted for something that we did not do. We couldn't very well have issued warnings to the servicemen who used the drug, since the government bought the bulk and distributed it themselves. In short, I think that you must find as a matter of law that there is no case. Not where we were forced to make the sale, and prevented from warning its users."

"What do you say to that, Mr. Sabotnik? There are cases that do hold that a government contractor and especially a defense contractor cannot be liable for injuries caused by their products if they were compelled to make the products by the government, and if the product was made to government specifications?"

"No. But I do not accept, your honor, that Lefcourte Labs is the innocent victim of government misconduct that Mr. Regis paints it to be. I believe that if I am allowed to go forward here, I will be able to show you and a jury that Lefcourte Labs was hand in glove with the Army, that it promoted and profited by the sale of the drug, maybe even induced it. I don't think that it was at all innocent."

"Are you suggesting that there was criminal conduct in the Trioxsone contracting?" Mary Ann asked.

"Maybe there was," Sabotnik answered. "That would be for the Justice Department and a grand jury to determine. All that I'm saying is that I should be given the chance to show that Lefcourte Labs has dirty hands in this business."

They went on and on for almost three hours. Mary Ann asking questions. The give and take of answers moving back and forth over the complex subject matter of the lawsuit. Mary Ann kept probing, looking for weaknesses in the arguments, worked hard at trying to avoid giving the appearance of favoring one side or the other. She masked her views with an unfailing politeness that had always been her trademark. In this case it was easy. She had three good lawyers before her and they were performing well. She was enjoying herself, and the hours rushed by. But in the afternoon there was a hearing scheduled on a motion for an injunction in a labor union case. In the end, she had to move to take control.

"Look," Mary Ann said. "The more argument I hear in this case, the more I wonder whether it might be possible for us to agree to work something out. It seems to me that nobody here disagrees that there may, and I emphasize the word may, be some dangerous long-term effects from ingesting Trioxsone. The defendants deny that Mr. Daniels can show by a preponderance of evidence that it caused his cancer; but I do not think they deny that it is now known to be a potentially dangerous drug which may cause some cancer.

"I wonder whether you all might not agree, before I decide

this motion, to issue the warning that is sought by the class action part of this lawsuit. It would have to be a carefully worded warning, so as not to create undue alarm or to frighten otherwise healthy veterans half to death with cancerphobia. But I am sure that we could arrive at a form of warning that would be appropriate; and I am sure that it would not be outrageously expensive to notify the veterans, and as a practical matter, the Veterans Administration should be in a position to provide those soldiers who desire it with free checkups, and if appropriate, with treatment.

"I suggest this because I have often found that it is desirable to have the parties settle cases where possible rather than to have the court issue an opinion and an order. I'll do that if I am forced to. That is my responsibility. But I am not sure that my decision will be any wiser than what you might be able to work out between you on this. Only my decision, and the decisions of the appellate courts that review this case, will establish precedents that might be applied to numerous situations that none of us have ever given any thought to. And my decision thus could create problems for the government, or large corporations, or injured individuals that transcend even this important case. So I think that before I render a decision, I would like you to report back to me in three weeks on whether or not this aspect of the case can be settled. I would also like you to consider among you whether Cleveland Daniels' own case for damages might be settled as well. That might be more difficult to accomplish. But as far as I know, he is the only one who has, as yet, made a money damages claim for a Trioxsone-related injury. And maybe we can resolve the entire matter in one shot without being forced to render some major and avoidable constitutional decision. Report back to me in three weeks, and if you are unable to settle, then I will rule promptly."

"Your honor," Sabotnik added, as they were getting up to leave. "One last thing, if I may. Mr. Daniels is in rapidly declining health. I wonder if I may have your permission to take his deposition immediately, by videotape, so that we may preserve his testimony in that form for trial should we ever reach that stage."

Mary Ann looked at Sabotnik, an old look. "Yes, Phil," she said, "you can take your deposition."

Back in her chambers, alone, Mary Ann sat down and tried to face herself. She felt trapped, knew that she was fast approaching a moment of truth.

She could hit it lucky, she thought. Delay a few weeks, maybe a few months, and hope to work out a settlement. Or perhaps in the interim she might win the appointment to the Supreme Court. Or someone else might. Either way she would be able to avoid letting the Daniels case ruin her ambitions.

And it would ruin her. She knew that to a near certainty. There was no question in her mind of how she would rule if she had to. She might do further research, listen to more argument, delay. But she would rule for Cleveland Daniels one way or another. She would rule for him because she would not live with her name on an opinion that said that there would be no remedy for such as Cleveland Daniels. She would rule for him although she would likely be overturned on appeal. She would rule for him although in so doing, she would most certainly alienate the Justice Department and thus destroy her chances. She would rule for him though it would prove her radicalism and unreliability. She would rule for Cleveland Daniels because Phil Sabotnik was his lawyer, because Sabotnik was honest and she cared about him, because she would not want to spend the rest of her life thinking that he thought that she had sold out. She remembered the one night, over twenty years earlier, that she had spent with him. It was surprisingly vivid in her mind. Even the reasons why she had discouraged going on. He was possibly the best man she had ever known. Too good for her really.

Mary Ann sat down and began to write her decision. Slowly, word by word, in longhand on a legal pad. Hour after hour, without a break for dinner, into the night. She didn't speak to her clerk, was unaware even when her staff left at the end of the day.

It was past eleven o'clock when she left the courthouse. Almost midnight before she got to her apartment. Christine was waiting up for her, reading a novel, listening to the stereo. Mary Ann looked at her daughter. She was beautiful, Mary Ann thought. And almost grown up. She walked up to Christine and gave her a hug. And suddenly, for no reason that Mary Ann could quite understand, she found herself crying. Christine hugged her back.

Nancy Revering flew back to Washington on the shuttle, her emotions in a turmoil.

After the court session, Ed Regis had taken her aside, praised her work, and asked her if she might ever consider his firm after she left government service.

She had sensed a threat implicit in Ed Regis' job offer, an unstated threat that if she did not accept a job, or more to the point, if she did not lay off Transcontinental, she would be sorry. And she was frightened. And wondered whether she was paranoid. It would be no great thing for someone like Regis to spread the word that she was no good, to block all possibility of advancement, at least with this Administration, to deny her access to the big law firms and the big salaries. She had seen it before. Special prosecutors who had overreached themselves going after important government or business leaders, who had failed to bring home indictments and convictions. They had failed and then slowly, over years, had watched their careers wither and die. There would be no promotions, no job opportunities, no choice assignments. Instead there would be scut work and dead ends.

She thought about Ted Murcer. He would not protect her. Not now, she thought. He's going to stop loving me, she thought. He's going to be angry and hurt and those emotions are going to turn into something bad. And she knew that she would not go back to him, that she should really be looking for a new job, that it was not a good idea for her to still work with him.

She thought about Mary Ann Salisbury. She appeared to be everything that Nancy wanted to be herself. A woman who had made it without seeming to have compromised her ideals. She had been Ted Murcer's law school classmate. It made Nancy feel young, naïve, and vulnerable. She was out of her depth, she thought. A baby pretending to be able to hold her own against adults.

Finally, she thought about herself. About how she had argued the government's position to Mary Ann Salisbury even though she had not believed it. That was her job. To represent a client's position. But there was a compromise there. She would very much have preferred to have argued Phil Sabotnik's side of the case, would have been far more comfortable arguing for the veteran.

Sabotnik couldn't get to sleep that night. Marilyn dropped right off and he lay there staring at the luminous dial on the digital alarm clock . . . 12:45 A.M. . . . 1:15 A.M. He got out of bed. Quietly. Went downstairs, poured himself a glass of milk, grabbed a big handful of chocolate chip cookies, turned on the "Late Show." He watched the end of an old, terrible World War II spy movie, made sure that the FBI caught the Nazi saboteurs before they could blow up the Brooklyn Navy Yard. At a quarter to three he staggered back upstairs.

"What's the matter?" Marilyn asked, half asleep. Half asleep, but never too out of it to know when he was troubled.

"Nothing, Marilyn, go back to sleep."

"No. What is it?" She sat up in the dark.

"A case," he answered.

"The one you argued today?"

"Yes."

"The case of the veteran who got cancer from taking that drug?"

"Yes."

"Did he die yet?"

"No. But it's only a matter of time."

"The case isn't going well? Is that it?"

"Yes and no. I mean that I don't know if the case is going at all. Today's argument was all about whether we have a right to bring the case at all."

"And the judge wasn't sympathetic?" she guessed wrongly. "You drew some conservative old fart who forgot several decades ago that he used to be a human being. Right?"

"No. The judge is very sympathetic. And very smart. And she

wants to rule in my favor. I know that she does. But she's also scared. Because it would be a radical thing to do. It could hurt her chances for elevation to a higher court."

"She?"

"Mary Ann," he answered simply. She sat up straighter, fully awake.

"Salisbury?"

"Yes."

"She's the judge who got this case?"

"Yes."

"You were arguing before her today?"

"Yes."

"And you never told me she had the case."

"No."

"You thought that it would bother me?"

"I guess so."

"Because twenty years ago you went to bed with her for a night?"

"Maybe."

"Because I used not to like her?"

"You didn't like her."

"And you loved her," Marilyn shot back. "You probably still do."

"That's ridiculous, I haven't seen her in twenty years."

"Is it?"

"What?"

"Is it ridiculous?"

"Yes."

"I'll bet that she's aged well and looks terrific."

"Yes."

"And she's probably single, or divorced, or maybe a widow."

"One of those . . ."

"But you don't feel a thing."

"Nothing," he lied.

"And that's why you can't sleep tonight?"

There was no talking to her. "I can go to sleep," he said quietly. "And I'm going to."

And they said no more. And he did fall asleep. And it was Marilyn's turn to sit up. Feeling threatened. And feeling stupid about it. Stupid after all those years to feel a threat, to react sharply. After a time she too got out of bed, quietly, went downstairs for a glass of milk and cookies.

48

"We could have big trouble with your friend Mary Ann Salisbury," Ed Regis reported to Petrakis. "If this Trioxsone case isn't shut down fast, I'm afraid that it will get out of control. She'll decide the case against us and we'll have to appeal. That's not what's worrying me. We would win on appeal. What worries me is that young government lawyer who's working the case for Ted Murcer. I think that she's got it in for Transcontinental and I think that she knows a lot about what really happened. And what she doesn't know, she suspects. She's goddamned dangerous and so is your old classmate Sabotnik. If they ever get their acts together and start to cooperate they could become a major problem. I am sure that that young woman has asked for a go-ahead to empanel a grand jury to investigate the Trioxsone contracting situation. And I'd hate like hell to see Mary Ann Salisbury as the trial judge presiding over such a grand jury. I wouldn't like to have to try to get her to quash subpoenas asking for our old business records. I believe that she would come down on us like old Judge Sirica came down on the Nixon White House. She's just the wrong judge for us."

"You may be worrying too much," Petrakis cut in. "I mean, suppose that your worst fears come about. Suppose that in spite of our combined influence they do seat a grand jury. Suppose they do subpoena our old records. Suppose Mary Ann orders compliance. You know as well as I do that under the internal corporate procedures I established last year when this case was filed, I've had all of Lefcourte Labs business records from more than seven years ago destroyed since it was too costly to store all those old papers. So they'll get absolutely nothing. Nothing to base a prosecution on anyway."

"And you're ready to stake everything on the odd chance that there isn't a Xerox copy of something embarrassing that somehow escaped the shredder. How can you be sure that some secretary or maybe some junior executive on the make didn't make a few extra copies of something damning, somewhere along the way? And you're ready to go into the grand jury and possibly face a perjury charge because you contradicted something that was written down in a document the government wasn't supposed to have. I should think that by now you were too old and too experienced to risk everything on the presumption that everything on paper was destroyed. Maybe it was. But I would never rely on it."

"So we have to settle?" Petrakis asked.

"I should think so."

"No matter what the cost in dollars?"

"Yes."

"Do you think that there's any danger that Phil Sabotnik won't accept a settlement at any price? He's just idealistic enough, and he's just rich enough, to push this case as a matter of principle no matter what we offer."

"I don't think that's likely," Regis replied. "He's got his client to think of after all. So he's not really free to make a crusade out of the case at the risk of depriving that colored boy and his family of the chance for instant wealth. He'd be caught in a bind once we offered substantial dollars. It would be unethical for him not to accept."

"And if we settle the civil action, does that really get rid of my problem with the government and the possible grand jury investigation?"

"Probably."

"Why?"

"Because once the civil action is gone and the pressure is off, first of all it would mean that there was nothing pending before Mary Ann Salisbury, so we would be quits with her and that would be a big plus. A criminal investigation would almost certainly end up before a different judge and we would be bound to do better no matter who we might draw. Besides, once the civil action went away, a lot of the impetus for action at the Justice Department would dissipate. A great deal of interest would be lost when the whole mess got transferred from the Civil to the Criminal Division. I imagine that then we could pull some strings discreetly and see if we could get this young woman, Revering, pulled off the case and put to work on something harmless, like defending auto accident cases for the Post Office Department in say Montana and Idaho. Then the investigation could go on a back burner, and get assigned to one of the more inept or lazy prosecutors who could be relied upon to go nowhere with it."

"You can accomplish that?" Petrakis asked slowly, looking at Regis.

"I think so," he said without blinking.

"Okay, do it," Petrakis answered, also without blinking.

49

Three days later they were all back in New York, back at Sabotnik's office, for the purpose of taking Cleveland Daniels' pre-trial deposition. "We've got to get together anyway before we get back to Judge Salisbury," Ed Regis had reasoned in his phone conversations with Sabotnik and Nancy Revering. "So why don't we take the plaintiff's deposition while we're at it. After all, Phil, you said yourself that Mr. Daniels was in failing health, and that you needed to preserve his testimony for presentation before a jury in the event that he dies before trial. I suppose we ought to do it as soon as possible." There was no disagreeing with that.

Cleveland Daniels was well enough to come downtown to his lawyer's office. Just barely. He was having a good week, a week without side effects from the chemotherapy. He was horribly thin and emaciated though, without stamina, listless. His hands shook.

Nancy Revering flew up from Washington carrying two huge leather trial bags full of files. She was wearing an expensive mauve wool knit dress that enhanced her figure.

Ed Regis also arrived with two large trial bags full of files. However, he had two young associates, recent law school graduates (with law review credentials, and experience clerking for federal judges), carrying the bags for him. Both associates would sit quietly throughout the deposition furiously taking notes, handing files and documents to Regis as, or even before, he called for them. It was immediately obvious that the two of them had been thorough and had intensively analyzed every available document about Cleveland Daniels. Ed Regis took the lead in the questioning. He went right for the jugular.

"You're Cleveland Daniels," he asked.

"Yes."

"And you've sued Lefcourte Labs."

"Yes."

"And the United States Government."

"Yes."

"You claim Lefcourte Labs gave you cancer?"

"I guess so."

"And you know the cause of cancer?" Sarcastically.

"That's what Mr. Sabotnik tells me."

"And he knows what causes cancer?"

"I don't know."

"How old are you?"

"Thirty-four."

"And you live in the Bronx?"

"Yes."

"Born there?"

"Uh huh."

"How far did you get in school?"

"Through high school, that's all."

"Did you ever hold a steady job for longer than a calendar year?"

"No."

"Did you ever earn more than $4,500 in any year in your life?"

"I don't know."

"Let me show you the three federal income tax returns that you bothered to file in the last ten years. Do any of them show income over $4,500?"

"No."

"Is there any reason why you didn't file tax returns in other years?"

"I don't know."

"Was it because you didn't earn any money at all those other years?"

"Maybe."

"Or did you just forget to declare your income those years?"

"No."

"Of course there were four or five years when you were in prison, right?"

"Yes."

"You didn't file any returns those years."

"No."

"Now you were convicted of a felony and served a jail sentence, didn't you?"

"Yes."

"And that was for armed robbery and assault on a little seven-year-old girl."

"I didn't assault any little girl."

"You didn't?"

"No."

"Does the name Marie Gonzalez mean anything to you?"

"No."

"Suppose I were to tell you that that was the name of the little girl who you ran down trying to escape from the armed robbery of the supermarket that led to your imprisonment."

"Was that her name?"

"Yes. And are you aware that she is now almost 75 percent deaf because of the injury you inflicted?"

"I didn't mean to hurt her."

"But you did?"

"Yes."

"And that was while doing an armed robbery?"

"Yes."

"And you were also convicted years earlier of petty larceny."

"Yes."

"That was for some involvement with a stolen car ring."

"No."

"Well didn't you steal cars and give them to some crooked garage that used to strip them down?"

"Sometimes."

"And you got money for doing that."

"Yes."

"Okay. Now were you ever convicted of any other crime?"

"No."

"How about in the Army? Weren't you involved in some disciplinary proceeding in Vietnam?"

"Yeah."

"And that had to do with a racial brawl that occurred while you were on leave?"

"I had forgotten about that."

"In Saigon."

"Yeah, I got drunk with a bunch of my buddies."

"Who were also black?"

"Yes."

"And you got into a brawl with a group of white soldiers?"

"Yeah. They were southern crackers, and a couple of Australians."

"And you pulled a knife on them?"

"We were outnumbered."

"And you were sentenced to three weeks in the stockade?"

"Yes."

"So that's a type of conviction too?"

"I suppose."

"Now when you were in state prison, you got into trouble there too, didn't you?"

"Yes."

"There was a homosexual rape you were involved with, right?"

"No."

"Does the name Henry Milton mean anything to you?"

"Yes."

"Do you remember his being raped in prison in your cell block about six months after you entered prison?"

"Yeah."

"And you drew three weeks' solitary confinement over that incident?"

"Yes, but it wasn't for raping that kid. It was for not telling the screws who did rape him. And I couldn't do that. Not if I wanted to survive in prison."

"But you got solitary confinement for committing a homosexual rape?"

"Yeah, but I didn't do it."

The deposition went on mercilessly, hour after hour. Sabotnik had tried to prepare Daniels for the ordeal, but to no avail. Regis had an absolute right to question the plaintiff, and an absolute right to try to show that he was a bum. He had the right to try to show the jury that Cleveland Daniels would never have earned an honest living in his life, that his heirs could never reasonably have expected to receive money from him had he lived a normal life. There was nothing for Sabotnik to do but sit quietly while Regis went on at length destroying Daniels' character. There was nothing to do but sit back and suffer along with his client, sit and admire the thoroughness and the detachment with which Regis went about his business. It took a strong stomach to be able to verbally savage an obviously dying man. Ed Regis had the stomach for it though. He went on and on in a drab monotone, without changing expression, his face a mask. He moved on from Cleveland Daniels' past misdeeds to more prosaic matters. He questioned him closely about his medical history from birth onwards, the doctors he had seen, the illnesses, operations, medications. He asked about Daniels' family, tried to discover their health histories, probed to see if there might be a genetic propensity to cancer in the family. He asked about Cleveland's military years, probing to see if there were any undisclosed acts of heroism there, anything that might unexpectedly reflect well on Daniels at trial. He covered it all.

And it was all a charade.

"Might I have a moment with you and your client in private?" Regis asked Sabotnik, during a break in his questioning. The old lawyer cast a glance toward Nancy Revering and she absented herself from the room.

"I'm sorry about having to question you like that," Regis began, seeming sincere, looking squarely at Cleveland Daniels. "It's my job, of course. But it's a cruel job and there's no pleasure in it at all."

Daniels said nothing. He was hollow-eyed, exhausted, almost unable to comprehend what the lawyer was saying.

"But there's a point to it also," Regis went on. "And that point is that if I ever read this stuff to a jury, or if you ever take the stand and repeat what you said today, no jury in this country will give you very much money no matter how good your case is. In fact I think it more than likely that no jury will give you any money at all. Not with the kind of weak scientific case that you have here."

He's going to offer more money, Sabotnik said to himself, as he listened to Regis' preamble. He knew it instinctively. Over the years he had heard hundreds, maybe thousands of offers prefaced by a bad-mouthing of the plaintiff's case.

"I can beat you in court," Regis continued, turning to Sabotnik. "I can beat you on the law, if not in front of Mary Ann Salisbury, then certainly on appeal. And if I couldn't beat you on the law, and we had to have a trial, then I will beat you on the facts. I think that should be quite clear to you after today's deposition."

Still no answer.

"I think that it's time to end this case once and for all," Regis stated softly. "I have authority to settle this case for a sum equal to the anticipated expenses that Transcontinental would pay to my firm to defend this case. And at my hourly rate, and at the hourly rates of my associates, that is an awful lot of money. I have this authority not because we are worried about losing the case, but frankly because we would like to avoid more bad publicity, because we would like to put this behind us."

"How much?" Cleveland Daniels asked suddenly. "How much?"

"Three hundred twenty-five thousand dollars," Regis replied without blinking. "That should net you and your family after fees and expenses almost a quarter of a million dollars. Your mother could live very well on a quarter of a million dollars, very well indeed. She could invest it very conservatively at a ten percent return and have an income of twenty-five thousand dollars a year without even having to touch the principal. Do you understand what that means?"

"Yeah."

"And that's our final offer. An offer for today only. If we go forward after today, I promise you that you will never see a penny from us in settlement. What do you say?"

Sabotnik made a move to protest, to tell Cleveland Daniels not to respond, to tell Regis that it was outrageous to make that kind of offer, to insist that he have time to confer with his client. Cleveland Daniels cut him off.

"That's all there is, man?"

"Yes."

"No bullshit?"

"No bullshit."

"Tell your client to go fuck himself."

50

One week went by. Then another. Mary Ann went about her business and waited. She carried the draft of her opinion folded up in an envelope inside her pocketbook. Roughly once a day she took it out and read it. She could file the opinion any moment that she wished to. Or she could hold it up for months without anyone daring to criticize her. The temptation certainly was to delay. At least until the Supreme Court situation had become clarified.

"It's down to three candidates," Judge Anderson told her late one afternoon.

"There's you, a fellow over at the Justice Department, and a lady who's an intermediate appellate judge in one of the state systems out west."

"There are only two candidates," Mary Ann answered.

The old judge understood at once.

"I'm filing this decision tomorrow," she went on, reached into her bag and handed him the envelope. She watched the old man open up the envelope carefully, watched him put on his reading glasses, unfold the typewritten papers and begin to read. She sat silently while he slowly read each page, still carefully setting aside each sheet as he completed it. The decision was over twenty pages in length and the old judge read it through from start to finish.

"It's very pretty," he said simply when he was through.

"And it will end my chances."

"Yes, certainly."

"I shouldn't file it then?"

The old judge looked at her steadily. He seemed to be weighing his words. Then he shrugged.

"No one can answer that for you."

"That soldier is dying, I'm told. He may only have days or weeks left."

"He will die then whether you file that decision or not. He'll die no matter what your decision may be."

"Yes."

"And you'll most certainly be reversed by the circuit court. And if it gets that far, your decision is even more certain to be reversed by the Supreme Court. I would vote to reverse it myself. Better that than to expose the government to a flood of litigation over a decade-old scandal. I would send this soldier over to the Veterans Administration for benefits and let it go at that. My guess is that most of my colleagues would be even more harsh."

"So I would be making a futile gesture?"

"A gesture, anyway."

"And it will label me a dangerous, unreliable radical."

"You will not be considered for the high Court."

"I'm going to file it anyway," Mary Ann said finally.

"I know," the old judge said.

"But I wanted to tell you first. And I wanted to tell you how much I have appreciated everything you have tried to do for me. How honored and privileged I have felt to think that you should have tried to do this for me. And well, just that I love you."

51

Cleveland Daniels caught pneumonia only a week after the newspapers carried the story of Mary Ann's ruling in his favor, three days after the government and Lefcourte Labs had noticed their appeals to the circuit court. He was weak, his resistance was destroyed by the long losing battle against cancer.

He was taken to Memorial Hospital, pumped full of antibiotics, sustained on pain killers that clouded his consciousness. He was hooked up to monitoring devices, fed intravenously, and slipped in and out of a coma.

His lungs filled up with fluid and he could not breathe. They were drained and they filled up again. He struggled, did not go easily. He was too young.

His lungs filled up with fluid. He could not breathe, he tried to cry out for his mother, to cry out for her to make it stop.

It did stop that night. His heart failed and Cleveland Daniels died.

At almost the same moment, several hundred miles away in Washington, an old man also died of cancer, died in almost precisely the same way.

The old man was Associate Justice Andrew Smith of the Supreme Court of the United States.

He also tried to call for his mother just before he died. He tried even though she had been dead almost thirty years.

52

Cleveland Daniels' mother arrived in Sabotnik's office with her husband, Ralph. They were ill at ease, and remained ill at ease while the lawyer expressed his condolences.

"Your son died without a will," Sabotnik explained, "which means that I will have to go into the surrogate's court and have you named administratrix of your son's estate. It's a formality really, but it's necessary if your son's lawsuit is going to go on."

"That means we still got a lawsuit even though the boy is dead?" Ralph asked.

"Yes."

"And we can get money from it?"

"Maybe. Lefcourte Labs actually offered your son a substantial sum of money before he died. But he turned it down."

"How much?"

"Over three hundred thousand."

"What?"

"Over three hundred thousand."

"And he turned that down?"

"Yes."

"Then he was a fool."

"Cleveland didn't think so," Sabotnik replied. "I think he believed in this lawsuit. I think he believed that it was possible that by bringing this matter into court he might prevent what happened to him from happening to others in the future. I think that he wanted to see those who were responsible punished for what they did."

Cleveland's mother looked strangely at Sabotnik.

"You say my son wanted those things?" she asked. "You sure it isn't you that wanted them?"

No answer.

"My boy didn't want to be a hero. I loved him and I took care of him the best way I knew how. But I knew that he wasn't a good boy. He was gone all those years in the Army and he never wrote me. Not from prison either. He never gave me a penny. Not ever. Not when he was working and had money, when he was living with me and I was hard up. He never contributed for groceries. I never said anything to him about that. There didn't seem to be a point to it. But don't tell me now that my boy suddenly got all concerned about justice and stuff like that."

"So what do you suggest?" Sabotnik asked.

"Settle the case if you can. And get Ralph and me that three hundred thousand dollars. We've worked hard all our lives. Real hard. And we don't have much to show for it. So if we've got a few good years left before we get old or die, and if we can retire and go to California or someplace where it's sunny, then I want to do that. I'd like to buy us a nice house somewhere. And I'd like for Ralph to be able to go fishing and not have to work in the subways. And I'd like to take it easy myself. I'd really like that. So I want you to settle my case, Mr. Sabotnik. I'm sorry that that's not what you want. And I'm sorry that my boy is dead. But settle the case."

53

"I've made the case," Nancy Revering told Ted Murcer excitedly. "I've got a witness who gives me Lefcourte Labs on a platter. A conspiracy to corrupt federal officials. Bribery. Pentagon officials and FDA officials getting lucrative jobs in return for approving the use of Trioxsone and the payment of huge acquisition costs."

"Who will believe it?" Murcer asked.

"George Petrakis."

"And who is your witness?"

"Ellen MacCauley."

"Who's she?"

"The former wife of Lawrence MacCauley, who used to be with the surgeon general, and now is an executive at Lefcourte.

In fact, he's become president of the company. Anyway, Mac-Cauley divorced his wife a few years ago. Left her for a younger woman. And she's pretty bitter about it. But the point is that back in the sixties when this deal went down, MacCauley used to keep a diary. He kept it in his own hand in looseleaf notebooks. And apparently he was pretty troubled by the whole deal. There are pages and pages of his agonizing about whether or not to accept Petrakis' offer. Eventually he rationalized that the drug would probably help the soldiers anyway. And he was bitter because he was being passed over a second time for his next star. So he justified it all in his mind. It's beautiful."

"You have the diary?"

"Not the original. But Ellen found it sometime before the divorce, and Xeroxed the whole thing without letting on to her husband that she had. She's been holding on to it ever since because she figured it would have its use."

"And you've got the copy?"

"Yes."

"And she'll testify?"

"Yes. And she knows things that aren't even in the diary. She used to talk to her husband and he told most everything."

"Except about the younger woman," Murcer said dryly, looking at her.

"He told her about it, Ted. And she remembers. Her memory is good. She's credible."

"An embittered older woman, trying to get back at the man who wronged her? A sneak who steals someone's diary? Someone who knew all about Trioxsone but kept her mouth shut for years while she was still benefiting from the money her husband was earning. I'm not so sure how credible she really is, babe."

"Credible enough to get us indictments."

"How about convictions?"

"Maybe."

"I don't think so. Not yet. Maybe you might get MacCauley. But don't count on getting Petrakis. She's too slender a reed."

"But what if I haul MacCauley in and confront him with the diary? What if I scare the shit out of him and threaten him with taking the weight and then offer him a deal? Maybe I can get his cooperation and nail Petrakis."

Murcer looked at her. She was completely changed, like a shark with a smell of blood in her nostrils. He almost could believe that she had forgotten and was oblivious to what had been between them. It was all work to her. And he realized suddenly not only that he could hurt her, but also that he wanted to.

"I'm going to have to bring this to the Attorney General," Murcer said slowly. "And together the Attorney General and I will have to notify the White House. It will have to be cleared at that kind of level. But I'm going to recommend prosecution. I'm going to recuse myself from the case because George is an old friend of mine and I don't want anything to do with this.

"And I'm pulling you off the case too. Right now. And I'm going to transfer you out of this section. You can go wherever you want in the Justice Department but I'd prefer it was outside of Washington. In New York. Or on the West Coast. Wherever you want. Just not here."

54

Ted Murcer found himself sitting alone with the Attorney General of the United States. He was uncomfortable.

"The President is not going to be happy with this," the Attorney General said.

"I know."

"And he's not going to be happy with whoever breaks this to him."

"Yes."

"The Pentagon is going to be awfully unhappy too."

"Yes. And it's not going to thrill the party fund raisers either. Not with George Petrakis controlling I-don't-know-how-many hundreds of thousands, or is it millions of dollars, in contributions."

"It's millions, Ted. And I do know how much, even if you don't. He's been spreading it around for years. He's been spreading it around shrewdly too. Which means that he has very many friends indeed. In fact, you're one of those friends yourself, aren't you?"

"Yes."

"And you're going to ask me to recuse you from the case so that there will be no appearance of impropriety, right?"

"Yes."

"And the real reason is that you don't want to get yourself tarred with this brush. Let someone else try to throw George Petrakis in jail and fail. It's too risky, isn't it?"

"It is bound to be a chancy prosecution. I don't know if General MacCauley will turn on Petrakis when it comes to it. And if he does, even then it's hardly a sure thing. Petrakis' lawyers can be expected to cut our witnesses to shreds. And he'll be able to produce everyone from the Queen of England to Sister Teresa as character witnesses. He'll be very hard to convict. And I don't want any part of the efforts. The truth is that I like the guy. I always have. And I don't think that he's that bad a guy. I'm sure he did what he did with the sincere belief that the damned drug would actually be good for the soldiers."

"But he did it?"

"I must believe so."

"And it was wrong?"

"Yes."

"And we have a case that we can build before a grand jury?"

"Yes."

"And staff lawyers know the details of the case?"

"Yes."

"And are chomping at the bit to get started?"

"More or less."

"And we'll face a revolt in the ranks if we try to suppress the case. Or possibly we might face someone leaking the details to the press?"

"Possibly."

"So we have no choice except to go forward?"

"That's my conclusion."

"Very well, then do it."

"Me?"

"Yes. I think that you had better supervise the case yourself.

Pick your prosecutorial team, and have them report to you. I'll advise the White House of developments. You'll report to me."

Murcer got up to leave, knowing he had been had, saying nothing. As he neared the door, the Attorney General stopped him.

"Oh, by the way, Ted, I thought you might want to know that about that Supreme Court nomination. It's going to an appellate judge from out west. The President believes that it's time for a woman to get a seat on the Court."

55

It took Sabotnik a week to settle the Daniels case. He called Ed Regis and explained that Cleveland's mother was prepared to consider the possibility of settlement, but that the amount originally offered was inadequate. He suggested three quarters of a million as a fair price.

Regis replied that since he had never really contributed to the support of his mother, it seemed to him that the case was now less valuable than it had been before. But he carefully told Sabotnik that Lefcourte Labs was still very interested in settlement. Regis promised to get back to him in a few days. It was all part of the time-honored minuet of settlement negotiation. Both men knew what was bound to happen.

"I've spoken to my client," Regis reported back to Sabotnik. "And I have the following settlement proposal for you. But I must stress to you first that this is our final offer and that I will not negotiate further.

"First," he said, going on, "we are prepared to pay $425,000. However, in return for the settlement price, we must also insist on receiving not only the usual release from your client, but also I want a written undertaking from you personally and from your law firm that you will not undertake to represent any other serviceman or former serviceman making a Trioxsone claim against us. You must also promise that you will never voluntarily provide assistance to any other lawyer prosecuting such claim. You must never discuss this settlement and your files must never be made available voluntarily to anyone. And that holds true for the government, too. You are not to voluntarily cooperate with any federal attorneys whether they be from the Civil Division or the Criminal Division. And if the government, or anyone else for that matter, attempts to subpoena your files then you must notify me immediately. And you must vigorously resist that subpoena, or permit us to do so. We will, of course, pay for the expenses involved in doing so."

There was a pause as Sabotnik took it all in. He replied softly, suppressing his anger.

"You're really interested in muzzling me. You're offering this money, which we both know is more than the case is worth, because you're afraid of a criminal prosecution and want me out of the way. Or maybe you're afraid that the publicity over this case will flush out dozens of other cases. One way or another, I'm your problem, right?"

Regis did not reply.

"And you want me to abdicate my responsibility to the public, and my responsibility as an officer of the court, or to other individuals who might need my help. I'm supposed to just sit silently and watch what happens, which will probably be nothing except that your clients will continue to make unconscionable profits. I'm supposed to agree because I will earn a big fee from this settlement?"

"You will agree," Regis said dryly, "because your first responsibility as a lawyer is to your client. And whether you like it or not, your own personal interests or desires, or even your sense of right and wrong, have nothing to do with it. You have to do what is best for the Daniels family and you know it. That comes before your concept of what might be good for the public, or good for other people who aren't your clients, or good for yourself. So don't give me any crap about this being unconscionable, Phil. If your client wants this settlement, and I think that we both know that she does, then you have to take it."

Sabotnik wanted to hang up on him. But he didn't. Instead he ended the conversation politely, put down the receiver, and then threw his pen against his office wall. Regis was correct, of course. Sabotnik knew that he would never be able to persuade Cleveland's mother to reject the settlement. And then he would be obligated to cut the deal with Regis. He would have to sign some piece of paper that he would hate. And he would hate himself for signing it. And he would honor his signature on that piece of paper. He would earn a fee of well over a hundred thousand dollars though, when he signed that piece of paper.

56

It was four months before the government's indictment of George Petrakis became public. In the interim Ted Murcer left the Justice Department. That had been relatively simple. A few feelers, a word or two in the right ears, some interviews conducted discreetly over lunches at expensive French restaurants. Finally, an invitation to join a major Park Avenue law firm at $250,000 per year. The whole thing met with the complete approval of his wife. She was more than happy to get out of Washington.

It was Murcer who first broke the word to Petrakis. It was on the day that Murcer shook hands with his partners to be. He called Petrakis' office and made an appointment to meet him for dinner that evening.

"I'm leaving the government," Murcer began as they started their first cocktail. "I'll be joining Sloan, Reeves, Coolidge, and Masterman."

"Good firm," Petrakis said noncommittally. "Have you had a falling out with the Administration? Or are you positioning yourself for a run for office?"

Murcer smiled. "You're too polite to ask whether the money might have anything to do with it."

Petrakis shrugged.

"It's you actually," Murcer said, "who caused me to leave. Or at least you are the catalyst."

Murcer hesitated, looked at his former classmate. Petrakis was perfectly composed, and perfectly groomed, waiting. Only an intensity in his stare betrayed him, a total concentration.

"I was directed to head up and supervise the investigation that's going to end up in your being indicted. Which is, in effect, the Attorney General's or the White House's way of politely telling me that my services are no longer required. Instead of firing me, I'm given an unpalatable, impossible job. Because no matter what I do, I lose. If I go easy on you, then I'm an old friend playing favorites for a former supporter. If I'm tough, then I'm an ungrateful bastard, and possibly a traitor to the party. The Attorney General knew that I would never allow myself to get set up that way. He knew I'd leave."

"Trioxsone?" Petrakis asked simply.

"Yes."

"MacCauley?"

"His wife. A diary."

"He's been turned?"

"Yes."

Petrakis stood up slowly. He offered Murcer his hand. Murcer rose.

"Ted, I think you will understand if I do not stay for dinner. I know you will understand."

Murcer nodded.

"And, Ted, thank you very much. Thank you very much."

Murcer answered slowly.

"Nothing to thank me for, George. Nothing at all. Because I never spoke to you tonight. Never even saw you. You understand?"

Petrakis shook his head, then turned and walked out of the restaurant. But first he put a twenty-dollar bill down on the table to cover the bar bill.

Later, home in his apartment, Petrakis placed two telephone calls. The first, and less important, was a long conversation with Ed Regis. The second was a long-distance call to Poughkeepsie, New York, to Diana.

"Di," he said when she answered. "It's Dad. Would you

please come down to New York tomorrow morning? It's rather important and I would like to talk to you.

"No, I'd rather not talk about it on the phone." He answered her question. "Let's talk tomorrow."

57

Sabotnik was surprised and flattered when he received Nancy Revering's resumé in the mail along with a handwritten note asking him for a job. His response was simple and immediate. "The job is yours, if you want it," he wrote. "Come up to New York and we'll discuss the details."

58

Mary Ann Salisbury testified as a character witness at George Petrakis' criminal trial. She would have preferred not to. But when he asked, she could only say yes. He had been a good friend to her, and she owed him too much to say no.

"I've known George ever since we were in law school," she stated.

"We served on the law review together when we were students, and I remember very well his integrity, not only academically and intellectually, but also as a human being. I remember how in those days when there was pressure on us to keep a young man off the review because of his left-wing background, George was in the forefront of seeing that the review behaved fairly to that young man. I remember that I didn't always agree with George on everything, but I always respected the complete honesty with which he took his positions."

"Well tell me, Judge Salisbury," Petrakis' lawyer asked, "have you had any contact with George Petrakis since you graduated from law school?"

"Yes."

"Will you tell us about it?"

"I lost touch with George during the time he was at the Supreme Court, and after he returned to New York for several years I did not really have anything to do with him. But back in the late sixties when I was promoting low-cost day care centers for working mothers, I met George again. He was instrumental at that time in providing funding for our projects. George was and is a dedicated and convinced supporter of women's issues. And again, I found in all of my many meetings with him, that George's word was always good. Whatever he promised, he delivered."

After she was finished, the prosecutor asked Mary Ann only three questions.

"Judge Salisbury, do you have any personal knowledge whatsoever concerning the events that led the United States Government to requisition Trioxsone from Lefcourte Labs for use on our troops in Vietnam?"

"No."

"And you have no personal knowledge concerning George Petrakis' role, if any, in those events?"

"No."

"So you have no personal knowledge one way or the other concerning whether George Petrakis is guilty or innocent of the crimes for which he is on trial?"

"That is correct."

"Thank you."

Mary Ann was the last witness to testify. She decided to wait around for the verdict. She had testified in the morning, and she sat in the back of the courtroom watching the lawyers sum up. The court was then recessed for lunch, with the judge's charge and the jury's deliberation scheduled to follow the recess. Mary Ann joined Petrakis and his daughter for lunch at the courthouse cafeteria.

There was nothing to say.

Petrakis sat silently, took a plate of food, ate it absentmindedly. He had a faraway look in his eyes, a look as if it didn't much matter. He would resign his position at Transcontinental one way or the other once this was done. That was inevitable. And one way or the other he would be financially secure. If convicted, there would be all manner of appeals. And a year or two would go by before he might go in to spend six months or a year in jail at a minimum security prison. There would be time off for good behavior. He would use the time in prison to catch up on his reading, to reflect, to write.

But there was Diana. And it did matter very much to her. Mary Ann could see that. She had cried, and was trying hard and successfully not to cry now. She reached every now and again for her father's hand, and he suffered her to hold it awhile. Then he would take it back. She was ready to comfort him. And he not quite ready to receive it.

Mary Ann felt uncomfortable. She was not sure why she was there. Her presence was an excuse for silence. A stranger, at least to the girl, they did not have to speak to one another while she was there. Not of anything significant.

Petrakis was guilty of course. Mary Ann had known that. So did the girl for that matter. And Petrakis himself. The defense was a charade. But a very good one. The prosecution had been indifferent. Mary Ann had not wanted to come. She had wrestled with it. Not wanting to lend her name to the defense of something she detested. She owed Petrakis though. And he was not asking her to lie. Because there was nothing in her experience but good to say of her classmate. So she had said it. For what little it was worth.

She sat through the summations. The judge's charge.

The jury went out to deliberate.

And they returned quickly.

Not with a question.

With a verdict.

Mary Ann watched the forewoman rise.

"Members of the jury," the judge inquired, "have you reached a verdict?"

"Yes, your honor."

"Mr. Petrakis, will you please rise."

"How find you, guilty or not guilty?"

"Guilty."